FAMILIES
&
FAMILY RELATIONS

AS REPRESENTED IN EARLY JUDAISMS
AND EARLY CHRISTIANITIES:
TEXTS AND FICTIONS

STUDIES IN
THEOLOGY AND RELIGION
(STAR)

EDITED ON BEHALF OF

THE NETHERLANDS SCHOOL FOR
ADVANCED STUDIES IN THEOLOGY AND RELIGION

NEDERLANDSE ONDERZOEKSCHOOL
VOOR THEOLOGIE EN RELIGIEWETENSCHAP
(NOSTER)

BY

JAN WILLEM VAN HENTEN

VOLUME 2

deo
PUBLISHING

FAMILIES AND FAMILY RELATIONS

AS REPRESENTED IN EARLY JUDAISMS
AND EARLY CHRISTIANITIES:
TEXTS AND FICTIONS

PAPERS READ AT A NOSTER COLLOQUIUM
IN AMSTERDAM, JUNE 9–11, 1998

EDITED BY

JAN WILLEM VAN HENTEN
&
ATHALYA BRENNER

deo
PUBLISHING

LEIDEN
2000

Studies in Theology and Religion series, 2
STAR

ISSN 1566-208X

Published by Deo Publishing
Scholeksterstraat 16, 2352 EE Leiderdorp, The Netherlands.

British Library Cataloguing-in-Publication data
A catalogue record for this book is available from the British Library

NUGI 632

ISBN 90 5854 014 6

Contents

Preface

The present volume contains papers read during a colloquium on aspects of families and family relations as represented in early Jewish and Christian sources. The editors are grateful to the Board of the Netherlands School for Advanced Studies in Theology and Religion for agreeing to publish this volume in the STAR series. They also wish to thank Professor Florentino Garcia Martinez and Professor Wim Weren and Dr Johannes Tromp for reading parts of the manuscript, Ms Mirjam Elbers for checking references and adapting part of the manuscripts to the STAR guidelines. And, finally, Mr Frans de Boer for refashioning the manuscript into camera ready copy. Apart from the STAR guidelines for authors, the handbook of the Society of Biblical Literature has been used for references and abbreviations. A list of additional abbreviations is given after this Preface. We have decided not to change the American or English spelling of the contributions, because forcing Americans to use English spelling or authors from the United Kingdom to use the American one is inappropriate in the context of an international volume. A bibliography and indices of modern authors, Bible and other ancient sources complete the book.

The editors

Abbreviations

All abbreviations of series, handbooks and journals in this volume are according to: P.H. Alexander *et al.* (eds.), *The SBL Handbook of Style: For Ancient Near Eastern, Biblical and Early Christian Studies* (Peabody, Mass.: Hendrickson Publishers, 1999). For the Books of the Bible and early Jewish or Christian works commonly accepted abbreviations were used. In addition the following abbreviations occur.

AJA	American Journal of Archaeology
AmA	American Anthropologist
CIJ	Corpus Inscriptionum Judaicarum
CPJ	Corpus Papyrorum Judaicorum
FJB	Frankfurter Judaistische Beiträge
PAAJR	Proceedings of the American Academy for Jewish Research
SBFLA	Liber Annuus
SCI	Scripta Classica Israelica
VC	Vigiliae Christianae

Introduction

Jan Willem van Henten and Athalya Brenner

(University of Amsterdam)

Genesis 1 presents humanity, from its inception, as a one-generational family. Genesis 4 adds a second generation of children to the primary couple, and introduces the concept of sibling rivalry. Humanity branches out of a single family, like a tree. The rest of Genesis focuses on a single family, Abraham and his descendants. This 'family' is depicted as later branching into other families, then a community and ultimately a people. Clearly, 'family' is a primary social structure for biblical authors. Kinship, even and perhaps especially also fictive/imaginary kinship, is perceived as representation and reflection of pragmatic as well as symbolical-metaphorical values.

In recent years at least four major publications dealing with aspects of the 'family' in the so-called biblical worlds appeared: *Families in Ancient Israel*,[1] *The Jewish Family in Antiquity*,[2] *Constructing Early Christian Families: Family as Social Reality and Metaphor*[3] and *Families in the New Testament World: Households and House Churches*.[4]

Previous publications, as is clear from their titles, proceeded from the assumption that a single model or concept of 'family' obtains for discreet time/place grids in antiquity, even if this does not obtain for contemporary life. The titles of such works – 'family', 'institution' (in the singular mode) – speak for themselves.[5] In

---

[1] L. Perdue *et al.*, *Families in Ancient Israel*, Louisville 1997.

[2] S.J.D. Cohen (ed.), *The Jewish Family in Antiquity* (Brown Judaic Studies, 289), Atlanta 1993.

[3] H. Moxnes (ed.), *Constructing Early Christian Families: Family as Social Reality and Metaphor*, London & New York 1997.

[4] C. Osiek, D. Balch, *Families in the New Testament World: Households and House Churches*, Louisville 1997.

[5] For instance: R. de Vaux, *Ancient Life in Ancient Israel* (in the original French from the early 1960's), Ch. 2; S. Safrai, "Home and Family", in: S. Safrai, M. Stern, *The Jewish People in the First Century*, Assen 1976,

the more recent publications, however, there is a growing awareness that a single model or concept of 'family' obtains no more for
antiquity than it does for contemporary life. Furthermore, it has
become increasingly clearer that attempts to present the 'family'
as a constant, unified, unchanging social entity are ideologically
and politically motivated by ancient authors as well as by their
interpreters. 'Families' (plural) rather than 'Family' (singular)
are now the topics for discussion. These starting points, rooted
as they are in the [post] modern predisposition to admit plurality and polyvalence at the expense of comforting generalizations,
are the hallmarks of the new publications, and numerous other
recent essays[6] that contain quite different views from former
publications. Undoubtedly, the change of perspective owes much,
explicitly as well as implicitly, to the social sciences as practiced
in Academe nowadays, to the New History and, especially, to
structuralist[7] and post-structuralist anthropology as well as to
the emerging trans-discipline of family studies.[8] The infiltration,
into biblical and related studies, of the more open debates about
sexuality, gender, sexual preferences and the status of women,
have also contributed to the shift – almost a paradigmatic shift –
in 1990's assessments of Families in the ancient worlds of Judaism
and Christianity.

The availability of the new textbooks motivated us to plan in
Amsterdam, for 1998, two activities linked to the renewed debates
about 'families': one, a course – a seminar, in fact – entitled
'Families in Biblical Times' for advanced students of biblical studies (both Hebrew Bible and New Testament) in our department of
Theology and Religious Studies; and two, a colloquium/workshop
entitled 'Families in the Ancient Near Eastern World, the Hebrew

---

728-92; S. Bendor, *The Social Structure of Ancient Israel: The Institution
of the Family (Beit 'ab) from the Settlement to the End of the Monarchy*,
Jerusalem 1996 – but originally a PhD dissertation in Hebrew, for the Hebrew
University, from the 1980's.

[6]For example S. Joubert, J.W. van Henten, "Two A-Typical Jewish Families in the Greco-Roman Period", *Neotestamentica* 30/1 (1996), 121-40.

[7]Cf. C. Lévi-Strauss, *The View from Afar*, trans. J. Newgroschel, P. Hoss,
New York 1985.

[8]For a useful introduction see J. Bernardes, *Family Studies: An Introduction*, London & New York 1997.

Bible and the Judaisms and Christianities of Early Antiquities'. Course students were required to attend the workshop/colloquium as part of their course plan. A cursory glance at the course plan[9] will show that the course was designated as an introduction to the discussion of 'families' in general, over a great time span and across the divides of Jewish/Christian religions, texts and cultures. We also wanted to examine certain issues related to family structures (such as consanguinity as against social relatedness, sexuality, labour and property, gender) in depth. The perspectives introduced were varied – sociological, anthropological, psychological, literary, biblical-classical. On the other hand, the colloquium/workshop, within the Dutch NOSTER context,[10] was to supply additional highlighting of other issues or relevant texts, developments or re-workings of seminal ideas mentioned in the recent publications indicated above.

The present collection contains several of the papers delivered during the colloquium, rewritten and adjusted to publication, together with the responses they elicited. However, it is *not* a 'conference proceedings' book in the usual sense. To begin with, some colloquium papers were omitted here, such as the major contribution by M. Stol[11] and the paper by B. Lataire.[12] So is the panel discussion on birth, pregnancy and related issues as well as Hachlili's slide presentation about the Goliath family.[13] Furthermore, if the papers here published are read against the background knowledge of the major publications mentioned above, as we hope they shall be read, a progressive learning chain will be established. In other words, the justification for this book lies not in its being a translation of a peer-meeting event into a book, but in its contribution

---

[9] Appendix A to this 'Introduction'.

[10] Appendix B to This 'Introduction'. NOSTER is the Dutch acronym for the Netherlands Research School for Theology and Religious Studies. The activities of its members, from PhD students to established scholars, are categorized into sections. This colloquium/workshop was organized for the Bible/Literary section.

[11] Prof. Stol's contribution is a summary of a chapter in a book, soon to be published.

[12] Ms. Lataire's contribution is part of a PhD dissertation in progress.

[13] These workshop events were, in our view, out of place in this publication.

to the newly opened debate over 'families' in the worlds habitually designated 'biblical worlds'. Building upon the groundwork established for the new Family Studies in Biblical Studies, it is now possible to examine issues in depth and anew. Broadly speaking, the issues reexamined and redefined in this volume are: marriage and its theological significance, brother-sister relations as a determinative element for reconstructing social structures, family continuity as expressed in non-literary sources, female domesticity as an unstable category, and kinship and identity in the context of Mediterranean honour notions. In most cases, issues of gender are highlighted. In this volume, moreover, distinctions between family structures in early Judaisms and Christianities are – consciously so – not emphasized. Rather, the focus is on dialectic processes of continuity and change in kinship/family notions, and the various social, political and ideological uses such notions are put to.

Two common denominators for all the essays are their thematic approach and wide scope. Discussion of 'families' rather than 'the family' necessitates awareness of changing historical circumstances and ideological engagements, as well as going back and forth across textual, material and chronological boundaries. Thus, it was difficult to arrange the essays either thematically or chronologically. We settled for a general distinction between essays dealing mainly with 'Jewish' concepts and ideas and between essays about chiefly 'Christian' issues. However, as readers will find, even such a distinction was problematic in some cases, since contributors did not confine themselves to the one or the other.

There are six units in this volume. Part I consists of four essays with a response to each one of them, and presents concepts of families and related issues in 'Some Cases of Early Judaisms: From Prophetic Books to Inscriptions'.

In "The Metaphor of Marriage in Early Judaism", Michael Satlow traces the reception of the biblical marriage metaphor, in which God is the husband or lover of Israel/Zion (as in Hosea, Jeremiah, Second Isaiah, Ezekiel and Malachi), among Jews in antiquity. His contention is that "Jews in antiquity by and large ignored, or even subverted, the biblical metaphor that compares the relationship of God to Israel as husband to wife. They did so

both because the metaphor made little sense to them in their own
social contexts, and because it clashed with several of their other
theological commitments". Satlow sees a diminishing use and devaluation of marriage as metaphor for the divine/human covenant,
from the Hebrew Bible through Jewish Hellenistic writings to
rabbinic literature, in favour of parental behavioural patterns, or
father-child relations, as a favourite metaphor for the relationship
between God and Israel. The divine husband is, increasingly, seen
more as a divine father, in accordance with changing theologies
and social contexts. This, in his view, might have reflected as well
as enforced a shift in early Judaisms, from an emphasis on marriage to a growing emphasis on parenthood. Satlow offers several
suggestions to explain this shift, and, in passing, also comments
on the acceptance and elaboration of the marriage metaphor in
the early Christian Church.

In "Why Would a Man Want to be Anyone's Wife?", Judith
Frishman takes up the significance of the marriage metaphor in
rabbinic literature through an extended example. She first discusses the potentially harmful implications of God-as-husband
and the feminized people-as-errant-wife, as in the biblical metaphor. Then through a reading of b. Pesaḥim 87b, she shows how
problematic the metaphor was for the rabbis, and what uses were
made of it. The Midrash contained in this talmudic passage connects the first chapters of Hosea – from which the marriage metaphor emanates – to the Songs of Songs. Frishman reminds us
that more research is needed for finding out in what ways its
problematics has been handled in Jewish sources before we proceed to determine the metaphor's influence on Jewish [rabbinic]
theologies on the one hand, and on marital relations in Jewish
families on the other hand.

In "'We have a Little Sister': Aspects of the Brother-Sister
Relationship in Ancient Israel", Ingo Kottsieper proceeds from
cautionary remarks about the difficulties of describing family
structures in 'Ancient Israel' according to biblical and extra-
biblical texts, especially difficulties concerning gaps between
utopia and realia, 'law' and praxis. He then reads several Hebrew
Bible texts – Song of Songs allusions to sisters and brothers,

Rebekah and her brothers (Genesis 24), Dinah and her brothers (Genesis 34), Tamar daughter of David and her brothers (2 Samuel 13-14) – and adds Proverbs 7:4 and two non-biblical examples to this list. Kottsiepper then moves to utilize sister-brother relations, and father-daughter relations, for explaining the development of Israelite patriarchal family structures. In his opinion, biblical patriarchy developed during Hellenistic times when, influenced by the changing political and social milieu, the position of women within family hierarchies were made inferior, whereas the position of men – the father especially, but also other male family members – was strengthened because of their outward-oriented authority.

In his response, "The Role of the Father", Arie van der Kooij picks up three points mentioned by Kottsieper. The first is that whereas a father figure is not mentioned in the Song of Songs, it is doubtful whether any theories about family structures can be gleaned from that text. Second, Van der Kooij asks whether the stories of Tamar and Dinah reflect "less" of a patriarchal structure than other biblical passages, that is, whether the developmental model Kottsieper presents for biblical families, from the historically more egalitarian to the more patriarchal in Hellenistic times, is valid. Third, the idea that the Jewish father, from the Hellenistic period onwards, assumes the decisive role in Jewish families deserves further consideration.

In "Hebrew Names, Personal Names, Family Names, and Nicknames of Jews in the Second Temple Period", Rachel Hachlili investigates names found on ossuaries and funerary inscriptions. In the Second Temple period papponymy (naming after a grandfather) and patronymy (naming after a father) were more common than matronymy (naming after a mother). This practice resulted in well defined (if somewhat relationally obscure) family units, with recurrent names across generations of the same family unit. The recurrence of names made nicknames necessary. Such nicknames reflected social standing in and outside the relevant family, milieu and sometimes occupation. Lack of names, such as in inscriptions of the type 'X and his wife', or the relational manner of designating women as 'wife of' and 'daughter of', also reflect

family hierarchy with regards to women. In short, the onomasticon
is a rich non-literary source for studying Jewish family structures,
relations and the management of economic resources. Hachlili's
essay is a case study of what can and should be gleaned from
such a source for families and Jewish and non-Jewish antiquity.[14]
We hope that more case studies can be done, so that eventually
our knowledge from the side of names helps us to understand in
what ways families operated.

Gerard Mussies responds, in "Source, Material and Percen-
tages", by drawing attention to the fact that, by comparison with
non-Jewish funerary corpora of names, Hachlili's Jewish corpus is
statistically rather small. Hence, findings based on this case study
might be misleading. Frequencies of name appearance and the
conclusions drawn from them, especially where women's names
are concerned, are the result of omission (of literary and other,
frequently occurring names) as well as inclusion (of names from
the relatively limited corpus of Jewish funerary names). The issue
of representability and data analysis is foremost in Mussies' critique, with the implication that, until the methodological issues
are settled, not much can be gleaned from Jewish names of the
Second Temple period for the study of any social issue, including
the issue of families.

In "Domesticity and the Spindle", Miriam Peskowitz[15] writes
about the material and economic relations in families after the
fall of the Second Jerusalem Temple, as imagined by the rabbis
– especially about the relations between [married] "women, labor
and home", often conceived of unquestioningly as matters of rou-
tine and essential natural categories. In Proverbs 31:10-31 there
is an image of a "woman of worth", an economically independent

---

[14]See also P.W. van der Horst, *Ancient Jewish Epitaphs: An Introductory
Survey of a Millennium of Jewish Funerary Epigraphy (300 BCE – 700 CE)*,
Kampen 1991.

[15]This is the only essay that is not an original publication. It is based
on Chapter 4 (pp. 95-108, 195-9) in Miriam Peskowitz, *Spinning Fantasies: Rabbis, Gender, and History*, Berkeley: University of California Press,
Copyright ©1997 The Regents of the University of California. Reprinted by
permission.

woman who uses her labour capabilities – especially insofar as textile production is concerned – to advance her family's welfare. Peskowitz traces the limits put on a married woman's economic independence by the rabbis, in Roman times, through an analysis of *Mishnah Ketubot*, chapter 5. She maintains that in rabbinic attitudes as exemplified in the *Mishnah* the traditional female occupation of wool-work underwent a shift, from indicating economic activity to acquiring the symbolic value of a woman's duty to her husband and acquiescence to his authority. Thus the spindle became an icon of the shift sought for regulating a married woman's domestic tasks, viewed by the rabbis less for their labour contents and more for their symbolic gender hierarchy value. In other words, the category of 'female domesticity' is fluid and unstable, rather than an essential constant.

In "Unraveling the Rabbis' Web", Lieve Teugels first summarizes Peskowitz's main points then makes comments about several issues: the analysis of rabbinic texts, Jewish attitudes from Roman times to their biblical legacy, the methodological problem of comparing a song of praise (Proverbs 31:10-31) to a halachic text (Mishnah Ketubot 5), Peskowitz's interpretation of Proverbs 31:10-31 itself, and her tendency, as perceived, to attribute the diminishing status of women to Rome as a scapegoat.

The second group (Part II), two pairs of essays and responses, presents "Some Cases of Early Christianities: New Testament Images". In " 'Keeping it in the Family': Culture, Kinship and Identity in 1 Thessalonians and Galatians", Philip Esler discusses 'families' within specific NT contexts against the wider context of Mediterranean family concepts, especially the concept of honour/shame. In group-oriented societies, honour/shame of an individual blood kin is shared collectively by the 'family' such an individual belongs to. A certain pattern of challenge and response exists. Following Malina, Esler distinguishes three degrees of group dishonour categories, and adds the issue of social 'limited good' to them. These features of Mediterranean culture apply, *inter alia*, also to the particular audience of Christ followers Paul addresses in 1 Thessalonians and in Galatians. When Tajfel's 'social identity theory' (social identity – cognitive, evaluative, emotional – is group-bound and group-motivated) is added, the question can be asked: how did Paul set out to create an identity for the specified congregations? Esler continues by exploring the language of kinship, metaphorical and fictive kinship in the Pauline texts – such as father, father-child and sibling imagery – and the aims that such language serves. Finally, Esler discusses the implications of his analysis for today's world.

In "The Family is Not All that Matters: A Response", Jan Willem van Henten critiques certain points in Esler's rich essay. His main criticisms are methodological. Does Esler take seriously notions of 'families', plurality, or does he remain – when all is said and done – with orthodox notions of structural Mediterranean family concepts, constant and unchanging, which he applies to the NT texts and the communities they refer to? What should be the space assigned to living accommodation? What is the significance of using kinship as against fictive kinship language? Van Henten then turns to 1 Thessalonians and Galatians in order to examine what means other than 'family' or 'kinship' notions are used, in these Pauline discourses, to establish group identity.

In "The Women in John: On Gender and Gender Bending", Sjef van Tilborg reads fully-fledged female characters in John on two levels: the text-continuum level and the story-construct level. In so doing, he wishes to understand better how Johannine woman characters – Jesus' mother, Martha and Mary, the Samaritan woman – that are often defined by relational kinship/family terms, show a mixture of dependence and independence. Van Tilborg anchors his reading in literary theories of characterization, historical considerations and feminist criticism. He reads John as a text indicating Jesus' attempt to create his own *oikos*, in which woman characters enjoy better status, and the Johannine text as potentially having an emancipatory value for woman readers. In other words, Van Tilborg opts for viewing John as having gender-bender features although he agrees that, ultimately, familiar patterns of prioritizing male characters are reverted to at the text's end.

Reimund Bieringer's response to Van Tilborg, "The Johannine Women and the Social Code of their Time", is the final essay in this volume. Bieringer classifies Van Tilborg's systems of reference for defining gender behaviour under three headings: characterization and plot; male and female virtues, especially courage and temperance; and spheres of life. After summarizing Van Tilborg's views, Bieringer critiques him on all three counts. On character and plot, Bicringer would like to have seen a comparative study of male and female contributions to the plot. On virtues, he takes exception to Van Tilborg's comparative usage of extra-biblical Hellenistic texts, claiming that a comparative method here might add little to the understanding of the Johannine text itself. On the ideology of life spheres, although Bieringer finds Van Tilborg's observations "stimulating", he raises again the issue of presuming that Hellenistic ideologies about public and domestic spheres are at the basis of biblical texts.

And we end, together with Bieringer, on this cautionary note. The Bible gives us only a glimpse of how communities organized their domestic (and public) spheres of life. The texts that have come down to us are *not* representative of actual 'families' of antiquity. The texts may be canonical or extra-canonical, literary sources or inscriptions or material remains, Christian or Jewish or Judeo-Christian. Be the texts we read for 'families' what they may, they dish up to us *virtual* families only. While trying to deconstruct these virtualities and coax them back into some kind of reality we can comprehend, we would do well to remember that our attempts, like those of our predecessors, are bound up with ideologies that are time-, status- and place-bound.

Part I

Some Cases of Early Judaisms: From Prophetic Books to Inscriptions

The Metaphor of Marriage in Early Judaism

Michael L. Satlow   (Indiana University)

Metaphors matter. On an individual level, we tend to describe the unknown in terms of the known; we use metaphor to construct meaning. On a communal level, we use metaphors for a wide variety of social purposes. In antiquity, for example, Page DuBois has brilliantly shown how Greek comparisons of a woman to a fertile field reflect and reinforce social values.[1] Similarly, Romans in the time of Augustus began to describe marriage in terms of civic relationships, and vice-versa, hence subtly altering the way in which both institutions were understood.

In theological writings, these two functions of metaphor frequently converge. On the one hand, metaphor is used to describe that which is by definition unknowable, the divine. The Hebrew Bible, for example, uses a rich variety of metaphors to describe God.[2] On the other hand, the metaphors that theological writers use must make sense in their contemporary context, both social and wider theological. The biblical metaphor that compares God to a king today rings flat, but not as flat as the comparison of God to a president would have rung to the Hebrews.

Because metaphors, by their nature, are socially contextual, the study of how these metaphors develop within a given culture or tradition presents a unique opportunity to the cultural historian. Early Judaism and Christianity inherited the biblical metaphors. These communities then made decisions, whether conscious or not, about what to do with them. Sometimes the metaphors made sense as they were; sometimes they made no sense and had to be ignored; more frequently these metaphors were brought

---

[1]Page Dubois, *Sowing the Body: Psychoanalysis and Ancient Representations of Women*, Chicago 1988.

[2]See Marc Z. Brettler, *God as King: Understanding an Israelite Metaphor*, Sheffield 1989.

into line with contemporary understandings. Almost a century ago, Ignaz Ziegler demonstrated that rabbinic "king parables" that compare God to a king reflect a contemporary setting within the Roman empire to a far greater extent than they do biblical monarchical institutions.[3]

This article is a short study of a different biblical metaphor, that of marriage. In the Hebrew Bible, the metaphor of God as the husband or lover of Israel or Zion occurs not infrequently. After briefly reviewing the biblical use of the metaphor, I will trace its reception among Jews in antiquity. My argument is that Jews in antiquity by and large ignored, or even subverted, the biblical metaphor that compares the relationship of God to Israel as a husband to wife. They did so both because the metaphor made little sense to them in their own social contexts, and because it clashed with several of their other theological commitments.

1   The Biblical Background

Hosea was the first biblical prophet to have explicitly and systematically compared human marriage to the relationship between God and Israel. God commands Hosea to marry a prostitute, bear children with her, and then send her away, thus reenacting the tumultuous relationship between God and Israel: God "married" Israel by means of the covenant, Israel was unfaithful to this covenant by means of her "whoring", and God sent her away. In later, happier, days, God will return to His people, "And in that day, declares the Lord, you will call [Me] Ishi, and no more will you call me Baali" (Hos. 2:18). The verse is a beautiful pun, for the word 'Baal' can mean the (false) god Baal, husband, and master. Not only does it imply that Israel will abandon Baal for the true God, but also that Israel and God will live in a kind of marital intimacy in which God is no longer her 'master'.[4] Isaiah 62:5, probably penned some two centuries

---

[3]Ignaz Ziegler, *Die Königsgleichnisse des Midrasch Beleuchtet durch die Römische Kaiserzeit*, Breslau 1903.

[4]For a less optimistic reading of this story, see Naomi Graetz, "God is to Israel as Husband is to Wife: The Metaphoric Battering of Hosea's Wife",

later, implies a similar intimacy: "As a bridegroom rejoices over his bride, so will your God rejoice over you".[5] By comparing the covenant to marriage, these prophets are suggesting that the covenant between God and Israel is intimate and reciprocal. The image of a 'whoring' Israel with which Hosea begins is also found in Ezek. 16, which describes such straying in almost pornographic detail.[6] Several of the other prophets also either mention or allude to the 'marriage' between God and Israel.[7]

While Hosea is the first to use this metaphor explicitly, it might also be lurking in the background of the earlier Pentateuchal sources. Gerson Cohen has argued that the prophets did not invent the description of the relationship between God and Israel as a marriage, "they had inherited it from more ancient circles of popular and priestly monotheism".[8] For support, Cohen points to the Pentateuch's description of God as 'jealous', a technical term applied also to a human husband; the Pentateuchal use of the metaphor of Israel 'whoring' after other gods; and the flowering of this sentiment, in his view, in Canticles.[9] Even if Cohen is not correct that the authors of the Pentateuchal passages to which he refers understood the relationship between God and Israel as a marriage, he has demonstrated that a reader – modern or ancient – who approaches the Hebrew Bible looking for the marriage metaphor will not be disappointed.

Despite the clear, if scattered, references to this metaphor

---

in: A. Brenner (ed.), *A Feminist Companion to the Latter Prophets*, Sheffield 1995, 126-45.

[5]The referrant of the "you" is not entirely clear. It appears to be Zion, but the previous verse refers to "your land" which implies that Israel is being addressed.

[6]Cf. Athalya Brenner, *The Intercourse of Knowledge: On Gendering Desire and 'Sexuality' in the Hebrew Bible*, Leiden 1997, 153-74.

[7]See, for examples, Amos 3:2, 5:2; Isa. 61:10; Jer. 2:20-25, 3:1-13; Mal. 2:14. Cf. G.P. Hugenberger, *Marriage as a Covenant: A Study of Biblical Law and Ethics Governing Marriage Developed from the Perspective of Malachi*, Leiden 1994, 280-338.

[8]Gerson D. Cohen, "The Song of Songs and the Jewish Religious Mentality", in: *The Samuel Friedland Lectures 1960-1966*, New York 1966, 1-21.

[9]*Ibid.*, 4-8, 13-15. For a theological interpretation of the biblical metaphor of 'whoredom', see R.C. Ortlund, *Whoredom: God's Unfaithful Wife in Biblical Theology*, Grand Rapids 1996, 15-136.

throughout the Bible, two qualifications should be noted. First, the marital metaphor is by no means the only or even most common way of describing the relationship between God and Israel. The Bible far more commonly describes God as king, among other things, than it does as husband.[10] Second, it is very difficult to ascertain if the marital metaphor was 'live' during the post-exilic period. That is, did the post-exilic Jewish communities themselves use the older biblical metaphor? Most, if not all, of the post-exilic writings completely ignore the metaphor; only Malachi might allude to it, but he more explicitly portrays the relationship between God and Israel as father-son.[11]

Before following the later trajectory of this metaphor, it is worth considering its practical implications. Human marriage should, at least to some extent, mirror the ideal of the relationship between God and Israel. A husband should be to God as his wife is to Israel. As the relationship between God and Israel is covenantal, specifying mutual obligations, so too should human marriage be reciprocal. But within this reciprocal relationship, the male partner (God or the husband) holds the upper hand. As God has the right to take as many nations as He desires as partners, so too should the human husband. And as Israel has no right to 'whore' after other men, so too should a human wife be forbidden from adultery. Because the relationship is mutual, either partner should have the right to divorce. Biblical law appears to confirm all of these implications.[12]

---

[10] Cf. Brettler, *God as King*.

[11] Mal. 2:14 refers to Israel's betrayal of "the wife of your youth ... your covenanted spouse". This might refer to God. But at Mal. 3:17 God refers to His coming kindness to Israel as a father toward a favored son. Deutero-Isaiah, as noted above, does compare the marriage of God and Israel to a married couple.

[12] Husband's obligations to his wife: Exod. 21:2-10; a woman's sexual fidelity: Exod. 20:14, Num. 5:11-31, Deut. 22:22; polygyny: Deut. 21:15. It is unclear whether a woman was, in biblical law, entitled to initiate divorce, although it seems likely. See Deut. 24:1; Yair Zakovitch, "The Woman's Rights in the Biblical Law of Divorce", *Jewish Law Annual* 4 (1981), 28-46; and David Instone Brewer, "Deuteronomy 24:1-4 and the Origin of the Jewish Divorce Certificate", *JJS* 49 (1998), 230-43, who argues that the purpose of

From a theological perspective, this metaphor contains three potential problems. First, it gives to God the right of divorce. What is to prevent God from sending away His covenanted spouse, Israel? Second, it gives God the right to take other nations as 'co-wives'. Within the strict confines of this metaphor Israel cannot be guaranteed a permanant place as God's first love. Finally, it implies a degree of intimacy between God and Israel that is not always compatible with an asexual and transcendent understanding of God. If Malachi 2:16 really does mean that God detests divorce, then it would reflect some awareness of the theological flaw of the marital metaphor by this late prophet.[13] The prophet wants to preserve the legal possibility of human divorce, but to voice the uneasiness with which this possibility coexists with the metaphor of God and Israel as a married couple. A more consistent way to preserve this marital metaphor would be to eliminate the possibility of human divorce, a strategy, as we will see below, adopted by some later Jewish groups.

2   Jewish Writing in the Second Temple Period

Among Jews writing in Greek, the description of the relationship between God and Israel as a marriage was stunningly uninfluential. With the exception of Paul (discussed below), no Jew writing in Greek uses this metaphor. These same writers do use marriage as a metaphor, but as one that describes other things. Jewish

---

the biblical divorce certificate was to abrogate a man's right to later reclaim his wife – the implication is that the divorce document itself did not affect the divorce.

[13]The meaning of Mal. 2:16 is highly contested. For a recent review of the question, see J. J. Collins, "Marriage, Divorce, and Family in Second Temple Judaism", in: L. Perdue (ed.), *Families in Ancient Israel*, Louisville 1997, 125-6, who states that "Malachi clearly intended to condemn divorce". But cf. A.S. van der Woude, "Malachi's Struggle for a Pure Community: Reflections on Malachi 2:10-16", in: J.W. van Henten (ed.), *Tradition and Reinterpretation in Jewish and Early Christian Literature: Essays in Honour of Jürgen C. H. Lebram*, Leiden 1986, 65-71, who contends that "Mal 2:10-16 does not deal with divorce at all" (66, original emphasis), and translates Mal. 2:16: "for he who neglects (his Jewish wife) puts forth his hand (in hostility)" (71).

Greek writers, for example, compare the relationship between an individual and Wisdom in erotic terms. Solomon's desire in Wis. (8:2-16) to make the personified Wisdom his mistress, with its manifest erotic overtones, goes far beyond the portrayal of Lady Wisdom in Proverbs 8. One of Philo's favorite metaphors is the description of the 'marriage' of one's soul to wisdom (*sophia*) or reason (*logos*).[14] The image in both Wis. and Philo relies more on Greek classical and philosophical precedents than on the biblical metaphor of covenant as marriage.[15]

An intriguing, and enigmatic, use of a marital metaphor occurs in the pseudepigraphical work Joseph and Aseneth. Putatively, this is a Greek expansion of the bald report in Gen. 41:45: "Pharaoh then gave Joseph the name Zaphenath-paneah; and he gave him for a wife Aseneth daughter of Poti-phera, priest of On". Jos. Asen. begins with the pagan heroine holding herself as superior to all men. This changes when she sees the magnificently handsome Joseph, who in turn scorns her: "It is not fitting for a man who worships God ... to kiss a strange woman who will bless with her mouth dead and dumb idols...".[16] Crushed by this rebuke, Aseneth begins a period of repentance and contrition, which culminates with her encounter with a heavenly being who transforms her, renaming her "City of Refuge, because in you many nations will take refuge with the Lord God, the Most High, and under your wings many peoples trusting in the Lord God will be sheltered, and behind your walls will be guarded those who attach

---

[14]See Philo, *Poster. C.* 78 (making *sophia* a spouse); *Congr.* 5-9 (acquiring culture is preliminary to the full marriage of the acquisition of virtue), 41, 59 (soul is the legitimate wife); *Fug.* 52 (God begats wisdom, to whom Jacob goes for a bride); *Somn.* 1.198-200 ('marriage' of different kinds of thoughts, gives good wise 'offspring', with a similar image at *Abr.* 100-1, where the union is between virtue and thought), 2.234 (wisdom is spouse); *Spec. Leg.* 2.30 (mind 'wedded' to *logos*); *Vit. Cont.* 68 (women remained virgins to 'wed' *sophia*). Cf. R.A. Horsley, "Spiritual Marriage with Sophia", *VC* 33 (1979), 30-54.

[15]Cf. D. Winston, *The Wisdom of Solomon: A New Translation with Introduction and Commentary*, Garden City 1979, 193-4.

[16]Jos. Asen. 8:5, trans. in: J. Charlesworth (ed.), *The Old Testament Pseudepigrapha*, vol. 2, Garden City 1983, 208.

themselves to the Most High God in the Name of Repentance".[17] The heavenly being informs Joseph of her transformation, and on Joseph's insistence, Pharaoh marries them, putting golden crowns on their heads and blessing them before he "turned them around toward each other face to face and brought them mouth to mouth and joined them by their lips, and they kissed each other".[18] The book then continues with only a vaguely related adventure story in which Pharaoh's son seeks to kidnap Aseneth for himself. Joseph is virtually absent from this part of the story.

Although the parallels between Jos. Asen. and Greek romance novels have been noted, the comparison should not be over-drawn.[19] Like all the Greek novels, Jos. Asen. begins with a chaste pair of lovers in a distant past and ancient, mythical land (but who nevertheless display good Greek values) who, after circumventing several intervening obstacles, eventually marry.[20] Jos. Asen. and the Greek romance novels share "the elite status of the lovers; their mutual chastity; their extraordinary beauty; their virtual identification with the gods; the role of the divine in ordaining the marriage; the relatively egalitarian quality of the marriage; and the linkages of death, initiation, and marriage...".[21] But whereas the Greek novels focus on the couple's ability to remain true to

---

[17]Jos. Asen. 15:7, trans. in: Charlesworth (ed.), *The Old Testament Pseudepigrapha*, vol. 2, 226; 15:6 in short version.

[18]Jos. Asen. 21:7, trans. in: Charlesworth (ed.), *The Old Testament Pseudepigrapha*, vol. 2, 235. The account is less elaborate in the short version (21:5).

[19]Cf. C. Hezser, "'Joseph and Aseneth' in the Context of Ancient Greek Erotic Novels", *FJB* 19 (1997), 1-40; R.S. Kraemer, *When Aseneth Met Joseph: A Late Antique Tale of the Biblical Patriarch and His Egyptian Wife, Reconsidered*, New York 1998, 9-11, 191-221. L.M. Wills, *The Jewish Novel in the Ancient World*, Ithaca 1995, 170-84 posits that Jos. Asen. is a combination of two distinct story lines, a love-adventure romance (that itself has at some point been spiritualized) and an allegorical story of conversion. The former story-line would resemble Greek romance novels more closely than the finished product.

[20]The Greek novels are marked by an emphasis on symmetrical erotic love. Cf. D. Konstan, *Sexual Symmetry: Love in the Ancient Novel and Related Genres*, Princeton 1994. Note that in Jos. Asen. only the heroine is stricken by love.

[21]Kraemer, *When Aseneth Met Joseph*, 201.

each other in the face of many external trials, the first part of
Jos. Asen. contains no external obstacles. Aseneth must surmount
only her own haughtiness and paganism, and ultimately requires
an angelic being to complete her transformation.[22]

An evaluation of the degree of similarity between Jos. Asen.
and the Greek romance novels is important for the interpretation
of the story. For our purposes, it is clear that the marriage of Aseneth and Joseph in this story is a metaphor. It is, however, not at
all clear what it is a metaphor for. Judith Perkins has recently argued that the erotic attachments and marriages within the Greek
romance novels are images for the relationship of the citizen to
his *polis* and class. By remaining faithful to each other despite
the attempts of others to 'penetrate' them, the lovers in these
novels symbolize the impenetrability of their social class. The
Greek romance, according to Perkins, reinforces social and class
cohesiveness and boundaries.[23] Catherine Hezser has recently
extended this argument to Jos. Asen., arguing that Jos. Asen.
"serves to confirm the particular religious identity of Jews living
within such *poleis*. Unlike the social and civic boundaries which
are presented as impermeable, however, according to Joseph and
Aseneth the religious boundaries between Jews and non-Jews can
be crossed from the gentile to the Jewish side".[24]

Both of Hezser's claims are implausible. The group boundaries
in Jos. Asen. are fuzzy: remember that it is *Pharaoh*, at Joseph's
urging, who sanctifies the marriage.[25] Erich Gruen, in fact, sees
in this book a story of permeable boundaries between Jews and
Gentiles, a combination of tales of harmonious relations and an
ironic view of Joseph's own haughtiness.[26] It is difficult to imagine
the 'intended reader' of such a work in its supposed context (in

---

[22] Cf. Wills, *The Jewish Novel*, 172.

[23] Judith Perkins, *The Suffering Self: Pain and Narrative Representation in
the Early Christian Era*, London 1995, 41-76, *contra* Konstan, *Sexual Symmetry*.

[24] Hezser, " 'Joseph and Aseneth' ", 2.

[25] Cf. E.S. Gruen, *Heritage and Hellenism: The Reinvention of the Jewish
Tradition*, Berkeley 1998, 95: "The fact that the wedding of Joseph and Aseneth takes place under the auspices of Pharaoh, who had not himself become
a convert, holds central symbolic significance".

[26] Gruen, *Heritage and Hellenism*, 89-99.

this interpretation), urban Egypt around the turn of the millennium. Jos. Asen. is clearly directed at an aristocratic audience, and a message preaching impermeable social and civic boundaries would hardly have been welcomed by a Jewish aristocratic community fighting a very bitter and public battle to gain civic rights.[27] The claim that a central message of Jos. Asen. is the openness of Judaism to true converts has a long scholarly history, but remains problematic.[28] Aseneth requires an encounter with an angelic being to complete her transformation. Even if this work was intended to be read by non-Jews, the potential convert could hardly be encouraged by this requirement.

While acknowledging the parallels between Jos. Asen. and the Greek romance novels, Ross Kraemer works from a radically different point of departure. She tends to see Jos. Asen. not as a Jewish work from Egypt produced sometime from the first century BCE to the second century CE, but as a Christian work written in (perhaps) third century CE Syria.[29] In this context, the marriage of Joseph and Aseneth represents the marriage of Christ and the Church. This interpretation nicely explains the use of marriage in this work: it both takes seriously Aseneth's new name as 'City of Refuge' and contextualizes well with Paul's use of this metaphor (see below). It is still unclear, however, whether Jos. Asen. can truly be seen as an entirely Christian composition. Following Larry Wills' suggestion, it is possible that the original 'love-adventure story' was Jewish, with a Christian allegorical addition.[30]

I have dwelt on Jos. Asen. because it contains the most

---

[27] Cf. V. Tcherikover, *The Jews in Egypt in the Hellenistic-Roman Age in the Light of the Papyri*, Jerusalem [2]1963, 116-59 (in Hebrew); Joseph Mélèze Modrzejewski, *The Jews of Egypt from Rameses II to Emperor Hadrian*, Philadelphia 1995, 161-83.

[28] Cf. V. Tcherikover, "Jewish Apologetical Literature Reconsidered", *Eos* 48 (1957), 169-93. Randall D. Chesnutt, *From Death to Life: Conversion in Joseph and Aseneth*, Sheffield 1995, 153-253 adheres to this traditional view of Jos. Asen.

[29] Kraemer, *When Aseneth Met Joseph*, 205, 253-72.

[30] Wills, *The Jewish Novel*, 184.

developed use of a marital metaphor of any Jewish literature
written in Greek, if it is indeed Jewish. The very centrality of
the metaphor, and its uniqueness when seen against other
Greek-Jewish literature, could support Kraemer's argument that
Jos. Asen. is essentially a Christian composition. However, if it is
Jewish, then whatever the meaning of this marital metaphor, it is
not a description of the relationship between Israel and God. Nor
does it appear to be a metaphor for civic and social harmony, as in
the Greek romance novels. When seen in a Jewish context, in fact,
the metaphor is so obscure that one wonders if an ancient Jewish
reader would not have been as perplexed at its interpretation as
the modern scholar.

Why did this biblical metaphor comparing the relationship
between God and Israel as a marriage fare so poorly? Four factors,
I believe, played a role in the rejection of this metaphor by Greek
speaking Jews in the Hellenistic and early Roman periods.

First, the biblical marital metaphor is at odds with the ideological understanding by these Jews of the purpose of marriage
as formation of an *oikos*. An understanding of marriage as patterned after or related to the relationship between God and Israel
would privilege the relationship of husband and wife over other
kinship relations. An *oikos* ideology, however, privileges the relationship of parents and children as primary.[31] Adoption of the biblical marriage metaphor would not have fit well into this valued
hierarchy of kinship relations. Nor would it fit well into a funda-
mentally androcentric understanding of marriage. Understanding
marriage as a covenant, with reciprocal obligations, would have
been too egalitarian for the comfort of most Greek men.[32]

---

[31] See the surveys of O.L. Yarbrough, "Parents and Children in the Jewish
Family of Antiquity", in: S.J.D. Cohen (ed.), *The Jewish Family in Antiquity*,
Atlanta 1993, 39-59 and A. Reinhartz, "Parents and Children: A Philonic
Perspective", in: *ibid.*, 61-88. Neither author directly compares parent - child
relationships to marital ones, but the evidence they cite does indicate a clear
valuation.

[32] Even Paul, who preached that "there is no longer male and female, for all
of you are one in Christ Jesus" (Gal. 3:28) does not abandon the traditional
understanding that "[man] is the image and reflection of God; but woman
is the reflection of man... For this reason a woman ought to have a symbol

A second reason why Jewish Hellenistic authors might have abandoned the biblical metaphor of covenant as marriage was that at least one large part of this metaphor would have been incomprehensible to them. Biblical texts draw a certain correspondence or equivalency between human fornication and abandonment of God. To fornicate is to act out, even participate in, idolatry. Post-biblical Jewish writers do not share this understanding. For them, the problem with human fornication was that it demonstrated a lack of control, which would in turn lead down the slippery slope to idolatry.[33] With this conceptual shift, the image of 'whoring' after other gods ceases to make much sense. Although he did not write in Greek (despite being thoroughly Hellenized) Ben Sira provides a nice example of this conceptual shift. At 26:10(11)-12(14) he writes in uncomfortable detail of the adulterous wife. Although he uses different metaphors, Ben Sira evokes Ezek. 16:25. Yet whereas Ezekiel only uses such language to denote Israel's betrayal of God, Ben Sira refers literally to an adulterous woman. Ben Sira, that is, uses the biblical images of a 'whoring' Israel as referring to the activities of human women while avoiding any hint of the biblical metaphor. He has totally leveled the metaphor, probably because it made little sense to him.

The third reason why Jewish-Greek authors might have rejected the biblical marital metaphor is that it presents God and Israel in too intimate a bond. The marriage-covenant metaphor implies a sexual intimacy with God that would have made these authors uncomfortable. The tendency of the Greek translators of the Hebrew Bible to expunge anthropomorphic images of God is well-known; the image of God and Israel making love would have seemed scandalous.[34] Whatever Philo's true opinion of the

---

of authority on her head..." (1 Cor. 11:7, 10). Paul appears to realize his contradictory position in the continuation of this passage, but hardly solves it. Cf. Eph. 5:22-24.

[33] See M. Satlow, "'Try To Be A Man' : The Rabbinic Construction of Masculinity", *HTR* 89 (1996), 19-40.

[34] For some examples, see the discussion of A.T. Hanson, "The Treatment in the LXX of the Theme of Seeing God", in: George J. Brooke and Barnabas Lindars (eds.), *Septuagint, Scrolls and Cognate Writings*, Atlanta 1992, 557-68. It is important to note that while the Septuagint *tends* to euphemize anthropomorphisms, it does not do so in every case. Cf. Sidney

nature of 'wisdom' or 'reason', even if he views it as an emana-
tion of God, Philo can far more easily use marital imagery when
describing their relationships to the human soul or mind.[35] The
Aramaic translations of the Bible (the *targum*) evince an even
stronger discomfort with the marital metaphor. Perhaps composed in Palestine in the decades or century immediately after 70
CE, the Aramaic translation of Hosea completely obliterates its
key metaphor.[36] Hence, the *targum* translates Hos. 2:18 as "And
at that time, says the Lord, you shall eagerly follow my worship,
and no more shall you worship idols".[37]

Finally, the social condition of the Jews may have played
a factor in the cold reception given to Jewish use of the metaphor. As noted, beginning around the turn of the millennium
both Romans and Greeks began to use marriage as a metaphor
for social relations. The Romans mapped ideals of harmony and
concord within the Empire onto marital relationships. Greek romance novels, at least on one level, use marriage to reinforce social
relationships between members of the aristocracy and the *polis*
and to increase aristocratic group cohesion. Most Jewish communities in *poleis* at this time, though, had a marginal and often
strained relationship with the host *polis*.[38] The metaphor would

---

Jellicoe, *The Septuagint and Modern Study*, Oxford 1968, 270-1. The Greek
translation of Hos. 2, for example, preserves the marital metaphor. Later
Greek translations and the Aramaic *targumim* more consistently eliminate
anthropomorphisms. See C. McCarthy, "The Treatment of Biblical Anthropomorphisms in Pentateuchal Targums", in: Kevin J. Cathcart, John F. Healey
(eds.), *Back to the Sources: Biblical and Near Eastern Studies in Honour of
Dermot Ryan*, Dublin 1989, 45-66.

[35] On Philo's understanding of the ontology of 'reason' see H.A. Wolfson,
*Philo: Foundations of Religious Philosophy in Judaism, Christianity, and
Islam*, vol. 1, Cambridge 1968, 200-94.

[36] See K.J. Cathcart, R.P. Gordon (eds.), *The Targum of the Minor
Prophets*, Wilmington 1989, 1-18 for a discussion of the characteristics and
provenance of the Targum to the minor prophets. But cf. E. Schürer, *History
of the Jewish People*, vol. 1, Edinburgh 1973, 101-2, which suggests a later
date.

[37] Translation in: Cathcart, Gordon (eds.), *The Targum of the Minor
Prophets*, 34. Text in: A. Sperber (ed.), *The Latter Prophets According to
Targum Jonathan*, vol. 3, Leiden 1962, 389.

[38] On Jewish communal organization and its relation to the *polis*, see E.

have fallen flat to Jews who were on the margins of the *polis* and
the Empire. The rejection of the metaphor on this ground may
then have led to a wider discomfort with applying it in any context
outside of the individual's relationship to knowledge or wisdom.

Comparison with one contemporary Jewish group that did
compare the relationship of God to His people to a marriage highlights the choices made by these more 'mainstream' authors. The
early Christians explicitly employed this metaphor, and as a sec-
tarian group believing itself to be on the cusp of the end of time,
had the luxury of dictating human marital practices that accorded
with their use of the theological metaphor.

Early Christians explicitly compared God's (or Christ's) relationship to the church with a human marriage. Jesus apparently
compared himself to the "bridegroom", and his disciples to the
"bride".[39] Paul appropriates this metaphor to much greater
effect. In 1 Cor. 6:15-17 Paul asserts that Christ is in everyone.[40]
He then goes on with an appeal to Gen. 2:24 that sex (or by ex-
tension, marriage) is the making of one flesh. Ergo, sex with a
prostitute is equivalent to uniting Christ with a prostitute. Elsewhere Paul asserts to the Corinthians that he "betrothed you to
Christ, thinking to present you as a chaste virgin to her true and
only husband" (2 Cor. 11:2).[41] In Romans, Paul develops a somewhat obscure marital analogy in which the only thing that really
is clear is that the Christian believer is "now" married to Christ.[42]

Schürer, *The History of the Jewish People in the Age of Jesus Christ*, vol.
3/1, Edinburgh 1986, 87-137.

[39]Mt. 22:1-14; Mk 2:19-20. Lk. 14:16-24 parallels Mt. 22:1-14, but the setting is not a wedding. Jn 3:27-30 puts the comparison in the mouth of John
the Baptist.

[40]Cf. Rom. 7:2-4 and J.D. Earnshaw, "Reconsidering Paul's Marriage Analogy in Romans 7.1-4", *NTS* 40 (1994), 68-88; R.M. Grant, "The Mystery of
Marriage in the Gospel of Philip", *VC* 15 (1961), 129-40.

[41]Probably a better translation would be '*married* you'. Greek legal sources
occasionally use this same verb (*armozo*) to denote marriage generally. Cf.
P. Oxy. 906, line 7.

[42]Rom. 7:1-4. Earnshaw, "Reconsidering Paul's Marriage Analogy", 68-
71 succinctly summarizes the interpretive problems of the analogy; his own
exegetical solution, though, is not entirely convincing. Note that in no reading
of Rom. 7:1-4 is Israel (or the singular Jew) said to have been married to God,

The perhaps pseudo-Pauline letter to the Ephesians (5:25-32) further develops this concept:

> Husbands, love your wives, as Christ loved the church and gave himself up for it, to consecrate and cleanse it by water and word, so that he might present the church to himself all glorious, with no stain or wrinkle or anything of the sort, but holy and without blemish. In the same way men ought to love their wives, as they love their own bodies. In loving his wife a man loves himself. For no one ever hated his own body; on the contrary, he keeps it nourished and warm, and that is how Christ treats the church, because it is his body of which we are living parts. 'This is why' (in the words of scripture) 'a man shall leave his father and mother and be united to his wife, and the two shall become one flesh' [Gen. 2:24]. There is hidden here a great truth, which I take to refer to Christ and the church.

Here human marriage, and conduct within marriage, is directly linked the metaphor of Christ's relationship to the church. A man should treat his wife as Christ treats the church. Moreover, human marriage itself is a "great truth", a "mystery" (as the Greek literally reads) patterned after the marriage of Christ and his church.[43]

Early Christian writers advocated marital practices that concord with this metaphor. As mentioned, the comparison of the relationship of God and Israel – or the church in this case – has some potentially thorny ramifications on marital practices, primarily divorce. For the metaphor to work, it should obviate the possibility of divorce: should a couple be allowed to divorce, the logic of the metaphor leads to the possibility that God can divorce His people, a theological nightmare. It is significant, and in my view related to their use of the marital metaphor, that

---

but only to God's Law.

[43] Rev. 21:2, 9-10 develop the prophetic metaphor of the marriage of Christ and Jerusalem.

early Christians foreclosed this human possibility. Jesus, apparently, cited both Gen. 1:27 and 2:24 in his prohibition of divorce.[44] Paul too subscribes to this prohibition.[45] A second potential problem is that of polygyny – might God have more than one 'wife'? Although the New Testament never explicitly condemns human polygyny, it does appear to assume monogyny. Here again human marital practice is brought into line with a theological metaphor.[46]

Just as looking at the earliest Christian uses of this metaphor highlights its absence among contemporary Jewish writers, so too its adaptation by later Christian writers will highlight its relative absence from rabbinic sources. Writing in the late fourth century, for example, John Chrysostom says on Eph. 5:31,

> [Paul] is showing that the person who has left those who begot him and nourished him will be joined to his wife. Then the "one flesh" is the father, the mother, and the child that is conceived from their intercourse. For the child is formed when the seeds mingle together; in this way they are three in one flesh. Similarly, we become one flesh with Christ by participation, and in an even greater way than the human child.[47]

Chrysostom goes on to develop this analogy, that marriage is a reenactment of the divine drama in which Christ "left his Father

---

[44]Mt. 19:1-12; Mk 10:1-12. Matthew glosses this prohibition to allow for divorce in the case of female adultery, probably in order to bring Jesus' dictum into line with contemporary practice.

[45]Cf. 1 Cor. 7:10-11.

[46]This is not to deny that there were other factors also at work. The use of Gen. 1:27 and 2:24 in these justifications points to an argument from nature. Paul's assumption of monogyny is certainly conditioned by his working within monogamous gentile communities. Nevertheless, the congruence between the use of a marital metaphor to describe the relationship between Christ and the church and of complimentary marital practices (which contradict the marital practices of the Hebrew Bible) is significant. Augustine noted the problem of the absence of any explicit prohibition of polygamy in the New Testament; see *The Good of Marriage*, 20-22.

[47]John Chrysostom, *Hom. 20 on Ephesians* 4 (translation in: D. Hunter [ed.], *Marriage in the Early Church*, Minneapolis 1992, 83, with minor stylistic modifications).

and came down and took a bride and became one spirit with her".[48] About twenty years later, Paulinus of Nola used the image of the integration of a married couple into Christ's body in a Christian epithalamium (marriage poem): "... a wife must in all humility receive Christ within her spouse, so that she may be equal to the holiness of her husband. Thus she will grow into his holy body and be woven into his frame, that her husband may become her head, just as Christ is his".[49]

By the Byzantine period, the Christian use of the marital metaphor had spread beyond theological circles. According to Gary Vikan, the art on marital items (e.g. rings, belts) reflects a Christianization of Roman and Stoic marital iconography.[50] The intention of the iconography on these items was "to convey symbolically the single, simple message that this marriage was one sanctioned by Christ".[51] The iconography seems to me not only to convey the notion that marriage is a divine gift, but also to link marriage to the theological metaphor of the marriage of the Church and Christ. This art, although confined to the wealthy, demonstrates the appeal of the New Testament marital metaphor.

The Christian use of this metaphor highlights the lack of any equivalent metaphor, as we will see, in the classical rabbinic literature. At the same time, as we will also see, it might also inform the increasing Jewish use of this metaphor in Palestinian sources in the Byzantine period.

3 The Rabbinic Period

In all of tannaitic literature the metaphor of the relationship of God and Israel as a marriage appears very infrequently.[52] One

---

[48] *Ibid.*

[49] Paulinus of Nola, *Carmen* 25 (translation in: Hunter, *Marriage in the Early Church*, 35).

[50] Gary Vikan, "Art and Marriage in Early Byzantium", *Dumbarton Oaks Papers* 44 (1990), 145-63.

[51] *Ibid.*, 160.

[52] In addition, m. Ta'an. 4:8 (ed. H. Albeck, *The Mishnah*, vol. 2, Jerusalem and Tel-Aviv 1988, 345) has been seen as containing the metaphor in the form of a commentary on Cant. 3:11. The verse reads "his mother crowned him

tradition glancingly compares God coming from Sinai to a groom comes toward a bride.[53] A second midrash appears in the Tosefta, and asks about the difference between the two sets of tablets that Moses brought down from Sinai. According to the account in the Hebrew Bible, the first tablets were the work of God (Exod. 32:16), but the second tablets were made by Moses, although the writing was that of God (Exod. 34:1). The midrash illustrates this with a parable:

> To what is the matter similar? To a human king who betrothed a woman. He brings the scribe, the pen, the ink, the contract, and the witnesses. [But] if she sins, she brings everything, [and] it is enough that the king gives to her clear writing [i.e., his signature] [in] his own hand.[54]

When God gave the first tablets, He was like a man betrothing a woman. God arranged the entire betrothal ceremony. After Israel sinned with the golden calf, though, it was she who brought the betrothal contract to her groom, asking only that he sign it clearly. The midrash compares Israel to a woman who cheats on the man to whom she is about to be betrothed.[55] In the parable, God

---

[King Solomon] on his wedding day"; the midrash interprets "his wedding day" as referring to the day of the giving of the Torah. This midrash, however, is a late gloss. See H. Albeck, *The Mishnah*, vol. 2, 344-5, notes *ad loc.*

[53]Mek. *Yitro* 3 (ed. H.S. Horowitz, I.A. Rabin, *Mekilta d'Rabbi Ishmael*, Jerusalem 1970, 214). Cf. Mek. SbY to Exod. 19:17 (ed. J.N. Epstein, *Mekilta d'Rabbi Shimon b. Yohai*, Jerusalem n.d., 142-3). The midrash itself keys off Deut. 33:2, but is not found in the Sifre's commentary on this verse. Exod 19:17 says that Moses brought the people *toward* God. By using using Deut. 33:2 here, the *darshan* implies a certain reciprocity, generating the image of bride and groom approaching each other on their wedding day.

[54]t. B. Qam. 7:4 (ed. S. Lieberman, *The Tosefta*, vol. 4, New York 1955-88, 29).

[55]Note that a parallel at ARN, ver. B., ch. 2 (ed. S. Schechter, *Avot d'Rabbi Nathan*, Frankfurt 1888, 10-1) makes a different point. In that version, Moses deliberately breaks the tablets so that Israel should not sign them. If she did sign them and then continue to worship the calf, she would be liable for punishment as an adulteress.

is compared to the husband, Israel to the wife, the Torah is the contract, and Moses lurks in the background as the scribe. The use of this metaphor to illustrate Israel's past transgressions appears also in the Sifre Deuteronomy, and, as we shall see, is in many ways typical of the rabbinic use of the metaphor.[56]

Later rabbinic sources use the marital metaphor with only slightly greater frequency. Ofra Meir, surveying the monumental collection of 937 rabbinic king parables made by Ziegler, found only sixty that involve marriage.[57] Only ten of these parables both date from the talmudic period and compare the marriage of God and Israel to human marriage, and nearly all of these are from later Palestinian homiletical midrashic works. To my knowledge, the metaphor does not occur at all in the Palestinian Talmud.[58] Prior to the homiletical midrashic works, midrashim tend to use the marital metaphor to illustrate God marrying off a son or daughter rather than God actually marrying. *Genesis Rabbah*, for example, contains parables that identify either the world, the Sabbath, or humankind as the daughter (or son) that God is marrying off.[59] A *baraita* in the Babylonian Talmud also contains the latter

[56]See Sifre Deut. 306 (ed. L. Finkelstein, *Sifre on Deuteronomy*, New York 1969, 330). S.D. Fraade, *From Tradition to Commentary: Torah and Its Interpretation in the Midrash Sifre to Deuteronomy*, Albany 1991, 131-2 understands this midrash as expressing hope for the ultimate reconciliation between God and Israel, but the metaphor itself is used here only to illustrate the initial relationship between them. For the assertion that the midrash's denial that Israel and God are actually divorced is a response to Christian polemics, see R. Hammer, "A Rabbinic Response to the Post Bar Kochba Era: *Sifre Ha'azinu*", *PAAJR* 52 (1985), 37-53, and the bibliography in Fraade, *ibid.*, 267-8, n. 35.

[57]O. Meir, "Nose' ha-ḥatunah b'mishle hamalakim b'agadat ḥazal", in: I. Ben Ami, D. Noy (eds.), *Studies in Marriage Customs*, Jerusalem 1974, 9-51; Ignaz Ziegler, *Die Königsgleichnisse des Midrasch Beleuchtet durch die Römische Kaiserzeit*, Breslau 1903.

[58]See, for example, the metaphor of a king marrying his son at y. Soṭ. 1:10, 17c, which is not applied to the relationship of God and Israel.

[59]Gen. R. 9:4 (ed. Theodor, Albeck, *Midrash Bereshit Rabba*, Jerusalem 1965, 69), 10:9 (*ibid.*, 85); 28:6 (*ibid.*, 265). Traditions (apparently Palestinian) that associate the Sabbath with a bride are also found at b. Shab. 119a; b. B. Qam. 32b. Cf. N. Tuker, "Shabbat v'yisrael k'ḥatan v'kalah: Hashabbat k'brit ben H' l'yisrael v'kesreah l'inyane ḥatunah", *Mahut* 18

identification.[60] A few parables advance the metaphor that Israel 'married' God's daughter, Torah.[61] One tannaitic interpretation of Cant. 3:11 asserts that "Solomon's wedding day" refers to "the day that the *Shekina* dwelt in the Temple".[62]

In the very few places outside of the later homiletical works that the image of God's 'marriage' to Israel does appear, it is transformed. A midrash on Hos. 2:18, for example, changes the message of the intimacy of God and Israel in future days into a teaching about the conduct of a human couple; God has no part in this new teaching.[63] One *sugya* that contains this midrash then continues with a sustained analysis of the beginning of Hosea that radically changes the prophet's meaning. In Hos. 1:2 God commands Hosea to marry a prostitute who clearly represents Israel's unfaithfulness to God. The Babylonian Talmud presents a series of exegeses of her name (Gomer) that emphasize her promiscuity, but do so in a fashion that completely obliterates the fact that she represents Israel.[64] By emphasizing her *human* promiscuity this *sugya* also emphasizes Hosea's lot: he has sinned and is punished, in part, by having to marry a woman "who is as sweet in the mouth of all as a fig-cake".[65] The Babylonian Talmud's leveling of Hosea's marital metaphor is even clearer in the continuation. In Hosea, Hosea's divorce and remarriage of Gomer symbolizes God's relationship with Israel. The marital relationship is primary. When, in the midrash, God orders Hosea to divorce Gomer, the prophet responds:

(1989), 53-61.

[60]b. Sanh. 108a.

[61]See Lev. R. 20:10 (ed. M. Margulies, *Midrash Wayyikra Rabbah*, New York 1993, 468); Cant. R. 8:11. Sifre Deut. 343 (ed. Finkelstein, *Sifre on Deuteronomy*, 398) uses a parable of a man marrying off his son, who appears to represent Israel.

[62]Sifra *Shemini, petihta* 16 (ed. Weiss 44c).

[63]b. Ket. 71b; b. Pes. 87a (ascribed to Rabbi Yohanan).

[64]b. Pes. 87b. Cf. Sifre Deut. 270 (ed. Finkelstein, *Sifre on Deuteronomy*, 291), which offers a hyperliteral reading of Jer. 3:1, erasing the biblical metaphor.

[65]*Ibid.*, attributed to Shmuel.

"Master of the universe, I have children from her and I am able neither to send her away nor to divorce her". The Holy One said to him, "And you – whose wife is a prostitute and whose children are the children of whoring and you don't know if they are yours or of other men – [say this]; then Israel, My children, the children of my tested ones, the children of Abraham, Isaac, and Jacob, one of my four worldly possessions … and you say, 'Exchange them for a different people' ".[66]

The precise meaning of the passage is obscure, but its exegetical thrust could hardly be clearer.[67] God has become Israel's *father* rather than *husband*. Perhaps this accounts for the tortuous syntax of God's response. The analogy that the *darshan* wants to make, between Hosea being unable to send his wife away and God not wanting to send His children away, simply does not work very well. Thus he buried this lack of correspondence in a cumbersome sentence, hoping that his readers would not notice. In any case, Hosea's metaphor is completely transformed: Israel is the child, not the wife. In the first half of the metaphor (before this breaks down as well), Israel is child of adultery rather than the adulteress.

A second example of rabbinic sources subverting the metaphor of God's marriage to Israel is more complex. In a *sugya* that ends up discussing how disheartening it is for a man to lose his first wife we find the following four traditions:[68]

---

[66] *Ibid.*, According to MS Munich 95 Israel is one of *three* of God's possessions, a difference that is not relevant to this discussion.

[67] The meaning of the connective "and" in Hosea's protest is not clear: does it really mean "because" here, or does it indicate that there is a second reason that Hosea is unable to divorce her? Is Hosea unable or unwilling to divorce her? What is implied by using both clauses, "send her away" and "divorce her"?

[68] The progression that leads to this discussion is not entirely clear. The Talmud here apparently interprets the first part of the Mishnah, which prohibits a man from riding on a king's horse, sitting on his throne, or using his scepter euphemistically: what is the status of a woman "used" (but not

A. Rabbi Eleazar said, "Anyone who divorces his first wife, even the altar sheds tears for him as it is written, 'And this you do as well; You cover the altar of the Lord with tears, weeping, and moaning, so that He refuses to regard the oblation any more and to accept what you offer' [Mal. 3:13], and it is written, 'But you ask, "Because of what?" Because the Lord is a witness between you and the wife of your youth with whom you have broken faith, though she is your partner and covenanted spouse' [Mal. 2:14] ...".[69]

B. Rabbi Yoḥanan also said, "For any man whose first wife died while he was alive, it is as if the sanctuary was destroyed in his day, as it is said, 'O mortal, I am about to take away the delight of your eyes from you through pestilence; but you shall not lament or weep or let your tears flow' [Ezek. 24:16], and it is written, 'In the evening my wife died, and in the morning I did as I had been commanded' [Ezek. 24:18], and it is written, 'I am going to desecrate My Sanctuary, your pride and glory, the delight of your eyes...' [Ezek. 24:21] ...".

C. R. Shmuel bar Nahman said, "To everything there is a recompense, except the wife of one's youth, as it is said, '... Can one cast off the wife of his youth?' [Isa. 54:6] ...".

D. Rav Shmuel bar Onia said in the name of Rav, "A woman is a golem [i.e., unformed lump] and she only makes a covenant with the one that forms her [into a] vessel, as it is written, 'For He who made you [bo'alayik] will espouse you – His name is 'Lord of Hosts' ...' [Isa. 54:5].[70]

---

widowed, which is dealt with at m. Sanh. 2:1) by a king? The discussion then turns to Abishag and the suggestion that David would have married her had he not already reached his limit of eighteen wives. David is then said to have been forbidden to divorce one of his other wives to marry her. The reason behind this prohibition is never clarified, but it does lead into the passages here.

[69] This is paralleled at b. Giṭṭ. 90b.

[70] b. Sanh. 22a-b.

The first three traditions explicitly ground sorrow at the loss of a first wife in the metaphor between human marriage and the covenant between God and Israel.[71] Each of these traditions uses a different biblical base for its marital metaphor. (A) uses the metaphor found in Malachi; (B) the one found in Ezekiel; and (C) the one in Isaiah. Despite its prominence, the metaphor is not developed in these traditions. The traditions use the metaphor to illustrate the grief that a man might feel on losing his first wife, but they do not articulate any theological ramifications. That is, they do not understand this grief as stemming from a broken covenant. Nor do the rabbis understand from these verses that man should not divorce his wife, just as God would not divorce Israel. Covenant language becomes a convenient 'hook' for these traditions, but they are formulated independently of any notion or metaphor of covenant.

The fourth tradition cited here is significant for both its midrashic brilliance and logical incoherence. Sex with her husband, Rav says, transforms a woman ontologically, 'creating' her, as it were. The Hebrew word *b'l* means master, husband, and lover. Rav reads the verse as meaning "the one who has sex with you makes you". On one level, the analogy works. Just as God made a covenant with His people, so too does a woman make a covenant with her 'creator' (her husband). But on a deeper level, it too falls apart. First, the analogy is not symmetrical. What does it mean that the woman makes the covenant, and what is the meaning of "only"? Second, the temporal succession does not work: does the woman make a covenant (i.e., marry) only *after* she has sex? The thrust of the tradition is that man 'creates' his wife just as God created man. The midrash obliterates any trace of intimacy or reciprocity that the comparison of marriage to covenant might apply, focusing instead only on a wife's subordination

---

[71] The 'specialness' of a first wife is alluded to in a non-midrashic context also at b. B. Bat. 144a (Rabbi Ḥanina). S. Baron, *A Social and Religious History of the Jews*, vol. 2, New York ²1952-76, 226, deduces from this source that "[t]here was a slight idealistic preference for the 'wife of one's youth', but legally it resulted, at most, in the advice of the Jewish sages ... to refrain, as far as possible, from divorcing her".

to her husband.

Before considering the later Palestinian homiletic midrashim that do describe the relationship between God and Israel as a marriage, it is worthwhile to consider another kind of rabbinic marital metaphor. The substance, if not the identical wording, of the "grooms' blessing" is most likely Palestinian. Two of these blessing, four and six, evoke a metaphor of marriage to describe the relationship of God to Zion:

> 4. Let the barren one rejoice and cry out when her children are gathered to her in joy. Praised are You, Lord, who causes Zion to rejoice with her children.
> 6. Praised are you, Lord our God, king of the universe, who created gladness and joy, groom and bride, rejoicing, song, mirth, delight, love, friendship, peace, and companionship. Lord our God, may there soon be heard in the cities of Judah and in the streets of Jerusalem the voice of gladness and the voice of joy; the voice of the groom and the voice of the bride; the joyous shouts of grooms from their bridal chambers, and of youths from their [marriage] celebrations. Praised are You Lord, who causes the groom to rejoice with the bride.[72]

These blessings present a pastiche of biblical citations and allusions that evoke the metaphor of the relationship between God and Israel as a covenant. The fourth blessing uses the language of Isa. 54:1 ("sing, barren one") as a reference to Zion, and strongly alludes to Isa. 61:10 and 62:5. The blessing is more or less faithful to the image from Deutero-Isaiah, which here uses the metaphor of marriage to describe the relationship between God and Zion. The blessing is apparently included here in order to underline the (somewhat unclear) connections between human marriage, procreation, Israel's Diaspora, and ultimate redemption. Zion should rejoice for her (and God's?) children when they marry, in anticipation of the day in which God will gather her children to her. The

---

[72]b. Ket. 7b-8a.

sixth blessing returns to this theme, connecting human marriage to the divine redemption of Zion, citing the consolation passage of Jer. 33:10-11.[73] Only in restored Zion can humans celebrate marriage to its fullest. Significantly, however, even in the six blessings that comprise the grooms' blessing there is no description of the 'marriage' between God and Israel.

The description of God and Israel as married is not totally absent from rabbinic literature. Some relatively late Palestinian homiletical midrashic compositions do contain coherent forms of this metaphor. Most typically, these works use of the marital metaphor to illustrate Israel's unfaithfulness to God, much in line with the example that we have already seen from the Tosefta. The metaphor, and its message, can be quite complex. Lam. R. for example, contains a parable comparing God's behavior to Israel to a king who abandons his wife for a long period of time; only her marriage contract (i.e. the Torah) and the material comforts contained in it comfort her in his absence.[74] David Stern has shown that the use of this metaphor here is far from innocent, pointing to an implicit critique of God's abandonment and "a critical interrogation of God and His treatment of Israel".[75] A parable that might have been formulated as a response to Christian supercessionist teaching compares Israel to an imperfect, but still loved, wife.[76] Deut. R. contains several marital parables in which Israel

---

[73] The blessing might also draw on Ps. 19:6, which compares the rising of the sun (!) to a groom leaving his chamber, or Joel 2:16. Cf. G. Anderson "The Garden of Eden and Sexuality in Early Judaism", in: H. Eilberg-Schwartz (ed.), *People of the Body: Jews and Judaism from an Embodied Perspective*, Albany 1992, 59, who points to the "eschatological significance" of the sixth blessing.

[74] Lam. R. *ad* 3:21, text in D. Stern, *Parables in Midrash: Narrative and Exegesis in Rabbinic Literature*, Cambridge 1991, 281-2.

[75] D. Stern, *Parables*, 56-62, 180-3, quote at 60. A similar interpretation can apply to Lam. R. *ad* 1:56, a parable of a king who gets angry at his wife and evicts her from her home, leaving her no place to go because she has followed his directives by ceasing contact with her former cronies.

[76] Cant. R. *ad* 1:6 (3), 9b, attributed to R. Yitzḥak. On this story see E. E. Urbach, "The Homiletical Interpretations of the Sages and the Expositions of Origen on Canticles, and the Jewish-Christian Disputation", in: J. Heinemann, D. Noy (eds.), *Studies in Aggadah and Folk-Literature* (Scripta

marries, is unfaithful, and then is brought back into a covenantal relationship with God.[77]

Expectedly, the few unambivalently positive uses of this metaphor in rabbinic literature appear in Cant. R. While patristic writers read Cant. as a sustained allegory for the relationship between Christ and the Church, the rabbis, even in Cant. R. read the same biblical book far more episodically. Hence, Cant. R. devotes relatively little space to understanding Cant. as a metaphor for the marriage of God and Israel. One tradition, ascribed to a third generation Palestinian amora, identifies the ten places in Scripture that Israel is called a "bride", and concludes from this that Israel "wears" the ten commandments like a bride wears her ornaments.[78] Other traditions talk of Israel as bashful before God's courting her, or of the newly-betrothed couple praising each other's physical attributes.[79]

Rabbis were not the only Jews in fifth and sixth century Palestine to be using the marital metaphor homiletically. Yannai, a Palestinian liturgical poet who probably lived in the sixth century, wrote one poem comparing the marital relationship of Jacob and Leah to that of God and Israel.[80] In two much longer compositions for the seventh day of Passover, Yannai develops Canticles as a metaphor for the love between God and Israel, their meeting at Sinai, the establishment of the Temple, and God's unquenchable and irrevocable love for His people.[81] On the verse "Before I knew it, my desire set me mid the chariots of Ammi-nadib" (Cant.

Hierosolymitana), Jerusalem, 1971, 262-5.

[77]See, for examples, Deut. R., *Ekeb* 3:7, 106a-b; 3:10, 106c. A similar use of the metaphor is attributed to Rav Nahman at b. Yom. 54a, that compares Israel's unfaithfulness upon entering the land to a bride entering her new husband's house.

[78]Cant. R. *ad* 4:10, 27c-d. This tradition is paralleled at Deut. R. 2.37, 104d-5a, but this appears to be a late addition.

[79]Cant. R. *ad* 1:2 (3), 4d; *ad* 5:16 (6), 33a.

[80]Yannai, *Piyut* 27. Text in Z.M. Rabinowitz, *Mahzor piyute Rabbi Yanai la-Torah vela-moʻadim*, Jerusalem 1985, 171-5, with a translation of the fourth stanza in T. Carmi, *The Penguin Book of Hebrew Verse*, New York 1981, 215.

[81]*Ibid.*, vol. 2, 265-72, 272-89.

6:12), for example, Yannai writes,

> Like bride bound up / with jewelry adorned
> She sits in a chariot / bedecked and perfumed.[82]

The language in the first line alludes to Isa. 49:18, in which God consoles Zion. Yannai, though, has transferred the metaphor to Israel: in this reading Israel, not Zion, is God's bride. Just as God and Israel once enjoyed a marital intimacy, so yet again, God says, "you will be Mine, and I will be yours".[83]

Yannai's student (?) Eleazar ben Kallir, who most likely worked in Palestine close to the time of the Moslem conquest, also used the metaphor of God's marriage to Israel. In one *piyyut*, Kallir describes a dialogue between Zion and God:

> My husband has abandoned me and turned away,
> And has not remembered my love as a bride.
> He has scattered and dispersed me far from my land;
> He has let all my tormentors rejoice at my downfall.
>
> He has cast me off like an unclean woman, banished
>   me from his presence;
> He has harshly ensnared me, given me no respite;
> He has chastised me till my eyes failed.
> Why has he forsaken me, forgotten me forever?
>
> O my dove, O plant of delight in my garden bed,
> Why do you cry out against me?
> I have already answered your prayer, as I did in days
>   of old,
> When I dwelt crowned in your midst...[84]

The putative female here is Zion, but Kallir blurs the lines between Zion and Israel, mother and wife. In the first stanza (not cited), Zion is compared to a mourning mother, while the second is the

---

[82] Rabinowitz, *Mahzor*, vol. 2, 284, lines 124-25.
[83] *Ibid.*, vol. 2, 287, line 165.
[84] Translation from Carmi, *Hebrew Verse*, 223, modified slightly.

lament of the bride, exiled "far from my land". God, again, assures Zion or Israel that He still looks out for her, and concludes "I shall not forsake you or forget you".[85]

In a poem that Kallir composed for a marriage, his use of this metaphor, and its assimilation into human marriage, is even more striking. This lengthy poem was to be recited during the first Sabbath after the marriage, during the *Qedusha* prayer (which is embedded in it). In the middle of this long composition, he turns to the married couple:

> Bound by affection, may your joy increase,
> In love and in gladness today with your marriage;
> Be glad and rejoice in the Lord your God.
>
> Delight, groom, in your glorious *huppah*,
> Excel in beauty among your companions,
> And may your heart rejoice in the wife of your youth.
>
> Your radiant face [O bride] shall glow like wine;
> Your enemies shall be as nothing;
> My [silver] parapet, your love is sweeter than wine.
>
> Like one drinking wine
> Or hearing the song of a swallow or a crane,
> I will rejoice in the Holy One!
>
> I shall crown My dove with grace and kindness, as
>   once I did
> When I revealed myself in the flame of the consuming
>   fire,
> For you have ravished My Heart, My sister, My bride...
>
> Arise, My beloved, and be married in love,
> Give hymns and thanks to your [f. sing.] King;
> Sing and make music in my bridal *huppah*:
> "Under the apple tree you have roused me"
>   [Cant. 8:5].[86]

---

85 *Ibid.*, 224.

The opening stanza links human marriage to divine joy. The next
two stanzas praise the groom and bride, respectively, with a string
of biblical allusions. Now the poet turns away from the human
couple and recites the strophe, a set of verses that recurs throughout this poem and which brings attention back to the theme of the
Qedusha, holiness. Here, the strophe also divides the poet's praise
of the human couple from his next subject, the praise of Israel
by God. First God is portrayed as promising His future 'wedding' with Israel, which will rival the one that God and Israel
had on Mt. Sinai. Finally, the last stanza blurs the line between
the human wedding and the 'wedding' of God and Israel, each,
as it were, melting into the other. Human marriage is a kind of
representation of the marriage between God and Israel.

These *piyyutim*, like the patristic writings, illustrate the
choices that the rabbis did *not* make. Like their counterparts in
the pre-rabbinic period, the earlier rabbis did not use the metaphor of the marriage of God and Israel for both social and theological reasons, sometimes tightly intertwined. For these rabbis,
the primary human relationship was that between parents and
children; marriage ranked a distant second. As the Babylonian
Talmud's reinterpretation of Hosea shows, the rabbis were far
more comfortable using the parental metaphor to represent the
relationship between God and Israel. Alon Goshen-Gottstein has
demonstrated that at least the tannaim preferred to see the relationship between God and Israel as that between a father and a
son.[87] However one understands the correspondence between the
valuation placed on this relationship among humans and its use
as a theological metaphor, it is clear that the father - son metaphor may have offered to the rabbinic mind certain theological
advantages. As a biological fact, the parent - child relationship
was undoable; it did not offer the possibility of God's divorce of
Israel and His remarriage to another people, a consideration that

---

[86]The entire poem is found in Ezra Fleischer, *Shirat-haqodesh ha'ivrit
b'yame-habenayim*, Jerusalem 1975, 154-64, the part cited is at 159-61. The
translation is slightly modified from Carmi, *Hebrew Verse*, 221-3.

[87]Alon Goshen-Gottstein, *God and Israel as Father and Son in Tannaitic
Literature* (diss. Hebrew University), n.p. 1987 (in Hebrew).

may have gained importance as Christian claims to be the 'true Israel' increased. By making Israel a 'son' rather than a 'wife' the rabbis do not have to deal with reconciling the image of a feminized Israel with their own self-image as 'masculine'.[88] The relationship was hierarchical, thus allowing in the metaphor the preservation of a sufficient distance between God and His creation. Finally, the father - son metaphor places the covenantal onus squarely on the son, rather than the more reciprocal relationship implied by a marital metaphor.

Despite the points of theological and social dissonance that the marital metaphor would have raised, the metaphor continued to have a poetic appeal. The metaphor was one of many stock images that the rabbis could use to present a rich picture of Israel's unfaithfulness. The marriage metaphor may have posed certain theological problems when used to indicate the intimacy between God and Israel, but was far less dangerous when used as an image of distance. Later homilists and *paytanim* would return to the positive associations of the metaphor because it offered enormous poetic potential. Moreover, the possibility of Christian influence, and its own popular use of the metaphor, cannot be excluded. What the metaphor offered to them in their creation of popular homilies and religious poetry outweighed the deeper theological disadvantages inherent in it.

4   Conclusions

In tracing the metaphor of God's relationship to Israel as a marriage through Jewish literary sources in antiquity, the focus has more often been on how this metaphor was ignored than on how it was used. Yet this finding is not insignificant, and from it we can draw some more general conclusions:

1. The biblical metaphor of marriage was not blindly determinative. Just because the Bible contains a description of God's relationship to Israel as a marriage, does not mean that later Jews had to as well. Jewish use of tradition was informed by

---

[88] Cf. Satlow, " 'Try to be a Man' ".

a complex interaction of different forces. When a tradition was incomprehensible, or simply unsavory, Jews – including the rabbis – either ignored or adapted it. 'Jewish' marriage, in other words, does not mean 'marriage as described in the Hebrew Bible'. Jewish understandings of marriage were informed by a serious engagement of texts and traditions within a given social, cultural, and theological context.

2. I could only suggest reasons for the wide (if not total) rejection of the marital metaphor by Jews in antiquity. If correct, these suggestions provide some insight into Jewish theological commitments. The metaphor of marriage was in many respects theologically problematic for these Jewish communities. Some of these problems – as well as popular use of the metaphor in Palestine after the fourth century – might be linked to the rise of Christianity. This area deserves further investigation.

3. On a material level, the metaphor points clearly to a devaluation of marriage among these Jews when compared to the parent-child relationship. The frequent use of this latter metaphor as a description of God's relationship to Israel indicates the primacy of this biological relationship in the eyes of these writers. Marriages can come and go, but biology is forever. If correct, this should prompt a reevaluation of the often repeated but rarely supported claim that Jews in antiquity divorced less frequently (or at least thought less of divorce) than their non-Jewish contemporaries.

Why Would a Man Want to be Anyone's Wife?

A Response to Satlow

Judith Frishman   (Catholic Theological University of Utrecht)

The metaphor of God as the husband of Israel is indeed but one of many metaphors, such as that of father and son or king and servant, which describe the relationship between God and the people of Israel. Yet it is this metaphor of husband and wife, most graphically depicted by the latter prophets,[1] which is said to convey best the intimate and reciprocal nature of the covenant.[2] Reciprocity may certainly pertain to the essence of a covenant, yet reciprocity need in no sense entail equality. In the prophetic texts marriage is presented as a legitimate relationship in which sexuality is expressed in the appropriate form.[3] Fidelity is demanded of the wife and it is *her* adulterous behaviour that is grounds for divorce. Her faithlessness releases the husband of his obligations, i.e. the provision of food and clothing, as Hos. 2:9 scathingly confirms: "Therefore I will take back my corn at the harvest and my new wine at the vintage, and I will take away the wool and flax which I gave her to cover her naked body".[4] While divorce could thus be devastating to the woman who had no one to turn to, it was also of consequence for her children. The legitimacy of children born to a wanton woman would certainly be called into question;[5] but even the inheritance rights of the child of a banished woman were at stake, as the story of Ishmael and Hagar would seem to indicate. Whether or not a woman could divorce her husband is a moot point. Yair Zakovitch[6] asserts that at certain

---

[1]Cf. A. Brenner, *The Intercourse of Knowledge*, Leiden & New York, etc. 1997, 153-74 on the "pornoprophetic" nature of these depictions.

[2]See Satlow, p. 15.

[3]So H. Eilberg-Schwartz, *God's Phallus and Other Problems for Men and Monotheism*, Boston 1994, 99.

[4]The English translations of the bible in this response are derived from *The New English Bible*, Oxford & Cambridge 1970 unless indicated otherwise.

[5]Such was the case of Jeptha in Judg. 11 as well as the children Jezreel, Lo-Ruhamah and Lo-Ammi in Hos. 1.

[6]Y. Zakovitch, "The Woman's Rights in the Biblical Law of Divorce",

stages in Israelite history a woman could divorce her spouse if he
failed to supply her basic needs, or if he deserted her. The biblical evidence, however, would seem to point almost exclusively to
the male prerogative in such matters, as Zakovitch's list of terms
in which women's passivity (i.e. divorced, abandoned, be hated)
is contrasted with male activity (he divorces, he sends away, he
hates) attests.[7]

If the marriage between God and Israel reflects human
marriage, what are the implications for both human marital
relationships and for the relationship between God and Israel?
It would seem, firstly, that the dominant position of men is
reinforced by God's role as husband, for no one could contest
the inequality between God and his creatures, including Israel.
God's rejection of idolatry, when expressed in terms of "whoring",
supports the social order in which sex outside of marriage for a
married woman is illegitimate. An enigma arises, however, because
the Israelite male is not only expected to identify with God in
this metaphor but also with Israel as God's wife. Looking from
the vantage point of the biblical male, and not simply from that
of the Jewish male in the Hellenistic and early Roman periods
as Satlow would have it,[8] one might wonder why any man would
want to be someone's wife!

Howard Eilberg-Schwartz, in his book *God's Phallus*, goes a
step further than Satlow in identifying the problems raised by the
metaphor under discussion. Satlow notes that a degree of intimacy
between God and Israel is not always compatible with an asexual
and transcendent God,[9] yet his remark begs the question as to the
date and setting of the development of the notion of an asexual
(even incorporeal) transcendent deity. Was it – pace Satlow[10] – the
Jewish-Greek authors who were the first to have felt uncomfortable with the sexual intimacy of the bond between God and Israel,
or did others do so earlier? Eilberg-Schwartz pinpoints awareness

---

Jewish Law Annual 4 (1981), 28-46:46.
    [7]Y. Zakovitch, *art. cit.*, 34.
    [8]Satlow, p. 22.
    [9]Satlow, p. 17.
    [10]Satlow, pp. 23-24.

of what he calls the "homoerotic dilemma"[11] in the prophetic texts themselves. He observes that in both Hosea and Jeremiah "the metaphors of God married to Israel [the collective representation – J.F.] spill over into other symbolic registers where God is imagined in relationship to individual men".[12] Thus Israel is meant to identify at times with the children – be they of the adulteress or of God –, at times with the adulteress, and at times with the male voice represented either by the narrator or by God himself. In a close reading of Malachi, Eilberg-Schwartz perceives that the erotic imagery of the marital metaphor has been displaced.[13] It is now a male Israel who has espoused daughters of alien gods (Mal. 2:11) and broken faith with the wife of his youth. God, according to Eilberg-Schwartz's interpretation of Mal. 2:15-16, voices strong disapproval of divorce.[14] But it is not God's divorcing Israel but a male Israel's abandonment of a feminine God, Israel's covenanted spouse, against which God protests.

The feminising of God was but one of the solutions to the problematic intimacy of the marriage metaphor. In the course of time several other solutions were found, among them the transformation or subversion of the metaphor.[15] One such instance of transformation pointed out by Satlow[16] is a *sugya* in b. Pes. 87b. The *darshan*, apparently confounded by God's commanding Hosea to take a wanton woman and beget children of her wantonness, feels compelled to offer an explanation. He provides the biblical book with a prologue in which Hosea, having been informed by God that his sons had sinned, not only refused to ask for mercy upon them as children of God, children of Abraham, Isaac and Jacob, but also requested that God simply exchange them for others. God, wishing to put Hosea to the test, subsequently demands that he marry a promiscuous woman, have children with her and then dismiss her. If Hosea is able to do so, God in turn will

---

[11]H. Eilberg-Schwartz, *op. cit.*, 99.
[12]*Ibid.*
[13]*Op. cit.*, 129.
[14]For the contested meaning of Mal. 2:16 cf. Satlow, n. 13.
[15]So Satlow, pp. 31-32.
[16]*Ibid.*

dismiss his own children. The prologue thus completed, the
darshan proceeds to quote literally from Hos. 1:2-3. Several
exegetical explanations of the names Gomer and bat Diblaim
briefly interrupt the discourse. According to Satlow the Babylonian Talmud, in these explanations, obliterates the fact that the
woman represents Israel and thereby levels Hosea's marital metaphor. I would argue, to the contrary, that the *darshan* is a close
reader and realises that, in the biblical text, both the mother and
the children represent Israel. Moreover, the *darshan* is also aware
that the first time Hosea appeals to his audience directly it is
not as God's wife but as the children of that promiscuous wife
(cf. Hos. 2:2: "Plead my cause with your mother; ... plead with
her to forswear those wanton looks ... "). It is not until Hos. 2:18-
22 that the woman is no longer spoken of in the third person, i.e.
as "she", but is addressed as "you": "On that day you will call
me *Ishi* and you will no longer call me *Ba'ali*" (Hos. 2:18).[17] The
listener or reader does finally identify with the adulteress, but
only at the point where she is restored to her husband. Thus the
Talmud does not simply level the marital metaphor; it intertwines
the themes of the repudiated children and the wanton woman.

In the continuation of the midrash Hosea is told to separate
himself from his wife, as Moses did when God spoke to him. Yet
this the prophet cannot do because she has born him children.
God then pointedly remarks that if Hosea, who can't even be sure
that the children are his, is still attached to them, how could he
(i.e. God) in turn reject Israel, his very own children, offspring of
Abraham, Isaac and Jacob, God's tested ones and one of his four
earthly possessions? The midrash concludes with Hosea's request
for mercy, firstly upon himself and then upon Israel. Hereupon
the punishment is removed and Hosea commences to bless the
children. This explanation accounts, among other things, for the
sudden shift from rejection in Hos. 1:9 ("... for you are not
my people and I will not be your God") to benediction in Hos.
2:1 ("The Israelites shall become countless as the sands of the

---

[17] The NEB reads, "On that day she shall call me 'My husband' and shall
no more call me 'My Baal'.", ignoring the grammatical change of person.

sea...". I would thus posit that it is not the *darshan* whose syntax is tortuously cumbersome but, rather, the biblical text with its fluctuating themes and subjects which is problematic and which the midrash attempts to resolve. On the other hand, the addition of the prologue does favour the father-son metaphor in Hos. 1 while the biblical text remains ambiguous, hovering between the husband-wife and father-children metaphors.

Of some interest perhaps for the evolution of the marriage metaphor is the context in which the midrash above is placed in b. Pes. 87b. The starting point of the *sugya* concerns the question as to where a married woman should eat the Passover offer, in her husband's home or in her father's home? The *Gemara* answers the question by quoting Cant. 8:10: "... so in his eyes I am as one who brings contentment". R. Yohanan explains further that she is a woman who is content in her father-in-law's house, and wishes to tell her own family. This is then supported by Hos. 2:18, "On that day you will call me *Ishi* and you will no longer call me *Ba'ali*", interpreted as follows: when a woman lives with her husband she calls him *Ishi* [my man], but as long as she remains in her father's house and the marriage has not been consummated she speaks of *Ba'ali* [my husband].

Having established a relationship between Canticles and Hosea, the *Gemara* reverts to Cant. 8:8, "We have a little sister who has no breasts", by way of association with the first half of Cant. 8:10, "I am a wall and my breasts are like towers". A prominent theme of Cant. R. – love as *talmud torah*[18] – is briefly touched upon and then followed by the midrash discussed above. In the final section, the repudiation of Hosea's children is ameliorated in two ways. Firstly, God, according to both R. El'azar and R. Ḥaninah, never remains angry with Israel for a long time but is merciful (Hos. 1:6). Secondly, exile is not only preferable to living under the Roman decrees, it also serves the purpose of having the peoples join with Israel.

Thus we see that the *sugya* in b. Pes. 87b employs the

---

[18]This theme is the subject of a forthcoming Ph.D. dissertation being prepared by Birke Rapp, Catholic Theological University of Utrecht (The Netherlands).

marriage metaphor in several ways. The texts of the Song of Songs and Hosea are combined, first in order to solve a logistic problem, i.e. where a woman should celebrate the Passover meal. Hos. 2:18 has indeed been levelled here, representing the differing degrees of intimacy experienced by an engaged and a married woman. The loaded nature of the original text has become quite mundane. Next the metaphor represents the love of torah, much as the marriage metaphor was used to express the love of wisdom in the Hellenistic period (torah and wisdom both being female and desired by the male rabbis). From love of torah the Talmud continues with God's love of his children in a midrash which, of all those found in b. Pes. 87b, is closest to the tenure of the original biblical book of Hosea. Yet the *darshan*, led by Hos. 1, chooses to place additional emphasis on the father-son metaphor instead of on the marriage metaphor. Lastly, the threat of repudiation voiced in Hosea is softened, whereby no specific attention is paid to the biblical metaphor which stands for Israel's being repudiated by God.

This passage certainly deserves more detailed study than allowed for in a brief response. Nevertheless, I hope that my presentation has contributed to the varied and complicated views and interpretations of the marriage metaphor in early Judaism, as surveyed by Michael Satlow in this volume.

"We Have a Little Sister":

Aspects of the Brother–Sister Relationship in Ancient Israel*

Ingo Kottsieper (University of Münster)

1 Introduction

The main subject of this contribution is to present some observations and considerations concerning the relationship between brothers and sisters in the broader context of family structures in Ancient Israel. Consciously, the title mentions just 'aspects' of this relationship and uses the plural 'family structures'. We must not assume *a priori* that there was only one family structure in the different societies of Ancient Israel, and we also possess only a small amount of sources, which does not allow a comprehensive analysis of all aspects of our theme.

After some short notes about the methodological problems our subject presents to us, some texts of the Old Testament will be examined which offer valuable information about the subject of this contribution. The discussion will start with some observations on the Song of Songs and then deal with the stories about the rape of Tamar and the fate of Dinah, and the reactions of their brothers to what happens to their sisters (2 Sam. 13–14; Gen. 34). Afterwards some suggestions are made concerning the role of the brothers in the negotiations about the marriage of their sister, which will be based mainly on Gen. 34 and 24. The sister as a helper and a saviour of her brother will be discussed on the basis of Prov. 7:4 and two non-biblical examples.

Since a family is a complex social structure, it is obvious that the relation between brothers and sisters cannot be discussed apart from the function of the other members of a family, in particular the father and the mother. Thus at some points this issue

---

*I thank Mrs. Claudia Mustroph who did a great deal to improve the language of my manuscript.

will also be pursued. Finally I will try to draw a more complete picture of a family structure which can be found in Ancient Israel and its development in the Hellenistic period.

2   Preliminary Methodological Considerations

An examination of the relations between different groups in the context of a family or a clan of Ancient Israel is faced with some fundamental problems:

The term 'Ancient Israel' which has been chosen here for the sake of simplicity covers a period of several centuries, in which some radical changes took place. Likewise, it does not describe a geographically homogeneous area. The two independent states into which Israel was divided both developed their own traditions. And of course, the special situations of the exilic, postexilic, and Hellenistic periods had their impact on the social structure of Israel and the traditions which were formed and transformed in those times.

For these reasons we are not allowed to generalise the statements of one text concerning a specific family structure for all of Ancient Israel. Only if we find such a structure in several texts which are independent from each other and date from different times we may assume that this structure was common in Ancient Israel. But even this does not mean that each family was shaped according to this structure.

A second difficulty for our discussion derives from our sources. The literature of the Bible is not only a small selection of the texts of Ancient Israel, but also – at least in the literary form in which we read them – mainly formed by authors from the upper strata of society. So it does not reflect all aspects of the real life in Ancient Israel. And in particular, family structures are normally not the central themes of these texts. Thus we are forced to extract the data from the indirect information given in these texts which normally only imply a specific family structure.

Otherwise the fact that our sources offer us mainly indirect hints also gives us a chance. By a direct discussion an author perhaps wanted to provoke his audience or to propagate a new and not commonly accepted structure which did not exist in reality. But if a specific family structure is not the central theme of a text, but only forms the background against which the story is told, we may assume that this structure reflects the real situation of the society for which the story was told.

The same holds true if a given text was not created by only one author, but developed in a longer redactional process. A redactor or a reviser of a text also wants to be understood by his audience and by this is forced to bring his texts in line with the ideology and the reality of the society he lives in.

The fact that our sources normally offer us only indirect hints of the family structure also means a danger. They can easily be misunderstood against the background of our own social experience and problems as well as the commonly held view of a patriarchal society in Ancient Israel.

The following example may illustrate this danger of misunderstanding. Since our societies are strongly influenced by the official law, some people think that this is also true of the societies of the Ancient Near East. So it is often assumed that the laws of the Old Testament reflect the normal situation of a real society, though it is obvious that in the Old Testament most of the cases which occur in normal life are not discussed. And because the legal tradition of the Old Testament shows that there was obviously no problem for a man to get divorced from his wife, the opinion can be found that this was typical of the patriarchal society of Ancient Israel.[1] But proverbs like Prov. 21:9 and 25:24 tell us that it is better for a man to stay on the roof then to be in a house with a nagging wife – there is no thought of getting rid of such a wife by divorce. In contrast, Prov. 13:19 states that the wife's quarrelling drives the man out and not the man his wife![2] This fact can

---

[1]Cf. e.g. Fr. Crüsemann, "'... er aber soll dein Herr sein' (Genesis 3,16): Die Frau in der patriarchalischen Welt des Alten Testamentes", in: Idem, H. Thyen, *Als Mann und Frau geschaffen: Exegetische Studien zur Rolle der Frau* (Kennzeichen, 2), Berlin & Stein 1978, 23, who on the one hand points to the fact that the biblical laws mainly deal with controversial cases and not with questions of everyday life, but on the other hand continues: "Immerhin läßt sich die übliche Praxis der Scheidung von hier aus erschließen".

[2]Cf. also Prov. 21:19.

only be explained by the assumption that the legal possibility of
sending a wife away does not reflect the real situation of matri-
mony which, in fact, normally was ruled by free contracts between
the families and by social pressure but not by an official law.

Therefore, to learn about real family structures it is best to
start with the literary texts and draw the picture mainly by the
help of the hints these texts give us. The data found in the legal
texts are then to be compared with these results, and we have to
judge wether they fit into the picture or not. If not, this does not
mean that the results are wrong but only that the legal texts faced
a more theoretical situation, not typical of the normal family in
Ancient Israel.

3   Brothers and Sisters in the Song of Songs

The assumption that there was a strict patriarchal structure in
the societies of Ancient Israel clearly does not fit into the picture
given by the Song of Songs.[3] As many commentators did observe,
the girl's father is never mentioned throughout the whole book.[4]
In contrast, we meet not only her mother but three times her
brothers also.

We find the first reference to them at the beginning of the
book:

> (5) Dark am I and beautiful,
> oh daughters of Jerusalem,
> like the tents of Kedar,
> like the pavilions of Salma.

> (6) Stare not at me
> that I am dark
> because the sun has espied me.

> The sons of my mother were angry with me,
> they made me a guard of the vineyards —
> my own vineyard I had not guarded!   Cant. 1:5-6

---

[3]Cf. F. Crüsemann, art. cit., 83.

[4]Cf. e.g. O. Keel, Das Hohelied (ZBK, 18), Zürich 1986, 251-252; A.
Brenner, "Das Hohelied: Polyphonie der Liebe", in: L. Schottroff, M.-Th.
Wacker, Kompendium Feministische Bibelauslegung, Gütersloh 1998, 238.

The girl explains her dark skin by the statement that she was exposed to the sun because her angry brothers sent her to the vineyard. The context makes clear that the last sentence gives the reason for her brothers' anger. As she had not guarded her own vineyard, she was sent away from the town, which serves as a background for most of the following texts. It is obvious that this statement refers to the sexual intercourse the girl had with her friend.

We find the brothers mentioned a second time in Cant. 8:8-10, which corresponds to 1:6:

> (8) We have a little sister
> and she has no breasts.
>
> What shall we do for our sister
> when they court her?
>
> (9) If she is a wall
> we will build on her a silver buttress.
>
> If she is a door
> we will strengthen her with a cedar board.
>
> (10) I am a wall
> and my breasts are like towers —
>
> now I already have become like one
> who surrendered.   Cant. 8:8-10

This section consists of two units (8:8-9 and 8:10) which, both, use the motif of the girl as a wall. Cant. 8:8-10 shares the idea with 1:6 that the brothers reject the permissiveness of their sister. But whereas 1:6 describes their reaction to something which has already been done, 8:8-10 focuses on their vain effort to prevent such behaviour.

It is not just by chance that these two corresponding texts are located near the beginning and the end of the whole book. Only several verses precede or follow them, which both contain the motif of King Solomon. This motif appears again in Cant. 3:9,

where the only Greek word of the book is found.[5] On the other
hand, Cant. 1:5 offers a good introduction of the girl and can be
understood as the beginning of the book. So it may be assumed
that Cant. 1:1-4 and 8:11-12 belong to a late, Hellenistic addition
which introduced the motif of King Solomon into an older collection of songs which was originally framed by Cant. 1:5-6 and
8:8-10.[6]

The assumption that Cant. 1:5-6 and 8:8-10 were consciously
chosen by the redactor of an older pre-Hellenistic collection as
a frame can be supported by some observations concerning the
two units which are placed just before Cant. 8:8-10. The first
one (8:5b) connects the arousing activity of the girl with what
happened in the previous generation also. What the girl is doing
was already done by her friend's mother. The following section
(8:6-7) sings the praise of the love which cannot be extinguished
and which supercedes everything else by its value. Together with
the frame (Cant. 1:5-6; 8:8-10), these sections provide a background for the texts of the pre-Hellenistic collection. The introduction (1:5-6) makes clear that the behaviour of the girl contradicts the commonly accepted moral standards. This is the reason
why the brothers became angry with their sister. But the last
sections show that the behaviour of the girl is not a special case.
She acted like women did in former generations (8:5b), and the
reason for this is not that she and the other women are wicked, but
rather the outstanding power of love (8:6-7). Thus all attempts
at preventing such behaviour will be in vain (8:8-10). The adoles-
cent sister acts in the same way, too. The observation that the
older collection's end points back to the opening section makes
clear that the speakers of Cant. 8:8-9 are also the brothers, not
brothers and sisters as Keel assumed.[7]

These observations show that the redactor of the pre-
Hellenistic collection lived in a society in which the brothers of a
girl in particular and not her father were expected to watch over
her sexual behaviour.

---

[5] אַפִּרְיוֹן, which stems from Greek φορεῖον.

[6] Cf. also further down, p. 79.

[7] O. Keel, *op. cit.*, 252.

Cant. 8:1-2 shows another aspect of the relation between brothers and sisters. This text expresses the wish of the girl that her friend would be as her brother, so that she could caress him in public and take him with her into the house of her mother:

(1) Who gives you to me as a brother
who nursed at my mother's breast?

I would find you in the street and kiss you
and none would scorn me.

(2) I would lead you
to my mother's house who taught me.

I would make you drink spiced wine,
the juice of my pomegranate.   Cant. 8:1-2

The section shows a tender relation between sister and brother which, obviously, was commonly accepted – nobody would scorn a girl who caresses her brother even in public. This corresponds to the phrasing of Cant. 8:8-9, which reveals a more careful attitude of the brothers and a less authoritarian relationship: "What shall we do for our sister so that she will be able to resist the attack of love and a lover?" The humorous way Cant. 8:10 states that this attempt is in vain, and the fact that the idea of a ban is completely missing, show that the brothers do not simply pull authority. The relationship between brother and sister is clearly based on emotions like affection, fondness and responsibility. These are the reasons why the brothers try to prevent their sister from acting in a way which was condemned by the common moral code. This becomes even more clear by a comparison with Cant. 5:7, in which the reaction of the city guards, the representatives of common morality, is described. They bring the girl's nightly search for her friend brutally to an end when they hit and humiliate her.

A further observation offers a deeper insight into the family structure which is presupposed by the pre-Hellenistic collection of the Song of Songs. The girl is always connected with her mother. It is her mother's house she wants to bring her friend to and it is her mother who taught her (Cant. 8:2). The motif of the mother's house is also found in Cant. 3:4, and 6:9 calls the girl "unique to her mother". But also her brothers are connected with her through their mother. They are called "sons of her mother" (Cant. 1:6), and in Cant. 8:1 they are those who were nursed at her mother's breasts.

Summing up the observations made so far, the following picture of a family structure which is presupposed by the pre-Hellenistic collection of the Song of Songs can be depicted. The girl belongs to the sphere of her mother, in which the father was not very important. The male members of the family whom she mainly deals with are her brothers, because they too belong to her mother's sphere. Although they exercise some authority over their sister – they are able to send her away into the vineyards – their relation to their sister is full of affection and responsibility. The humorous way the texts describe the failure of their efforts to prevent their sister's permissive behaviour reveals that their authority was by no means absolute or even feared by the girl. Only the power of the city guards and the fear of public contempt are a real hindrance for the girl to enjoy her love freely.

These results face us with the question whether this picture corresponds to the real situation of the society in which the redactor of the collection worked, or whether it is just a fiction of love songs.[8] Keel explains the silence about the father with the assumption that the Song of Songs would simply ignore "die mit spontaner Liebe häufig im Widerstreit liegenden Ansprüche der Gesellschaft, welche im Kontext des Alten Testaments primär durch den *pater familias*, durch Ehe und Nachkommenschaft konkretisiert werden".[9] But this argumentation overlooks that the

---

[8]Cf. the statement of A. Brenner, *art. cit.*, 239, who depicts the family structure proposed in the Song of Songs in a similar way as I did above: "Ob diese Sachlage anzeigt, daß die Gesellschaftsformen, die sich im Hld widerspiegeln, durch matrilineare oder fratrilineare Prinzipien geprägt werden, ist jedoch bei weitem nicht sicher".

[9]O. Keel, *op.cit.*, 42; cf. also p. 251.

The assumption, that the brothers took over the function of the old or dead father (thus e.g. F. Delitzsch, *Hoheslied und Koheleth* [Biblischer Commentar über das Alte Testament, 4/4], Leipzig 1875, 28, and G. Krinetzki, *Kommentar zum Hohenlied* [Beiträge zur biblischen Exegese und

problem of public disapproval of the girl's behaviour is an important theme of the collection, as its frame sections show.[10] So, it
opens more questions than it answers. Why then should the Song
of Songs at all deal with the question that the behaviour of the
girl was not in line with the common moral code – but never
mention the father if he really was the prime representative of
this morality for the girl? Why then are the brothers' reactions
mentioned? And the argumentation of the frame would be sense-
less if the presupposed family structure was totally unrealistic.
Obviously the redactor himself did not expect any objections by
his audience to his view of family life. If there really had been
a patriarchal structure we should expect that the author could
not make the family relationships a theme of his collection and
keep silence about the father at the same time.[11] So the problem
lies in the assumption of modern commentators that there was a
strict patriarchal family structure in which the father had all the
responsibility for and power over his daughter.

But the Song of Songs is not the only source which reveals that
the relationship between brothers and sisters played a dominant
part in the family structure of Ancient Israel, and that the father
did not have as strong a function as it is normally assumed.[12]

Theologie, 16], Frankfurt a.M. 1981, 225), is purely speculative.

[10]Cf. also the reference to the city guards in Cant. 5:7.

[11]Compare, for example, the Egyptian love songs, which do mention the
father beside the mother, e.g. S. Schott, *Altägyptische Liebeslieder*, Zürich
[2]1950, 40, 69.

[12]H.-P. Müller, *Das Hohelied* (ATD, 16/2), Göttingen 1992, 87, like many
other exegetes, points to Gen. 24; 34 and 2 Sam. 13f., where the brothers
are depicted in a function comparable to the one they have in the Song of
Songs and with which we will deal further down. But he questions, whether
a section like Cant. 8:8-10 are "den Normvorstellungen einer älteren Zeit
wirklich noch nahe, oder versetzt es nostalgisch – scherzhaft vielleicht auch
– in längst vergangene Zeiten?" Thus H.-P. Müller also assumes, that such
sections really point to a society in which the brothers were expected to
look after their sister's sexual behaviour and to deal with the question of
her marriage. But the pre-Hellenistic collection of the Song of Songs gives
no hint for the assumption that the author wanted to place his audience in
some bygone time. Such hints are only found in the Hellenistic additions, as
I shall argue later (cf. p. 79). The observation that such additions are needed

However, here we have to stop looking at the bright side of love
and turn instead to some dark stories about rape and humiliation.

4 2 Sam. 13–14 and Gen. 34: The Brothers and Their Humiliated Sister

The sad stories of 2 Sam. 13–14 and Gen. 34 illustrate the specific
responsibility of the brothers for their sister, which was grounded
in their intimate relationship. Let us first take a closer look at
2 Sam. 13–14.

4.1 2 Sam. 13–14

This story tells how Amnon fell in love with his sister Tamar and
wanted to sleep with her (2 Sam. 13:1-2). To reach this aim he
pretended to be ill and asked his father to send Tamar to him so
that she would look after him (13:3-6). After she had reached his
house, he sent all other people away and called his sister to come
into his bedroom, where he raped her (13:7-14).

This story presupposes that neither the wish of a sick man to
be looked after by his sister, nor the fact that his grown-up sister
was together with him alone in his bedroom, were uncommon or
rejected by the moral code. On the contrary: the plan which was
proposed by Amnon's cousin and dubious friend Jonadab depends
on the naturalness of such a situation. This aspect offers us a sad
parallel to the wish of the girl in Cant. 8:1-2 not only to caress her
friend in public but even to bring him to her own room, where she
could take care of him tenderly as she would do with her brother.

The difference in the reactions of David, Tamar's father, and
Absalom, another brother of hers, is significant. The fact of the
rape makes David angry (13:21), but there is no reaction by him
either towards his daughter nor towards his son Amnon. It is
Absalom who takes care of his raped sister. He speaks to her and
takes her to his house, where she then lives in seclusion (13:20).
And it is he who waits two years for an opportunity to take
revenge for her (13:22-29). So it is Absalom who sees to the issue

---

to transform the book into a depiction of older times clearly shows that,
without those, the texts are not to be understood in this way.

of his sister. His advice to Tamar that she should be silent (13:20) is not based on a wrong family solidarity,[13] as it is often the fact in modern societies, but means that she could not react on her own to the crime, in contrast to Absalom.

Instead, Absalom's words in 2 Sam. 13:20 are to be understood as an answer to the cry of Tamar in 13:19. The Verb זעק denotes a "Notschrei der Anklage oder Appellation, mit dem ein Bedrohter oder Vergewaltiger in auffälligster Weise das Eingreifen der gemeindlichen Rechtsinstanz (2 Sam. 13,19 [...]) oder deren obersten Richter (...) heischt".[14] The fact that Absalom himself carried out the revenge implies that we cannot understand his answer as a sign that he took the crime less seriously because the rapist was the brother of Tamar. Thus his command, "Now be silent, [for] he is your brother", means that Tamar should stop her cries; and the second admonition, not to pay attention to this matter, is the advice that Tamar should no more try to react herself to what happend. שִׁית לֵב ל has the connotation of reaction to something (cf. Exod. 7:23; 1 Sam. 4:20; Ps. 48:14; 62:11; Prov. 24:32) or to act in a special respect (cf. Job 7:17; Prov. 27:32).[15] The reader has to keep in mind that our story does not refer to a society in accordance with the ideal of a constitutional state, in which even family affairs are subject to official laws. On the contrary, the story is to be understood against the background of a society in which family conflicts were normally a matter for the family alone. Especially in the case of the story of Tamar in which she and her rapist are children of the king, who himself represents the law, it cannot be expected that Tamar as an unmarried woman had a real chance to appeal to an independent court against her royal brother![16] To judge that Absalom's

---

[13]Cf. e.g. S. Bar Efrat, *Narrative Art in the Bible* (JSOT.S, 17), Sheffield 1989, 271; H. Schulte, *Dennoch gingen sie aufrecht: Frauengestalten im Alten Testament*, Neukirchen–Vluyn 1995, 126; E. Seifert, *Tochter und Vater im Alten Testament: Eine ideologiekritische Untersuchung zur Verfügungsgewalt von Vätern über ihre Töchter* (Neukirchener Theologische Dissertationen und Habilitationen, 9), Neukirchen–Vluyn 1997, 109.

[14]G.F. Hasel, *art.* "זעק", in: *ThWAT*, Bd. 2, Stuttgart 1977, 633.

[15]Cf. I. Müllner, *Gewalt im Hause Davids: Die Erzählung von Tamar und Amnon (2 Sam 13,1-22)* (Herders Biblische Studien, 13), Freiburg & Basel, etc. 1997, 310: "Sie [the phrase שִׁית לֵב, I.K.] meint das Beachten eines Gegenstandes und impliziert, daß dieser Akt der Beachtung Konsequenzen zeigt".

[16]It should also to be kept in mind that 2 Sam. 13 is not in accord with the mosaic laws as a comparison of 13:13 with Lev. 18:9; 20:17 and Deut.

answer "zielt also darauf, daß Tamar Handlungsfähigkeit abgibt"[17] and is
to be labeled a "verbaler Gewaltakt" which ends in the (social) death of
Tamar,[18] means to misunderstand the answer of Absalom completely. Obviously Tamar had no real possibility to act against Amnon or to get back to
her old social status. But Absalom, her brother, wanted to take revenge for
her and he takes care of the further life of the woman, as far as it was possible in his society.[19] Thus H. Hagan is correct in stating that the "seeming
insensitivity of the statement (...) fits well enough with Absalom's plan of
delay and disguise".[20]

27:22 shows. Thus the story presupposes a society where such laws are not
accepted (or even known), cf. e.g. S. Bar Efrat, *op. cit.*, 239f.

[17] Thus I. Müllner, *op. cit.*, 319.

[18] Idem, *op. cit.*, 321.

[19] This is the meaning of the last part of 2 Sam. 13:20, which – by the way
– gives an answer to Tamar's question in 13:13: "Where should I go with
my shame?" ושממה is not a verb as I. Müllner, *op. cit.*, 323, takes it, but
an adverb which is introduced by a *w-explicativum*. Thus ושממה explicates
that Tamar lived in Absalom's house in the status of a woman who has to
stay alone and cannot be married to another man because of the crime she
was a victim of (cf. S. Bar Efrat, *op. cit.*, 267; R. Burrichter, "Die Klage
der Leidenden wird stumm gemacht: Eine biblisch-literarische Reflexion zum
Thema Vergewaltigung und Zerstörung der Identität", in: Chr. Schaumberger, *Weil wir nicht vergessen wollen...: ... zu einer Feministischen Theologie im deutschen Kontext* [Anfragen: Diskussionen Feministischer Theologie,
1], Münster 1987, 16; E. Seifert, *op. cit.*, 107). One may blame a society, in
which a raped girl got such a status, but not a figure like Absalom, who gave
his humiliated sister a home to live in. Cf. also Ph. Trible, *Texts of Terror:
Literary-Feminist Readings of Biblical Narratives*, Philadelphia 1984, 51-3.
The suspicion of R. Burrichter, *art. cit.*, 35f., that the phrase 'Absalom's
sister' denotes in some way Absalom's ownership of Tamar, because his advice
was a preparation for *his* revenge and he used Tamar's suffering for his own
plans to get rid of a rival (cf. also Idem, *art. cit.*, 31, where she refers to
Budde and Rost, who interpreted the story in connection with Absalom's
revolt), does not only overlooks the fact that Tamar had no chance for her own
revenge, but is also methodologically questionable. By this Burrichter changes
from the level of textual interpretation to psychological speculations, what
the *personae dramatis* might have thought or felt. And it even contradicts
the story itself. Explicitly it is stated in 13:22 and 32 that Absaloms hate and
murder of his brother is motivated by Amnon's crime and not by Absalom's
attempt to get rid of Amnon as a rival; cf. also S. Bar Efrat, *op. cit.*, 274:
"Thus it was family affairs, not political objective which according to the
narrator, led to Amnon's murder".

[20] H. Hagan, "Deception as Motif and Theme in 2 Sam. 9–20; 1 Kgs 1–2",

David's distance from his daughter, which is revealed by his poor reaction to her rape, is further illustrated by his completely different reaction to Absalom's revenge and Amnon's death.[21] He mourns for Amnon for a long time, and Absalom is forced by his father's wrath to flee (13:36-39). Only by a ruse of Joab and the wise woman from Tekoa could David be convinced to give up his wrath and let Absalom come back (14:1-22). Even then David denied Absalom access to him for two years (14:24, 28).

The story by which the wise woman from Tekoa illustrated David's behaviour (14:5-7) reveals that not the poor reaction of David to his daughter was considered as a fault.[22] It depicts the conflict just as a matter between the two brothers. Accordingly, the fact that Absalom killed Amnon because he had raped his sister is of interest for David only in one respect: it was not an attempted coup to get rid of all other sons of the king (13:32-33), but only Absalom's revenge for his sister. David's fault is only seen in his very harsh reaction against Absalom (14:13-14).

Absalom's sympathy with Tamar's fate is grounded on the fact that he was her full brother in contrast to her half-brother Amnon, as many commentators observed.[23] Already the story's introduction refers to this fact by calling Tamar explicitly a sister of Absalom but Amnon only a son of David and not her brother (13:1). Accordingly, Amnon calls Tamar not his, but his brother's sister in his dialog with Jonadab (13:4). By stating that Tamar

---

Bib 60 (1979), 310; cf. also J.P. Fokkelman, *Narrative Art and Poetry in the Books of Samuel* (SSN, 20), vol. 1, Assen 1981, 111.

[21] This distance is also made clear by the fact that at no point is Tamar called David's daughter or he Tamar's father. Tamar herself calls him "the king" (13:13). "No familial language relates father and daughter" (P. Trible, *op. cit.*, 42; cf. also 53). In contrast, Amnon and Absalom are called David's sons (e.g. 13:1, 21, 25, 37) and David their father (13:5). Cf. also R. Burrichter, *art. cit.*, 34f.

[22] Thus it is not correct that 13:21 "enthält (...) aber sicher den unausgesprochenen Vorwurf, daß David seine Autorität und seine Funktion als Richter nicht wahrnimmt". (Fr. Stolz, *op. cit.*, 247).

[23] Cf. e.g., Fr. Stolz, *op. cit.*, 245; E. Seifert, *op. cit.*, 104; S. Schroer, *Die Samuelbücher* (Neuer Stuttgarter Kommentar: Altes Testament, 7), Stuttgart 1992, 171.

was the full sister of Absalom and not of Amnon, the exposition
of the story prepares and gives the reason for the different behaviour of the brothers toward their sister. Accordingly, verses 22
and 32 account for Absalom's wrath and revenge because that
Amnon raped Absalom's sister. Thus, obviously, it was clear for
the audience of the story that it was to be expected from a full
brother of a girl, not her father, to take revenge for his sister who
was raped.

The difference between the relations of full and half brothers
in respect to their sister recalls the fact that the girl's brothers
in the Song of Songs are always connected to her through their
mother and, by this, are depicted as full brothers. And the poor
reaction of David to the fate of his daughter corresponds to the
absence of the father in the Song of Songs which deals with a girl's
sexual and emotional experiences of love, a girl who was attached
to her mother but not to her father and, through her mother, to
her full brothers.

The emotional connotation of the brother-sister relationship
and the ambivalent status of a half brother is reflected by the
fact that the story calls Tamar the sister of Amnon: only in the
context of his 'love' for her (2 Sam. 13:2, 11) and the wish that she
should attend him (13:5, 6),[24] Amnon reminds David that she is
his sister as an argument to send her to him – so here he is acting
like a brother. But the fact that he has to ask David, her father,
to send her to him, depends on his status as her half brother,
who does not belong to her mother's house and does not stand
in direct contact with her – in contrast to her brother Absalom,
who speaks directly to her and takes her into his house without
asking David (13:19-20).

---

[24] Additionally, in 13:20, the speech of Absalom, Amnon is called Tamar's
brother; but there this phrase has, as shown above, the meaning that this
special connection between the rapist and his victim makes it impossible,
that Tamar could react against Amnon by herself, and that she should leave
it to her brother Absalom.

4.2 Gen. 34

These results are corroborated by Gen. 34. As this text is a product of a longer redactional process, first we have to clear its history. By this we are offered a chance to see what different authors or redactors, who worked on this text at different times, thought about our subject.[25]

Two stories are connected in Gen. 34. The first tells about the reaction of Simeon and Levi to Shechem's deed who treated Dinah, their sister, "like a prostitute" (34:31). For that reason they killed Shechem (34:25-26*), which caused a rebuke by Jacob. He feared that by the deed of these two sons he and his family would come into the serious danger of being destroyed by the "inhabitants of the land" (34:30). Hence this story will be called the 'Shechem story'. The second story, which will be referred to by the name 'Hamor story', tells about a negotiation between Hamor and Jacob and his sons. Hamor offers them to become inhabitants of the land (34:10). The reason for this proposition is revealed by 34:23. The property of Jacob's clan would enrich Hamor's people. But Jacob's sons take Hamor's offer as a chance to outwit the town's inhabitants. Deceitfully, they tell them that they could only agree on the condition that the people of the town would circumcise themselves. After this has happened and the men of the town are defenceless because of the pain of circumcision, Jacob's sons attack the town and loot it (34:25*, 26*, 27-29). Since this second story does not deal with our subject – a girl's relationship

---

[25]Most of the commentators agree with the assumption that Gen. 34 has a longer history of development. But there is discussion whether one story was later reworked (thus e.g. E. Blum, *Die Komposition der Vätergeschichte* [WMANT, 57], Neukirchen–Vluyn 1984, 213-27), or whether Gen. 34 is a composition of two independent stories by a redactor who created his own story from them (thus e.g. C. Westermann, *Genesis* [BKAT, 1/2], Neukirchen–Vluyn 1981, 651-4). I take the latter position, but differ in some details from the older attempts. As in this article there is no room for a detailed discussion, I shall just present a short outline of my opinion and the main arguments without a discussion of the literature. For different opinions the reader can consult the aforementioned books and the literature quoted there.

with her brothers (and father) – I leave it aside.

These two stories were united by a Deuteronomistic redactor (hence called D), who connected Hamor and Shechem by the assumption that they were father and son. This historical view is found only in the Deuteronomistic History (DtrH), which deemed the people of Shechem as Hamor's descendants (Josh. 24:32; Judg. 9:28).[26] Also the connection of non-circumcision with the motif of disgrace (חרפה, Gen. 34:14) is found in Josh. 5:7-9.[27] Hamor's offer that the alliance between his people and the Jacob's clan should also include intermarriage between the two groups (34:9, 16, 21b), by which they would become 'one nation' (34:16b, 21b), is formulated according to Deut. 7:3.[28] By this allusion to Deut. 7, D could explain the strange behaviour of Jacob's sons, for Deut. 7:2 states explicitly that Israel is not only forbidden to make an alliance with the seven people of Canaan, but also to have mercy on them. Thus D explicitly declares that Shechem had wrought folly in Israel (Gen. 34:7bα), a phrase which is also found again only in Deuteronomistic context.[29] Also the phrase לא יעשה (34:7bβ) with

---

[26] The fact that Judg. 9:28 calls the old inhabitants of Shechem as "Hamor's men, the father of Shechem" shows that the connection between (the town) Shechem and Hamor was a fixed historical fact for the DtrH – the mentioning of Hamor has no function in Judg. 9. Thus it can be assumed that Gen. 39:19, which expresses the same fact as Josh. 24:32, is not the source for Josh. 24:32 (and Judg. 9:28) but a reference to it which was added by D.

[27] Cf. also 1 Sam. 17:26, 36, in which it is the ערל Goliath, who reviled (חרף) Israel. Even if this connection is not so close, it reveals that the association between being not circumcised and being a חרפה for Israel was a motif of DtrH. The only other text in which such a connection appears is Jer. 6:10; but there the connection is even looser.

[28] This becomes obvious by a comparison of Gen. 34:9 (והתחתנו אתנו בנתיכם), 34:16 (תתנו לנו ואת בנתינו תקחו לכם ונתנו את בנתינו לכם ואת בנתיכם נקח לנו וישבנו), and 34:21b (את בנתם נקח לנו לנשים ואת בנתינו נתן להם אתכם), with Deut. 7:3 (ולא תתחתן בם בתך לא תתן לבנו ובתו לא תקח לבנך). The connection between חתן and נתן בת appears also in 1 Sam. 18:27 and is obviously a Deuteronomistic phrase; cf. also E. Blum, op. cit., 221.

[29] Cf. Deut. 22:21; Josh. 7:15; Judg. 20:6, 10; Jer. 29:23. W. Thiel, Die deuteronomistische Redaktion von Jeremia 26–45 (WMANT, 52), Neukirchen–Vluyn 1981, 18, shows that Jer. 29:23 was rewritten by the Deuteronomistic redactor of Jer.; but he finds his additions only in Jer. 29:23aβb. But the fact that עשה נבלה בישראל is only found in Gen. 34, Deut., Josh., and Judg. argues

the meaning "(such a crime) should not be done" has parallels
only in the Deuteronomistic literature.[30]

Probably, D alludes also to Deut. 22:28-29. The formulation
of Gen. 34:2 (וירא אתה שכם בן חמור החוי נשיא הארץ ויקח אתה
וישכב אתה ויענה) reminds one of the phrasing of this law:

כי יִמצא איש נער בתולה אשר לא ארשה   28a

ותפשׂה ושכב עמה ונמצאו   b

ונתן האיש השכב עמה לאבי הנער חמשים כסף   29a

ולו תהיה לאשה תחת אשר ענה לא יוכל שלחה כל ימיו[31]   b

The function of this allusion is clear. The Shechem story faces
a reader who knows Deut. 22:28-29 with the problem that the
reaction of Dinah's brothers were not in line with this legislation.
Shechem offered a price for the bride and wanted to marry her –
this is what Deut. 22:28-29 demands. Obviously D did not ignore
this problem, but he gave an answer to it: Shechem was not an
Israelite but belonged to the seven nations Deut. 7 speaks of –

---

for the assumption that at least also עשׂו נבלה בישראל in Jer. 29:23aα belongs
to the Deuteronomistic redaction of Jer. 29.

[30]Cf. 2 Sam. 13:12, in which a connection between these two phrases occurs
in a slighly different form: כי לא יעשה כן בישראל אל תעשה את הנבלה הזאת.

Probably Gen. 34:7aγ (ויחר להם מאד), a common phrase which occurs 3
times (of 8) in DtrH (1 Sam. 18:8; 2 Sam. 3:8; 13:21), was also added by D.
It repeats the statement of 34:7aβ. There the unusual עצב (Dt) is used which
occurs again in Gen. 6:6 only. Thus 34:7aγ may be an interpretation of this
word.

[31]Deut. 22:28-29 is a reformulation of an older form of this law, as it is
found in Exod. 22:15: וכי יפתה איש בתולה אשר לא ארשה ושכב עמה מהר ימהרנה
לו לאשה. But in this text the idea of humiliation is absent. The formulation
of Gen. 34:2 is not to be labeled a direct quotation of Deut. 22:28-29, as the
differences show; thus it is just an allusion. It has to be kept in mind that
Gen. 34:2 is only a reformulation of the statement of the old Shechem story,
which told that Shechem slept with Dinah. But as Gen. 34:31 shows, he did
not rape or force her.

The observation that the phrase שכב – לקח in the sense 'to take (a woman)
and sleep with her' has its counterparts only in Deuteronomistic literature (2
Sam. 11:4; 12:11) and the fact that the description of the deed of Shechem as
ענה associates it with Deut. 22:29, leads to the assumption that the Shechem
story told only that he saw Dinah and slept with her (וירא אתה שכם נשׂיא הארץ
וישכב אתה).

thus D labels him a Hivite (34:3)![32] And with those an Israelite must have no mercy (Deut. 7:2).[33]

But the interpretation of Shechem's deed in the light of Deut. 22:28-29 causes another problem: Why did Dinah stay in his house, as Gen. 34:26 presupposes? D gives an answer also to this question through the addition of 34:3bβ: He did not only fall in love with her, but also spoke to her heart, which means he consoled and convinced her. The phrase דבר על לב in this sense is not uncommon in DtrH, cf. Judg. 19:3 and 2 Sam. 19:8.[34]

The observation that the connection between the Shechem story and the Hamor story depends on the Deuteronomistic view that the Shechemites were descendants of Hamor, argues for the assumption that Gen. 34:4 and 8b belong to this redaction too.[35] These verses unite the two stories and explain why not only Shechem, but also Hamor appear in the negotiation.[36]

Probably 34:19 is also an addition of this redactor. It calls Shechem a

---

[32] Cf. also Gen. 34:30, in which the Canaanites and Perizzites are mentioned as the inhabitants of the land, who also appear together with the Hivites in Deut. 7:2. The fact that the term ישב הארץ for the people of Canaan occurs especially (but not only) in Deuteronomistic contexts is not a sufficient argument for the assumption that all of Gen. 34:30-31 belongs to D, as E. Blum, *op. cit.*, 218, states. But the addition of the "Canaanites and Perizzites" brought these verses in line with Deuteronomistic language.

[33] Maybe D had in mind also a text like Deut. 9:4, where it is stated, that the people of Canaan are dispelled because of their crimes.

[34] Probably also Gen. 34:3bα belongs to the Deuteronomistic redaction. This part serves as a commentary to the uncommon phrase דבק נפש ב (34:3a) in the sense 'to fall in love with'. The word נער instead of נערה occurs again in Gen. 34:3bβ and Gen. 24:14, 16, 28, 55; probably Gen. 24 was also formed by a Deuteronomistic redaction, and it shares the motif of the (forbidden) marriage with a non-Israelite with the Deuteronomistic edition of Gen. 34, cf. E. Blum, *op. cit.*, 383-9.

[35] With 34:4 the problem remains why the term ילדה instead of נער is used (cf. 34:3, 19; for 34:3 cf. further down and for 34:19 n. 44). Otherwise this word occurs only in the postexilic texts Joel 4:3 and Zech. 8:5; thus probably it did not belong to the original Shechem story, but to a later addition. The question remains what D wanted to express with this term – or did he just choose another term to avoid a third repetition of נער after it was used twice in the preceeding sentences?

[36] Accordingly, the mentioning of Shechem in Gen. 34:13 (את שכם), 18 (ובעיני שכם בן חמור), and 20 (ושכם בנו) and the mentioning of Hamor as Shechem's father in 34:2, 6, 13, 26 belong to this redaction.

'young lad' (נער), in contrast to the Shechem story in which he is the chief of the land (נשׂיא הארץ, 34:2a).[37] The function of this verse is to explain better why Hamor and Shechem accept the proposal Jacob's sons made: Shechem is in love with Dinah and the most honoured man in the house of Hamor. This assumption is in accordance with the observation that the term נער is quite common in DtrH; more than 60% of the occurrences of this word are found in Josh. through to 2 Kgs.[38]

Probably, the Deuteronomistic redaction was not the last step in the history of Gen. 34. Especially the motif that Shechem made Dinah unclean, which is found just in three supplementing sentences (Gen. 34:5aα, 13bβ, 27b), adds to the text an idea which reminds one of the discussions about marriage between Jewish and non-Jewish people in later postexilic times. Thus Ezra 9:11-12 explains the prohibition of intermarriage between these two groups by the argument that the people of Canaan defiled the land by their uncleanliness.[39] But, in contrast to Ezra 6:21, no hint is found in Gen. 34 that Shechem could really convert to Judaism by circumcision. Thus the author of these additions still shares the opinion of D that a connection between Israel and the 'Canaanite' people is strictly forbidden. As we can also find the influence of P in 34:1aβ,[40] it is best to assume that these later

---

[37] Nowhere else in Genesis a Canaanite ruler is called נשׂיא. The term occurs only again in 17:20, 23:6, and 25:16, which all probably belong to P, as C. Westermann, *op. cit.*, 655, observed. But there it refers either to Abraham, the נשׂיא of God (23:6), or to the chiefs of the Ismaelite clans (17:20; 25:16). This shows that in P נשׂיא designates not the chief of a land, but of wandering clans. Thus this term in 34:2 cannot belong to P.

[38] Also the rest of the verse is in accordance with the language found in Deuteronomistic literature. Thus חפץ ב in the sense 'to love/like someone' is found e.g. in Deut. 21:14; 1 Sam. 18:22; 19:1; 2 Sam. 15:26; 20:11, and the term נכבד 'honoured' in 1 Sam. 9:6; 22:14; 2 Sam. 23:19, 23.

[39] Cf. Ezra 9:11, הארץ אשר אתם באים לרשתה ארץ נדה היא בנדת עמי הארצות בתועבתיהם אשר מלאוה מפה אל פה בטמאתם.

[40] Compare 34:1aβ, "whom she had born to Jacob" with Gen. 16:15-16; 25:12, and the mention of the land's daughter in Gen. 27:46.
Another addition of P may be seen in 34:10bγ (והאחזו בה), which is "offensichtlich der Terminus für das Ansässigwerden Israels in Kanaan bei P" (C. Westermann, *op. cit.*, 657). Also the phrases לנו/לכם כל זכר in 34:15, 22 which is typical after מול (N) in P (cf. Idem, *op. cit.*, 658) may be an addition

additions belong to P, who explains the prohibition of intermarriage with non-Israelites by the argument that Israel becomes
unclean through sexual contact with them.[41]

Thus the old story of Shechem and Dinah runs as follows:

> 34:1*[42] Dinah, Leah's daughter, went out. (2*) And Shechem,
> the chief of the land, saw her. And he slept with her. (3a) But
> he fell in love with Dinah, Jacob's daughter. (5) When Jacob
> heard (of it), while his sons were on the field together with their
> flock, he kept silent until they came back. (7aβ) When they
> heard (of it), the men became indignant.[43] (11) But Shechem
> spoke to her father and her brothers: "May I find favour in
> your eyes. And whatever you declare, I will give. (12) Make the
> price for the bride and the gift I have to give great – I will
> give whatever you will say. [But give me the young girl to be
> my wife!]"[44] (25aα*)[45] But two of Jacob's sons,[46] Samuel and

---

of P.

[41] The idea that forbidden sexual contact makes someone unclean is also
found in Lev. 18:20, 23; cf. also Lev. 18:24. This motif was obviously common
in priestly circles, as Ezek. 18:6, 11, 15 shows. Thus the argumentation of Ezra
9:11-12 is a later adaptation of this earlier priestly ideology.

[42] 34:1 was of course not the beginning of the story, which could not start
with a ויקטל-form and presupposes knowledge about the family of Jacob. But
the episode we are interested in began with 34:1.

[43] Cf. for the syntax W. Groß, *Die Pendenskonstruktion im Biblischen
Hebräisch: Studien zum althebräischen Satz*, vol. 1 (Arbeiten zu Text und
Sprache im Alten Testament, 27), St. Ottilien 1987, 45-8.

[44] The use of נער for 'young girl', as in the Deuteronomistic additions to
Gen. 34:3, could serve as an argument for the assumption that 34:12b was
also formulated by D. In fact, this sentence could be skipped, because the
context makes it clear that Shechem wanted to marry Dinah. Also, the story
is told quite shortly. But maybe it is just a reformulation of D or a later
assimilation of an original נערה to the formulation in 34:3.

[45] The Shechem story probably did not give an answer to Shechem's proposal but this 'answer' was seen in the reaction of Simeon and Levi. 34:14 was
obviously formulated by D as especially the connection between ערל and חרפה
shows, cf. above, p. 64. Also, the plural introduction (ויאמרו אלהם) shows the
redactional character of this verse. While it cannot be excluded completely
that there was a short answer which was substituted in the redactional process by the answer to Hamor (and D's addition to it), the observation that D
obviously took the Shechem story as the basic text and added to it aspects
of the Hamor story and his own additions makes it more probable that he
did not skip parts of the Shechem story.

[46] The text of 34:25 is probably a combination of parts of the Shechem and

Levi, Dinah's brothers, took both their swords. (26*) And after they had killed Shechem with the sword,[47] they took Dinah away from Shechem's house, and went away. (29b*) And they plundererd everything which was in the house.[48] (30*) Then Jacob spoke to Simeon and Levi: "You have brought trouble on me by making me odious to the inhabitants of the land. I own only few men, and they will gather themselves against me and attack me, and I shall be destroyed, I and my house!". (31) But they answered: "Should he treat our sister as a prostitute?"[49]

The parallels of the Shechem story with 1 Sam. 13 are obvious: Shechem treated Dinah in a way which was considered as treating her like a whore.[50] Her father did not react to this deed, because he cared about himself and his family's position as foreigners.[51] Obviously his daughter's fate is of less interest to him. But his sons, and especially Simeon and Levi, "Dinah's brothers" (34:25),

the Hamor story, which told that after three days Jacob's sons attacked the city and killed all men including Hamor (26a, first two words).

[47] The words of Gen. 34:26a, ואת שכם הרגו לפי חרב, probably belonged to the Shechem story. As Gen. 34:5, 7aβ show, the author of the story liked to use different syntactically features to mark the logical hypotaxis of sentences.

[48] Read with the Samaritanus and the Peshitta ויבזו את instead of ויבזו ואת, which is obviously a dittography.

[49] Whether this was the real end of the story is a matter of debate, but obviously the episode which is to be discussed in our context ends here.

The parts of the Hamor story D took over are 34:6* (without אבי שכם), the first two words of 7 (the sentence made of 34:6* + these two words were split into two by D's addition of באו מן השדה), 8a, 10abαβ (without the first ו), 13a (without ואת שכם ו and אביו), 15 (without לכם כל זכר), 17 (without ולקחנו את בתנו [D]), 18a, 20 (without ושכם בנו and with singular forms in 20aβb), 21a, 22 (without לנו כל זכר), 23-25*, 26aα (the first two words, cf. footnote 46), 27a, 28, and 29a (without יבזו).

A clear difference between these two stories is that the Shechem story always uses אמר (34:11, 12, 30, 31), while the Hamor story uses דבר (34:6, 8, 13, 20).

[50] Thus the Shechem story did not tell about a rape. It may be questioned whether even the Deuteronomistic redactor interpreted Shechem's deed in this way, cf. L.M. Bechtel, "What if Dinah is not Raped? (Genesis 34)", JSOT 62 (1994), 19-36.

[51] Note the clear connection between Shechem, the נשיא הארץ, and the ישב הארץ, whose revenge Jacob fears.

who were her full brothers – she was Leah's daughter as 34:1 explicitly states – are particularly interested in what happened to their sister and react to it. They reject Jacob's reproach explicitly with the argument that Shechem treated *their sister* wrongly.

Thus Gen. 34 presupposes the same family structure that we found in the Song of Songs and in 2 Sam. 13: the father is less affected by the fate of his daughter, his interest is focused on the fate and position of his family in the context of its broader neighbourhood. But the brothers, especially the full brothers, take a lively interest in what happens to their sister and feel responsible for her sexual honour and her being unmolested.

The fact that neither the Deuteronomistic redactor nor the additions made by P play down the distant attitude of Jacob to his daughter reveals that these post-exilic authors and their audience shared the view of the family structure which was presupposed in the pre-exilic story.[52]

This corresponds to the fact that also the pre-exilic story of 2 Sam. 13–14 was incorporated into the DtrH without any attempt to alter the reaction of David or to play down his being uninterested in Tamar's fate.

5 The Part of the Brothers in the Context of the Marriage of Their Sister

According to the Shechem story in Gen. 34 Shechem negotiates about the marriage not only with Jacob, but also with Dinah's brothers. This presupposes that brothers had the right to have a say in this regard.[53]

This is confirmed by Gen. 24, which tells us about the courtship of Rebekah. In this text not Bethuel, her father, but her brother, Laban, takes the main part in the marital negotiation

---

[52]Moreover, the additions of P in 34:13 and 27 clearly state that the reaction of the brothers are to be explained by the fact that Shechem (and the Shechemites) made "their sister" unclean. In contrast, P saw no necessity to add anything to Jacob's reaction in Gen. 34:5 and only adds there that Jacob heard that Shechem made his daughter unclean.

[53]It has to be remembered that Jacob also waited until the return of his sons (Gen. 34:5). Shechem could propose his offer only until they came back.

(24:33-60). Moreover, after Rebekah has met Abraham's servant she does not come back to her father's, but to her mother's house, where she tells about the things which happened at the well (24:28). The continuation in 24:29 presupposes that there, in her mother's house, Laban heard about the events. This exactly corresponds to our observations concerning the Song of Songs: that a girl belonged to the sphere of her mother and was linked to her brothers by this context.

Only at one point in the story do we also meet Bethuel. In 24:50 he agrees together with Laban to the marriage of Rebekah. But everything else concerning the fate of Rebekah is arranged only by Laban and her mother. They ask her if she wants to leave her family at once (24:54-58), and they bless her (24:60). Thus not Rebekah's father, Bethuel, but her brother and mother are concerned with the matters of Rebekah's own wishes and welfare.

That the mention of Bethuel was possibly added to the story later, as many commentators assume,[54] makes no difference in this respect. Even then the original story presupposes that there is nothing uncommon about the fact that a girl's mother and brother take the main part in this matter – the absence of the father is not explained in this broad story, not even in 24:23 where Abraham's servant asks Rebekah about her father and about the possibility of his stay in the house at night. Thus it can be assumed that the absence of the father in this matter meant no problem to the narrator and his audience.

The explanation given by some commentators that the original story had never mentioned the father at all because he was already dead,[55] is only grounded on the prejudice that families in Ancient Israel had a patriarchal structure which left no important place to other members beside the father. But if this explanation were correct, why then does this broad story at no point mention that Bethuel was dead? Also, the specific role that the mother plays in the story cannot be explained by the assumption that her husband was dead and that his son took over his functions.

If we assume that the mention of Bethuel is only secondary,

---

[54]Cf., e.g., G. von Rad, *Das erste Buch Mose: Genesis* (ATD, 2–4), Göttingen & Zürich [12]1987, 204f.; E. Blum, *op. cit.*, 387.

[55]Cf., e.g., C. Westermann, *op. cit.*, 475-76.

this would also mean that only in one passage of the story the later editor, who regarded Bethuel as the father of Rebekah and Laban (and clearly did not share the assumption that he was dead), missed a reference to the father. For him a father was indispensible only in respect to the basic consent to a girl's marriage. Thus even for the editor and his audience the idea was not unusual that not the father, but the brother of Rebekah invited the servant of Abraham and afterwards, together with his mother, managed the departure of Rebekah and blessed her.

The assumption that the father's part in a marital negotiation was to decide whether he wanted to give his daughter away to a man and, by this, into a different family is corroborated by Gen. 29 and Exod. 2:15-22. These texts only mention the father, but they skip the question regarding what the girl wished and what this marriage meant to her. They only deal with the negotiation between the husband-to-be and the bride's family, but do not mention at all what happens in the family of the bride in this respect.

6   The Relationships Between Father and Daughter and Brothers and Sisters

The observations made up to now allow us to draw a picture of the family structure and a girl's relations to the male members of her family, which form the background of the texts just discussed.

Although the motif of an emotional affection of the father for his daughter is not completely missing in the Old Testament,[56] usually a more distant relationship between father and daughter predominates. In contrast to his relation to the sons, the father seems to be astonishingly uninterested in the personal fate of his daughters. It seems that for a father the abuse of a daughter was less serious than the abuse of a male guest, as Gen. 19:4-8 or Judg. 19:23-24 illustrate. While in the context of marital negotiations the father takes an important part, he mainly acts as the representative of his family and their interests opposite to the groom's family in this matter. His daughter does not appear in

---

[56]Cf., e.g., 2 Sam. 12:1-4.

this context as a subject with her own interests, but as an object of legal negotiation – the father reacts to a wish of an outsider and decides whether he hands his daughter over to him or not.

This picture corresponds to the legal traditions of Exod. 22:15-16 and Deut. 22:28-29 which deal with the premarital intercourse of a girl, but mainly discuss the problems of the price for the bride, paid as a compensation for the girl to her family. In this context, in which the interests of the family and not of the girl are the main issue, the father takes the only part as the *pater familias*.

The fact that he was held responsible for representing the interests of his family as a whole and not of his daughter as an individual is also revealed by Deut. 22:13-21. The accusation of a man against his wife that she slept with another man while she was still living as his betrothed in her father's house is treated as a legal case between this man and his wife's father. If the man lies, the fine is handed over to the father (22:19); otherwise the woman is killed at the door of her father's house because her deed was held as a crime done in her father's house, as 22:21 clearly states. Thus her father's house was connected either with her deed or with the wrong accusation. Evidently the father himself was not responsible for the deeds of his daughter – when the accusation is right, only his daughter is punished.[57] Thus the father takes a middle position between his daughter and her husband and represents the interests of his family, which are affected either by the slandering of the man or by the crime of his daughter. That the girl was mainly connected with her mother and not with her father is shown by the fact that the proof for her innocence is produced also by her mother (22:15).

In contrast to the father the full brothers have a closer relationship to their sister, based not on legal terms but on an emotional proximity. They take care of her fate and represent her interests regarding an outsider. So they also act in the context of her

---

[57] That her punishment is carried out near her father's house, means that through her killing his house becomes clean from her crime. If the father was held responsible for his daughter, he should be accused too!

marital negotiation and are obliged to defend her and to take revenge for her. At the same time they support the common moral code against her, even though not as an absolute authority – as the humorous lack of the girl's concern about their attitude in the Song of Songs reveals. They meet their sister as an independent subject and she is not just an object of their interests. As Cant. 8:8-9 shows, their attempt at preventing their little sister from acting against the common moral code is motivated by the wish to protect her against her own blunders.[58] The emotional relation between brothers and sisters is grounded in their contact with each other in their mother's house.

The affection between brother and sister is reflected by the metaphor of brother and sister as a loving couple, found not only in the Bible but also throughout the literature of the Ancient Near East.[59]

This relationship must not be called *fratriarchy* in the sense of a legal term.[60] The criticism and reproach the brothers receive through their father (Gen. 34:30; cf. 2 Sam. 13:36-39) show clearly that it was by no means a common obligation for the brothers to take revenge for their sister.[61] The fact that they act on behalf of

---

[58]It should be noted that at no point the texts discussed give the defense of family honour as the brothers' motive. Where a reason for the brothers' action is given, it is always the girl's interest and never the family's interests, cf. especially Gen. 34:31. Thus the explanation of C. Westermann, *op. cit.*, 663, who sees in the reaction of Dinah's brothers the beginning of a "Nationalgefühl, für das das Töten um der eigenen Ehre willen etwas Notwendiges war", is to be rejected.

[59]Cf. e.g. Cant. 4:9, 10, 12; 5:1, 2; M.H. Pope, *Song of Songs* (AB, 7), Garden City, NY, 1977, 480-1; O. Keel, *op. cit.*, 152-3.

[60]Thus e.g. J. Hoftijzer, "Absalom and Tamar: A Case of Fratriarchy?", in *Schrift en uitleg* (FS W.H. Gispen), Kampen 1970, 54-61; C.H. Gordon, "Fratriarchy in the Old Testament", *JBL* 54 (1935), 223-31; cf. also A. Brenner, *art. cit.*, 239.

[61]Cf. also I. Müllner, *op. cit.*, 333. But Müllner is not right in her assumption that the reactions of Absalom and Dinah's brothers are to be understood as an attack against the authority of their fathers – the texts nowhere hint at this interpretation. In Gen. 34 Simeon's and Levi's defence is the last word of the episode and there is no attempt in the text at contradicting it. Cf. also n. 19 above.

their sister is grounded in their emotional relationship to her but not in any sort of power over her or a legal obligation.[62]

7 The Sister's Importance For Her Brothers

The reason why we find only some marginal hints for a positive importance of a girl for her brothers lies in that Old Testament texts are not written in and for the family sphere. If at all, they deal with family matters mainly from the outside. Thus an unmarried girl was represented to the outside by her father and her brothers, and her position inside the family was normally not the central theme of the texts. The only exception is the Song of Songs, and it shows a completely different picture than the other texts.

But there are a few more hints in the literature of the Old Testament and the Ancient Near East for the importance that a girl had for their brothers.

Thus Prov. 7:4 admonishes the young man to call wisdom, which can protect him from the strange woman, his sister. This metaphor is not only explained by the simple fact that Hebrew חכמה is a feminine noun, and thus the feminine אחות 'sister' was chosen to define her. In contrast, the parallel colon combines the feminine noun בינה with the *masculine* noun מדע, 'relative'. Thus אחות in Prov. 7:4 is to be understood literally as 'sister'.[63] The sentence presupposes that a sister had also a guiding and protecting

---

[62] In fact, Gen. 34 and 2 Sam. 13 depict a conflict between the interests of the family as a whole in the context of the enclosing society and the interests of a single member of the family. The father, as the representant of the whole family to the 'outer' world, was held responsible for it; the brothers' deeds depend on a totally different basis: their emotional affection for their sister, whose interests are implicated. But this conflict is just stated, not solved. It could not be solved in a society like the one of Ancient Israel – and is not solved totally in modern societies either, though they are more conscious of this conflict.

[63] Also the term מדע shows that Prov. 7:4 does not understand אחות in the sense of 'bride', as many commentators assume, cf. e.g. A. Meinhold, *Die Sprüche*, Teil 1, Sprüche Kapitel 1–15 (ZBK, 16/1), Zürich 1991, 125; R.C. van Leeuwen, "The Book of Proverbs", in: *The New Interpreter's Bible*, vol. 5, Nashville 1997, 84.

function for her brother, such as he has for his sister (cf. Cant.
8:8!) – but not only for a little brother, because the context of the
text speaks to a grown-up young man.

This corresponds to the function of Anat, the sister of Baal,
in the Ugaritic myths, in which she acts on behalf of her brother.
Not only does she demand a palace for Baal with her well-known
brutality (KTU 1.3 V, cp. 1.4 V 20ff.), but she also stands up
aggressively for him (cp. e.g. KTU 1.3 III 32ff.). Not by chance
is the brother-sister relation between Anat and Baal explicitly
mentioned in the context of her fight with Mot to rescue her
brother. After she had mourned for the dead Baal, searched and
buried his body, she attacks Mot with the words:

> You, oh Mot, give my brother! (KTU 1.6 II 12)

The preceding lines compare her love for Baal with the love of
a mother animal for its offspring and by this make it clear that
Anat is acting for Baal on the ground of her love as a sister and
not as his lover. Thus "brother" is to be taken in this context
literally.

Finally I would like to refer to the part which is taken by
Šeru'a–eterat, the sister of Šamaš–šum–ukin in the story about
his revolt against his brother Assurbanipal, as it is told in Papyrus Amherst 63, 18–21.[64] Before Assurbanipal uses his political
power against his brother, he sends Šamaš–šum–ukin's sister to
Babylon to persuade him not to carry on with his self-destroying
plans (19:15–21:13). This motif, which is missing in the Assyrian
sources, was obviously introduced by the West-Aramaic narrator,
who uses it without any further comments.[65] Evidently, he and

---

[64] Cf. R.C. Steiner, Ch.F. Nims, "Ashurbanipal and Shamash–shum–ukin:
A Tale of Two Brothers from the Aramaic Text in Demotic Script", *RB*
92 (1985), 60-81 (which count the columns as 17-20); S.P. Vleeming, J.W.
Wesselius, "Preliminary Observations on the Revolt of Babylon", in: Idem,
*Studies in Papyrus Amherst 63: Essays on the Aramaic texts in Ara-
maic/demotic Papyrus Amherst 63*, vol. 1, Amsterdam 1985, 31-42.

[65] For the fact that this text was formulated in the Aramaic communities
of the South Syrian or Libanese areas cf. I. Kottsieper, "Die literarische
Aufnahme assyrischer Begebenheiten in frühen aramäischen Texten", in: D.

his audience were familiar with the idea that a sister could have a protecting and guiding function for her brother even in such a serious matter as a revolt. These parallels show that such a relation between sister and brother was common in the Syrian-Palestine area throughout the 2nd and 1st millennium BCE.

8 Conclusion and Outlook

I would like to propose an outline of a family structure that can explain the specific relation between brothers and sisters. Furthermore, I shall make a suggestion as to why and when the family structure of Ancient Israel became patriarchal in the way it is often assumed to have been all the time.

Between an outside and an inside orientated sphere of the family in the societies of Ancient Israel should be distinguished. Men, and especially the father, represented the outside-orientated sphere, whereas the inner sphere was represented by women and especially by the mother as the term 'house of mother' shows. Prov. 31:10-31 gives a good example for this structure. It is the wife who is responsible and acts independently for the economic welfare and the well-being of the family. This also includes trade relations with the outside. So the assignment of the women to the inside orientated sphere of the family does not mean that they are excluded from the public domain. Not only Prov. 31:16 and 24 presuppose that women were active in public, but we also meet Lady Wisdom and the strange woman in the street (Prov. 1:20-21; 7:10ff.; 8:2f.; 9:13ff.). And, also, girls were free to go out in public as the Song of Songs and the story of Dinah show. The only place we do not find them is in the sphere of public administration, which was clearly a men's domain. Thus Prov. 31:23 locates the husband of the strong wife in the city gate. There he makes use

---

Charpin, F. Joannès (eds.), *La circulation des biens, des personnes et des idées dans le Proche-Orient ancien: Actes de la XXXVIIIe Rencontre Assyriologique Internationale (Paris, 8–10 juillet 1991)*, Paris 1992, 283-9; Idem, "Anmerkungen zu Pap. Amherst 63: Teil II-V", *UF* 29 (1997), 397-8; Idem, "Bäume als Kultort", in: U. Neumann–Gorsolke, P. Riede (eds.), *Das Kleid der Erde: Pflanzen in der Lebenswelt des Alten Testament*, Stuttgart 2000, part II.1.

of his power together with his sons, as Ps. 127:5 shows.

The daughters belong to the inner sphere of the family, the mother's house. Thus they had no direct relations to the father which explains the distance between him and them.

The sons' position was ambivalent. On the one hand they belong as men and the father's potential successors to his sphere, which explains the interest the father takes in them in contrast to his daughters. On the other hand they are as children of their mother connected with the sphere of the mother, and through this are in touch with their sisters together with whom they have grown up and are educated in their mother's house.[66] This explains the emotional relations between sisters and especially full brothers, which made the brothers representatives of their sisters to people outside the family. The brothers were the connecting link between the sisters as members of the inner-orientated sphere of women and the outside-orientated sphere of men.

In a society which centres mainly around the family this means a more even and less hierarchical family structure.[67]

---

[66]For the education of sons by their mother cf. especially Prov. 1:8; 6:20; 31:1.

[67]Thus it is questionable if one should label the society of Ancient Israel patriarchal in the common sense of this word. This term blurs the fact that the structure of this society was obviously more complicated and not simply hierarchical, with the father on top. Of course, he was the leader of the family so far as its connection with the outer sphere is concerned, but even there his sons played a certain part. But he clearly was not the main authority and not responsible for all matters within the family. E. Seifert (*op. cit.*, 98) has observed rightly that in a patriarchal society it should belong to the father's duties to protect his daughter from other men. He is "die zuständige Person, wenn sie sich von männlicher Gewalt bedroht fühlt". But, as she proceeds: "Wenn wir uns auf die Suche nach alttestamentlichen Erzählungen begeben, in denen Töchter in einer bedrohlichen Situation Schutz von ihren Väter erfahren, so kommen wir zu einer Defizitanzeige", where she reflects on the stories we dealt with. But is a society in which the father does not act patriarchally, patriarchal?

How misleading the modern approach to a society can be, I learned in a discussion with a friend from Benin. His society is often also labeled by Europeans as patriarchal and in fact, the men are the main persons who appear in public. But in his own family it was his grandmother who owned some land and she alone decided what to do with it. Even when some of

However, in the Hellenistic period there obviously occurred a severe shift in the society of Ancient Israel under the influence of Hellenistic society. Already in Greece of the late fifth and then in the political theories of philosophers of the early fourth century, like Plato and Aristotle, we find the strong tendency to subordinate the private sphere of the family to the realm and the interest of public society. Accordingly, the family was seen as an integral element of a hierarchical structure of power. Under the impact of Hellenism it was just a small step for the societies of Ancient Israel to change the old family structure, in which the father already was the representative of his family, to a hierarchical structure in which the father became an absolute leader and the women lost power.

This shift is reflected in some additions which were added later to two texts discussed above. In this new situation the distant relation of the father to what happened to his daughter in his family became problematic. Accordingly, the Septuagint and 4Q51 add an explanation to 2 Sam. 13:21 stating why David did not act against Amnon as it would be expected by him as the leader of his family: he favoured Amnon for he was his first born son.[68] And the pre-Hellenistic collection of the Song of Songs, which pictured the girl as acting independently of her father, was supplemented with the motif of King Solomon, which is connected with the motif of marriage.[69] By this the collection was moved on the one hand into the distant past – the time of Solomon – and on the other hand the editor could indicate that everything which was told there of course belonged to the officially sanctioned sphere of marriage. And it is not by chance that we find admonitions like

---

this land should be sold, it was her decision. But she never appeared in such negotiations; it was her husband who took over this part as if he were the owner. In fact, he asked his wife what to do and whether to accept the offers of the purchasers – but this happened in the family sphere not seen by outsiders. Thus, from the outside, it appears that the man has the power of decision even about the property of his wife; but this picture does not depict the real situation.

[68] The Septuagint adds at the end of 2 Sam. 13:21: ὅτι ἠγάπα αὐτόν ὅτι πρωτότοκος αὐτοῦ ἦν; 4Q51 reads for this passage: [כי א]הבו כי בכור[ו הוא].

[69] Cf. Cant. 4:11 and above, p. 54 for these Hellenistic additions.

Sir. 7:24-25 and 42:9-14 that demand of a father to take care of
the virginity of his daughter and act authoritatively with her not
before this book, written in Hellenistic times.[70] Now the father
is held responsible for the behaviour of his daughter. One could
add more texts from the Hellenistic period which reflect this shift
in family structure – but this would be another article. Let me
end here with the statement that it was this development that
deprived women of position and power in the societies of Ancient
Israel, and led to a patriarchal family structure that has shaped
modern societies even up till now.

---

[70]Cf. also Sir. 22:3-5, in which the motif is found that a good daughter
brings property to her father, but a bad one brings disgrace. Such admonitions, even a single reference to a daughter, are missing in the older wisdom
literature. In these texts a family seems to consist only of father, mother,
and sons. The comparison with Jesus Sirach, in which now also the daughters appear, illustrates the shift that happened in the Hellenistic period. Now
a father has also to deal with his daughter, who no longer belongs exclusively
to the realm of the mother.

The Role of the Father

A Response to Kottsieper

Arie van der Kooij   (University of Leiden)

Kottsieper's paper is of great interest because, among other things, it concerns an issue that is not given much attention: the relationship between brothers and sisters in Ancient Israel. It stands to reason that in dealing with this topic one should also address the role of the father and the mother in the setting of the family. As Kottsieper notes, it is not easy to give a fair picture, historically speaking, of family structures in ancient Israel because of the fact that our sources are very limited. Moreover, there is also the difficulty of how to reconstruct social realities of family life on the basis of written sources which are, first of all, of a literary nature.

Kottsieper concentrates his discussion on the following passages: Canticles 1:5f. and 8:8-10; Genesis 24 and 34, and 2 Samuel 13-14. From these texts the picture emerges that the brothers, particularly the full brothers, do care very much about their sister, whereas the father is depicted as someone at a distance (Gen. 34 and 2 Sam. 13-14), or is not mentioned at all (Canticles). The father, so Kottsieper argues, is mainly interested in the status of the family in public, and not so much in that of his daughter. At the end of the paper it is suggested that this ancient model changed, rather dramatically, into a family structure of a more hierarchic and patriarchal type in the Hellenistic period.

As a respondent I would like to raise the following questions:

(a) It is true that the father is not mentioned at all in Canticles, but it is doubtful whether this observation can be used as evidence for any type of a family structure. It may be part of the literary genre of love poetry not to mention the father, as, for instance, is the case in the same type of literature in the Sumerian language.

(b) It is to be asked to which extent the stories of Gen. 34 and 2 Sam. 13-14 provide or reflect a basis for the idea of a 'less' patriarchal family structure. It may well be that these stories attest to the idea that the father is primarily concerned with the status of his family in public. Or to state it this way: when an affair such as in 2 Sam. 13-14 takes place in private and does not affect the name of the family in public, the father is not inclined to act (to punish someone or the like). It is to be noted that this is fully in line with the notion of the ancient Near East that a crime accomplished indoors is not that bad as a crime carried out 'in the street', because of the public shame involved (Compare 2 Sam. 12:12). It therefore is doubtful whether the stories just mentioned can be used as evidence for a less patriarchal family structure.

(c) The idea that the dominating role of the father in Jewish family life dates from the Hellenistic period, very interesting though, deserves more underpinnings. It is difficult to use the additions of 4QSam-a and the LXX for 2 Sam. 13:21 as an indication of the supposed new social reality. The extra material of both witnesses is rather of a midrashic nature; it fills a gap by explaining why David did not punish Amnon for the rape of Tamar. Hence, it cannot be taken further.

Hebrew Names, Personal Names, Family Names and Nicknames of Jews in the Second Temple Period

Rachel Hachlili   (University of Haifa)

This study endeavours to give a general picture of major onomastic trends and elements of Jewish Hebrew names in the Second Temple period. Personal names, family names and nicknames are an important source for ancient Jewish life and society.

During salvage excavations in the Jericho necropolis the monumental Goliath family tomb was excavated (Hachlili 1979). It consists of two chambers on two levels. The walls of the upper chamber were decorated with wall paintings (Hachlili 1983); it had eight loculi, a central pit, and a side pit filled with a pile of skulls and bones. The lower chamber was smaller, its walls white plastered; it had six loculi and no pit. Inside the tomb 22 ossuaries were found, with a total of 32 inscriptions written or incised on 14 of them. The inscriptions usually include the name of the deceased and his or her family relationship, and sometimes some more data. These finds led to my research into the onomasticon of the names and nicknames common in the Second Temple Period. The tomb contained the remains of a family of three generations: the founders of the tomb, Yehoezer son of Eleazar and Shelomzion, their six sons and their wives, and 14 of their grandchildren.

The Hebrew and Greek names on the Jericho inscriptions are, in order of frequency: Yehoezer, Eleazar, Ishmael, Judah, Menahem, Nat[an]el, and Simon for men; and Mariah, Mariamme, Shlamsion and Salome for women. The name Yehoezer is found for the three consecutive generations of this family. The Goliath family tomb inscriptions reveal the characteristic features of names and nicknames in the Second Temple Period (from the second century BCE to the early second century CE).

The sources for names in the Second Temple period are vast:

non-literary sources such as funerary inscriptions mainly on ossuaries, but also on tombs, tombstones, sarcophagi; papyri and ostraca from Masada, the Judaean Desert, Wadi Murabaat, and the Bar Kochba letters; the Dead Sea Scrolls; Literary sources such as the Hebrew Bible, the New Testament, the Maccabean books, and the writings of Josephus Flavius. The research into the onomasticon of this period reveals an interesting historical and social picture. (For a study of the Jewish onomasticon and the question of identifying ancient Jews by their names, see Mussies 1994).

Names in the Second Temple period consist of several forms: full names in the patronymic form of 'X son of Y', such as יהועזר בן אלעזר Yehoezer son of Eleazar; single personal names, such as יהודה Yehudah; a full name with a nickname, such as יהועזר בן יהועזר גלית; patronymics, such as 'son of Y', בן יהודה 'son of Yehudah'; matronymics, such as בן החורנית 'son of the Horanit woman'; a single nickname, הגלילי 'son of the Galilean'; and a nickname as patronymic בן העני 'son of the poor'. A woman's full name was 'X daughter of Y', שלום בת יהודה Shalom daughter of Yehudah; a married woman is named 'X wife of Y', מרים אשת (אתת) יהודה Miriam wife of Yehudah. Sometimes a woman is named as 'X mother of Y', as in שלומציון אמה יהועזר Shelomzion mother of Yehoezer, or in an abbreviated form, שלמצין אמנה Shelomzion our mother. Sometimes the inscription includes a woman's name and her son's name: שלם ומתיה בנה, Shalom and Mattya her son.

The full name was the official and formal name of a person, commonly used in burial inscriptions, where it also served as commemoration, memorial for the dead. On jars the full names designated ownership; and on legal documents a formal name was required. The abbreviated names, where the personal name or patronymic is deleted, are found mainly in lists, but sometimes also in ossuary inscriptions.

1 Personal Names

The personal Hebrew biblical names שמעון, יהוסף, יהודה, יהוחנן, אלעזר, יהושע, חניה, יונתן, מתתיה (Shimeon, Yehosef, Yehudah, Yeho-hanan, Eleazar, Yehosua, Hananiah, Yonathan, and Mathathiah)

are the most common Jewish names in the onomasticon of the late
Second Temple period (Table 1; and see Hachlili 1984:188-91; Ilan
1987:138), including the names inscribed on ossuaries (Rahmani
1994:14), the personal names of the Qumran sect members (Eshel
1997:52), and the names at Masada (Hachlili 1998: Table 1).

In the biblical onomasticon, although enormous, the frequency
of the names is small. In the Second Temple period the onomasticon is much smaller but the frequency of the names is great.

The popularity and the frequency of the men's names, especially the five most common, is probably a result of their being
the typical names of the Hasmonaean dynasty (Hachlili 1984:188-
191; Ilan 1987:238-241; see especially her interesting suggestion
about Yehosef being another Hasmonean brother), as well as the
custom of patronymy – that is, naming a son after his father –
that was prevalent during this period among the Jewish population (Hachlili 1979:53; 1984:195). The two common names that
are not of the Hasmonaean dynasty are יהושע/ישוע Yehosua, and
חנניה/חניה Hananiah (Ilan 1984:17).

יהודה Yehuda was a common Hebrew name adopted by proselytes (see below), for instance Ariston of Apamea, who is also
named יהודה הגיור 'Judah the proselyte', as inscribed on an ossuary
from Akeldama, Jerusalem (Ilan 1991/2:154-5; 1996:69-70). Note
also that members of the Qumran sect were called יהודה Yehudah,
whereas opponents of the sect were given the names מנשה Manasseh and אפרים Ephraim (Eshel 1997:40). Some scholars maintain
that Manasseh could be identified with the Sadducees, and Ephraim with the Pharisees.

It is interesting to consider that names such as those of the
Patriarchs – Abraham, Isaac and Jacob – were rarely used in the
Second Temple period, for instance אתת יעקוב 'wife of Jacob' at
Masada (Yadin & Naveh 1989:22, no. 402). Equally scarce were
most of the Israelite tribal patronymics and names of the prophets (Klein 1930:325; see also the study by Cohen 1976; Hachlili
1984:188-9; Ilan 1984:11-6).

Proper names were those in full, that is, a personal name with
a patronymic, and many of the funerary inscription and other
sources have them. Most of the ossuary inscriptions refer to the

full name, whereas patronymics unaccompanied by the personal name of the deceased are rare (Rahmani 1994:15). However, at Masada full names such as שמעון בן יועזר and אלעזר בר יהוסף, Shimeon son of Yoezer, Yehosef son of Eleazar (Yadin & Naveh 1989:40, nos. 466, 470; Naveh 1990:115-6), are mostly inscribed on storage jars and are thus meant to indicate either the ownership or the person's responsibility for the contents of the vessels. Note that in the Second Temple period the names were used in their longer theophoric version, for example יהוסף Yehosef, יהושע Yehosua, יהוחנן Yehohanan. The reason is not clear; however, this might have been the correct, official form of the name.

In several name-lists the most common are patronymics such as בן ה.. 'son of Y' or 'son of' plus nickname, without a personal name. For instance, בן עזריה, בן הציר 'son of Azariah', 'son of the painter', in the list incised on an ossuary lid from Bethphage (Milik 1971; Naveh 1990:111-2); the name-lists on ostraca from Masada bear mostly patronymic or single nicknames, such as הגדריאן and בר ישוע 'from Gadara' and 'son of Yeshua' (Naveh 1990:112-5). On a similar list of officers in the temple, many of them are referred to by patronymic only, such as נחוניא חופר, בן אחיה שיחין 'Ben Ahijah', 'Nehuniah the trench-digger' (Mishna Sheq. 5:1; t. Sheq. 2:14; Naveh 1990:109-11). It seems that in daily life, among particular social groups, people might have called each other by a proper name, a nickname or 'son of Y', where Y was a personal name or a nickname (Naveh 1990:113).

2   Women's Names

A Woman's proper full Hebrew or Aramaic name was 'X daughter of Y' (the father): שלמציון בת אלעזר 'Shlamzion daughter of Eleazar'(Rahmani 1994: no. 342). However, frequently a woman's name included her husband's name: מרים אשת מתיה 'Mariame wife of Mattiah' (Rahmani 1994: no. 559) or son's name; or she was referred to only as 'wife of': אנתת אלעזר 'wife of Eleazar' (Rahmani 1994: no. 74). Women's names constituted about 11% of the named population in the Second Temple period. This adds to other evidence indicating the social status of women in the period (Ilan 1989:186-7). The most common female names in the

Second Temple period were מרים Mariame, Mariah מריה, Shalom/
Salome שלום, and שלמציון Shlamzion; about 50% of the entire
female population bore these names (Hachlili 1984:191; Ilan 1989:
191-2). Only 11 Hebrew names were used by the majority of
women in this period (see Table 1), and less than half the women
had names in Aramaic, Greek or Latin, Persian and Nabatean
(Ilan 1989:191). At Beth She'arim (3rd-4th century CE), six Hebrew women's names appear in this order of frequency: Sarah,
Miriam, Esther, Ruth, Rachel and Hannah (Hachlili 1984:191).

On the Masada ostraca the women were recorded only as 'wife
of' or 'daughter of', with only the husband's or father's name
inscribed in Hebrew and Aramaic: אתת [ז]בידא 'wife of [Ze]bida'
and בת דמלי 'the daughter of Domli' (Yadin & Naveh 1989:21-
2, nos. 399, 400, 402, 403, 405). The exception is שלום הגלי[לית]
'Shalom(or Salome) the Gali[lean]' (Yadin & Naveh 1989:22, no.
404), who was called by her personal name and an epithet.

מרים Mariame (Mariam), מריה, Mariah, שלום Shalom/Salome
and שלמציון Shlamzion were the most common Jewish women's
personal names of the period. They are not biblical names, and
their popularity is probably due to being typical names of the
Hasmonean dynasty (Hachlili 1984:191; Ilan 1987:240). However,
we do not know if matronymy was a custom practiced by women,
as the mother's name is not mentioned in the name of a daughter,
and only rarely in the name of a son. Ilan (1989:191-2, 196-200)
lists most of the examples and states that approximately 50% of
the female population had these two names. Almost all the funerary inscriptions have these names, with a few others recorded once
or twice. Scholars maintain that Salome and the longer version,
Shlamzion. are the same name. (Ilan 1989:196-97, 198-99 lists only
the two names, giving Mariah as a form of Mariame and Shlamzion as a form of Salome; but in her report on the inscriptions
from Akeldama she notes [1996:70] that Salome and Shlamzion
are not the same name). Indeed, Salome and Shelamzion were
apparently not the same name; Mariamme and Maria might have
been the same name, Maria a diminutive (Cohen 1974; Hachlili
1984:191, note 8; Mussies 1994:253).

Shlamzion does not appear at Masada, only Salome. Shlamzion was perhaps used most frequently around the time of the

reign of the Hasmonaean queen (1st century BCE), whereas Salome was used more frequently in the later Second Temple period (1st century CE). In later times these names were no longer in use.

2.1   Choosing a Name

Different customs determined the choice of name in the biblical and Second Temple periods. The reasons behind the choice in the Second Temple period were different from those in the First Temple period, when names were given in honour of special events that befell the family or the people. Examples for this are Isaac (Gen. 17:17-19); the sons of Jacob, where every name has its reason (Gen. 29:32; 30:23; 35:18); and Imannuel (Isa.7:14-17), among others (Hachlili 1984:192). By contrast, during the Second Temple period, naming children after an ancestor was prevalent. The most common was paponymy, naming a son after his grandfather. This custom was prevalent in the Egyptian, Phoenician and Greek worlds. The Elephantine and Asswan Aramaic papyri indicate that the custom first arose among the Jews in 5th century BCE Egypt (Buchanan-Grey 1914:163-4, 172). There is some indication that this custom was also common in Eretz Israel: the name טוביה 'Tubias' was a common paponymy in בית טוביה 'the House of Tubias' (from the 6th century to 200 BCE); and in prominent families such as the Hasmonaean dynasty (Hachlili 1984:192, Figure 2). One of the few literary sources for the custom of paponymy indicates that a child is being named Abram after his dead grandfather (Jub. 11:14-15).

The custom of patronymy was apparently common among the royal Hellenistic dynasties. From the 1st century BCE on this practice became increasingly prevalent among prominent Jewish families in Eretz Israel, resulting in a small number of personal names appearing for several generations in a single family (Hachlili 1979:53, Fig. 49; 1984:192-4).

2.2   Recurrence of Names in a Family

The custom of patronymy, even when the son was not born after the father had died, seems to have been prevalent during this period among the Jewish priesthood and aristocracy, especially among the families of the high priests and the Hasmonaean and Herodian dynasties. Originally it was a foreign custom, used by the Hellenistic royal dynasties, then it was evidently adopted by the Jews (Stern 1960:8, nn. 43-7).

As a result of the increasingly common use of paponymy and patronymy, the recurrence of names down three generations was prevalent in the Second Temple period.[1] It might even be possible to identify a family by its characteristic recurrent name (Hachlili 1984: Table 2).

Most of the material concerning names in families comes from literary sources and inscriptions in ossuary family tombs. These sources indicate an important trend, that is, the recurrence of names down at least three generations of the family. From the literary sources we gather that during the Second Temple period the prevalent custom among the royal dynasties was paponymy, apparently from the end of the 4th century BCE onwards. In the Hasmonaean dynasty the names Mathathiah, Yehohanan, Yehudah and Yonathan are repeated in ten generations, these being paponymics or names of some other kinsmen, usually uncles (Hachlili 1984: Figure 2).[2] In the House of Tubias (3rd century BCE) the name Tubias and the Greek name Hyrcanus are repeated in four generations, each individual being named after his grandfather (Maisler 1941:122). In the Herodian dynasty recurrent names are Herod, Joseph and Agrippa (Hachlili 1984: Figure 1). In the high priestly families the same feature is found: in the בית חוניו 'House of Onias' (332-165 BCE), the recurrent names are Onias and Shimeon for six generations, until in the last generation we find Onias, a paponymy (Hachlili 1984: Figure 5; cf. Josephus, *Ant.* 12.44, 224-225, 237-238; 13.26; 20.197-198; Buchanan-Grey 1896:2, and nn. 4, 5; 1914:165, n. 4). In the חנן Hanan (Ananus or Annas) family of high priests (1st century CE), the names are Hanan (Ananus), a repeated patronymy for three generations,

---

[1] A similar custom appears in Palmyra in the 1st century CE: see Ingholt 1974:43.

[2] It is interesting to note that the name Shimeon, the most common in this period, does not recur in the Hasmonaean dynasty after Shimeon the Hasmonaean.

and Matthias, after an uncle (Hachlili 1984:Figure 4; Josephus, *Ant.* 18.26; Stern 1966:250-1; 1976:606; Barag & Flusser 1986:42, Table 1). In the Boethus family (late 1st century BCE-1st century CE). the recurrent name is Shimeon son of Shimeon (*Ant.* 19.297; Stern 1976:604-6). The Phiabi family of high priests (1st century CE) has the name Ishmael son of Ishmael repeated (*Ant.* 18.34; 20.179; Stern 1976:607-8, n. 4).

Repeated names were customary also in priestly and other noble families, and might have been prevalent also among Jews of all classes. In the priestly family of Josephus Flavius (Yehosef son of Mattathiah), the repeated names are Mattathiah by patronymy, Shimeon, and Yehosef (Josephus, *Vita* 5.8; Schürer *et al.* 1973:43-6, n. 3; Hachlili 1984: Figure 6). In the priestly family of חזיר Hasir (a priestly course), buried in the Kidron valley tomb, the inscription found on the lintel describes a family of three generations, with the repeated names Yehosef, by paponymy, and Eleazar, after an uncle (Avigad 1954:61-2). With the Kalon priestly family (who belonged to the ישבאב Jeshebab priestly course), buried in a Jerusalem tomb, the names Yehoezer/ Joezar and Shimeon, and the female name מרים Miriam, occur in both the second and third generations. However, Kalon and Jeshebab, although mentioned by members of the family, are not found interred in this tomb (Grimme 1912:533; Klein 1920:8-11; Stern 1976:591). In the Goliath Family tomb the repeated names down three generations include seven different individuals named Yehoezer by patronymy, and Eleazar and Ishmael (Table 1; see also Hachlili 1979:53, 66, fig. 49). It is also evident that children were named after relatives: Eleazar by paponymy, and Ishmael after an uncle. In a Kidron valley tomb the repeated names are Shimeon and Eleazar in three to five generations (Mayer 1924 :56-9). In the Dositheus family, in a tomb near Jerusalem, the repeated name is Mattiah son of Mattathias (Sukenik 1928:121). In the Babtha family (of the Bar Kokhba Letters) the recurrent names are ישוע Yeshua and יהודה Yehudah (Yadin 1971:234). In a tomb in East Talpiot, Jerusalem the family repeated names are יוסה Yehosef/Yosé (a contraction of Yehosef) and מריה Mariah (Kloner 1996:17-20). In the Akeldama tombs the Ariston family contains two repeated female names, Shalom and Shlamzion, the daughters of Ariston, and two other females with the same names, all buried in the same tomb (Ilan 1996:91).

In the family of the president Hillel (1ˢᵗ century CE on) the custom of papynomy is evident, and the repeated names are הלל Hillel, גמליאל Gamliel, Shimeon, and Yehudah (Buchanan-Grey 1896:2; Klein 1929:327).

A few examples of the custom of patronymy among the Jewish general population is attested in ossuary inscriptions from Jerusalem: מתיה בן מתיה 'Mattiah son of Mattiah' (Sukenik 1928:121); 'Yehudah son of Yehudah' (Frey 1952: no. 1283c); from 1ˢᵗ-2ⁿᵈ century CE, 'Saul son of Saul' on an ostracon from the Judean Desert' (Aharoni 1962:196, Pl. 29A); 'Yehudah son of Yehudah' in letter no. 29, and 'Yehosef son of Yehosef' in letter no. 42 from Wadi Muraba'at (Benoit et al. 1961:156). On a marriage contract, the name of the groom is 'Eleazar son of Eleazar', and the name of a witness is 'Yehudah son of Yehudah' (Milik 1954:183).

2.3 Priests' Names

Most of the names are relatively common in this period, but some scholars suggest that several of the names occur frequently among priests and especially in high priestly families. For instance, the name Eleazar was used mainly by priests (Stern 1961:21, n. 119). Yehoezer is considered to be a name of priests (Grintz 1960). Other names, such as Yehosef, Yehoshua/Joshua, Shimeon and Mattathias, are common in high priestly families (see Table 1). The use of a name in consecutive generations in the family was a custom characterizing prominent and priestly families. The popularity and frequency of these names is possibly a result of their being the typical names of the Hasmonaean dynasty (Hachlili 1984:188-191; Ilan 1987:238-41), as well as the customs of paponomy and patronomy, which were prevalent during this period in the Jewish population (Hachlili 1979:53; 1984:195). In choosing the names for their children, members of the general public might have preferred the names of high priests, aristocrats and priests.

3 Family Names

Surnames (family names) were not common in ancient times
(Hachlili 1984:202-3). They appear usually in the form of the
word 'House' plus a name, 'son of Y', or an ancestor's name. A
family name could also be acquired by virtue of title, profession,
appellative or nickname, and could be inherited by subsequent
generations.

House בית. Many of the royal and priestly oligarchies of the
Second Temple period are referred to as the 'House of ' with the
name of the first ancestor, who was a prominent figure after whom
his progeny were named (Bichler 1966:138, n. 48), for instance the
royal House of the Hasmonaeans; the high priestly families were
frequently named 'House of' Boethus, Phiabi, Hanan (Annan)
and Cantheras, קנתרס or Cathros קתרס (*Ant.* 17.339, 341; 18.3, 26;
19.297; Jeremias 1969:194-8). The name 'son of Cathros' בר קתרס
was found inscribed on a stone weight in the 'Burnt House' in
Jerusalem (Avigad 1983:129-31). The priestly family name קיפא
Qypha, Qopha (or Caiaphas). on three ossuaries from the 'Caiaphas' tomb in North Talpiyot, Jerusalem, is possibly equated
with the high priestly house of Cathros. meaning 'basket-carrier'
(Reich 1992:75-6; also Peuch 1993; Horbury 1994). The 'daughter
of Cathra' בת קתרא found on an inscription from Masada (Yadin
& Naveh 1989:22, no. 405 ; Naveh 1990:117) might also belong
to this family. Sometimes the name was used for disgrace, for
example, בית הפגרים 'House of Corpses' (Klein 1929:348).

'**Son of X**'. The appellative 'son of X' or 'sons of X', where the
X is not a personal name but a family name, usually appears in
families of the twenty-four priestly courses (the full list is given in
1 Chron. 24:7-18). Genealogical lists of priest were kept and used
in the Second Temple period in order to maintain the priestly
customs and their purity of pedigree (1 Chron. 9:10-13; Josephus,
Vita 6; *Apion* 1.31-36; Jeremias 1969:275-83). 'Son of Hakkoz'
הקוץ, Meremoth the son of Uriah, son of Hakkoz (Neh. 3:4), are
a priestly family of the seventh course; they might have served as
the Temple treasurers, an inherited office in the family of Hakkoz
(Stern 1976:590-1; Benoit *et al.* 1961:223). The name appears

possibly also in an inscription on a stone found in Nazareth (Eshel 1991). It is possible that the name בן סירא 'son of Sira' also belongs to the same Hakkoz family (Klein 1929:341; 1930:267), as the meaning of both these names in Hebrew is 'thorn'. The family of the priests of 'sons of Hasir' בני חזיר, the seventeenth course, is inscribed in the Kidron valley tomb (Avigad 1954:59-61). The name מנחם בן בנא יכים כהן 'Menahem son of sons of Jachim', of the twenty-first course, is inscribed on an ossuary found in a tomb at Dominus Flevit (Bagatti & Milik 1975:89-92). On an Aramaic marriage contract from 117 CE appears the name מנשה מן בני אלישיב 'Manashe of the sons of Elyashiv' of the eleventh course (Benoit et al. 1961:112).

An ancestor's name. The name of a progenitor was occasionally used by subsequent generations as a family name. In the high priestly families, שמעון בן ביתוס 'Shimeon son of Boethus', ישמעאל בן פיאבי 'Ishmael son of Phiabi', מתתיהו בן חנן 'Mattathias son of Hanan' were named after an ancestor of some generations back. Some scholars maintain that a personal name (of an ancestor?) could also serve as a family name; on an ossuary is inscribed שמעון בוטון 'Shimeon of (the family of) Boethos', a priestly family; or עלי בן שמעון יהועזר 'Eli son of Shimeon Yehoezer'; the last name, Yehoezer, might represent a family name (Rahmani 1994:16, nos. 41, 151). Klein (1929:329) suggested that a family name deriving from an ancient ancestor is חניכת אבות 'ancestor surname' (Mishna Gittin 9), which might be kept for at least ten generations.

3.1 Nicknames as Family names

A surname could be a nickname given to one (or more) of the ancestors by virtue of title, occupation, place of origin, physical characteristic and defects, and positive or negative qualities (Goitein 1970; Hachlili 1984:203). Many families are known whose nickname evolved into a family name.

Surnames deriving from titles such as הכהן 'the priest' (1 Sam. 11:2-3; 22:11) or הסופר 'the secretary' or 'the scribe', for example, שפן בן אצליהו בן משלם הספר 'Shaphan the son of Azaliah, son of Meshullam the secretary' (2 Kgs 22:3), or גמריהו בן שפן הספר

'Gemariah the son of Shaphan the secretary' (Jer. 36:10) were acquired by virtue of an inherited office and title, so that it became the surname of successive generations. Place of origin was sometimes a nickname that turned into a family name, for example, הבשני 'from Beth Shean', a nickname appearing on ossuaries of three members of a family from Jeusalem (Frey 1952: nos. 1372-4).

Family names stemming from physical characteristic and defects are found in several instances. In the Goliath family monumental tomb, in each of the inscriptions where the name Goliath appears, it is added to the personal names and family relation of the interred individual (Hachlili 1979:52). The first-generation and second-generation Yehoezer had this name, Goliath, added to their personal name. It seems that 'Goliath' was not the name of an individual but a nickname describing a physical characteristic (at least four male members of this family were exceptionally tall; Hachlili and Smith 1979:69-70) that became a surname. Thus, both the physical characteristic, being tall, and the nickname were inherited in this family.

The nickname of an ancestor, קיפא 'Chaiphas', appearing in literary sources, and recently found inscribed on several ossuaries discovered in a tomb in North Talpiyot, Jerusalem (Reich 1992:74-6), is a nickname of a high priest family, acquired either through an occupation or as an appallative. An example of an appellative added to a personal name is הנזר 'the monk' (Avigad 1971:198), which probably became a surname.

Surnames evolving from appellatives, based on negative character qualities, appear in families returning from Babylon, for example בני חגב 'sons of Hagab' (locust, grasshopper, Ezra 2:46) and בני פרעש 'sons of Parosh' (flea, Ezra 2:3; 8:3; 10:25; Nehemiah 3:25; 6:8; 10:15).

The surname קלון 'Kalon', deriving from a derogatory nickname (meaning 'disgrace', 'shame'), is inscribed on ossuaries of three generations of the priest family of the Jeshebab course, interred in a Jerusalem tomb (Grimme 1912; Klein 1920:11; Frey 1952: nos. 1350-5).

Occupations are also found as nicknames that became

surnames. Examples are: a fisherman family from Jaffa is inscribed as בית החרמים 'House of Haharamim' (Schwabe 1937:86-9);
'house of linen workers' בית עבדת הבץ (1 Chron. 4:21), probably
weavers; 'Son of goldsmiths' עזיאל בן חרהיה צורפים, and 'son of
perfumers' חנניה בן הרקחים (Neh. 3:8).[3] 'The poor' העני is a family
surname carved on two inscriptions from Beth She'arim (Schwabe
& Lifshitz 1974: nos. 100, 206), probably indicating the family's
modest way of life.

4   Nicknames

Nicknames appear frequently during the Second Temple period;
they were added to personal names and were an organic part of a
person's name. Nicknames were given because of the frequency of
some of the personal names and distinguishing individuals bearing the same name especially in a single family. Another reason
was the need of a family to have the same identifying nickname,
sometimes down several generations. Frequently a nickname was
given as an endearment or a pet name, or in order to disgrace a
person. Nicknames often described a title, profession or physical
aspect of the individual, sometimes becoming a family name (see
above; also Hachlili 1984:195-204). Some families used a surname
deriving from their ancient ancestor nickname, using the חניכת אבות
'ancestor surname' (Mishna Giṭṭin 9; Klein 1929:329). Sometimes
a nickname was given after death in memory of an event, and the
next generations used this same nickname.

Special nicknames were given to priests, especially to those
who had a common personal name; sometimes they were
deregatory nicknames in order to denounce hated priests (Klein
1930:262). Others were called after their disabilities, or their office; for instance the nicknames given to the officers in the temple
(Mishna Sheq. 5:1; Tosefta Sheq. 2:14 (Klein 1929:330, 333, 338).
In some cases the nicknames were given in order of the alpha-
bet, such as בן הא, בן-גימל, בן אילפא; or according to their order of

---

[3]But see Mendelsohn (1940:18-19) who maintains that the term *ben* here,
does not refer to blood relation but means 'organization' or 'guild', thus 'the
guild of the weavers'.

birth, such as בן-לקיש, בן פטירא, בן בוכרי, בן-בוכרי (Klein 1929:334, 340). It is possible that a person's name with the addition of a matronymic – his mother's (grandmother's) name – is a nickname, as usually the proper name included the father (or grandfather) name. The name-form 'son of Y' – בן יהוחנן, בן הציר 'son of Yehohanan', 'son of the painter' – without a personal name might be a nickname. Such names appear on the Bethphage ossuary lid (Milik 1971:75-94, Fig. 1) and on several name lists on the Masada ostraca: for example, בר קרזלא, בן כנבון (see below; Yadin & Naveh 1989: nos. 420, 421, 429, 430, 435, 437). Some of the officers of the temple are also named in the same way: בן-גבר, בן-ארזה (Mishna Sheq. 5:1). Klein (1929:330) maintains these were the son's nickname rather than the father's. Others (Bichler 1966:127, n. 16; Clines 1972:282-7) contend that this form was a nickname of the young while the elderly were called by their full name; or that, similar to the First Temple period, this form meant that the person belonged to a guild. It also might have been a family name, as many of the guild professions were inherited (Mendelsohn 1940:18).

4.1 Nicknames of the Hasmonean Dynasty

In the early Second Temple period we find nicknames already in the Hasmonaean family: "At this same time there was a man living in the village of Modai (Modin) in Judaea, named Mattathias, the son of Yohanan, the son of Shimeon, the son of Asamonias, a priest of the course of Yehoyarib, and a native of Jerusalem. He had five sons, יוחנן הקרוי הגדי Yohanan called Gaddes, שמעון הקרוי התטי Simon called Thatis, יהודה הקרוי המכבי Yehudah called Maccabaeus, אלעזר הקרוי החורי Eleazar called Auran, and ויונתן הקרוי החפי Yonatan called Apphus" (*Ant.* 12.265-266; also with few changes 1 Macc. 2:1). השמונאים 'Hasmonaeans' is possibly a family name used as a nickname only by Josephus (instead of the name Maccabaeus; Jeremias 1969:188-9, n. 132). Other scholars (Abel 1949: pls. III-IV) maintain it was the nickname of the father or the grandfather of Mattathias.

Scholars are divided on the nicknames of Mattathias's sons. Some contend that they were given to them at birth. Others maintain that these nicknames were added as they grew up after their deed or characteristic (1 Macc. 2:2-5; notes to the Hebrew translation).

יוחנן הקרוי הגדי Yohanan called Gaddes, or Gaddis. According to some scholars Gaddes, or Gaddis might be the name Gad, the Semitic god of fortune (Abel 1949:31; Marcus, n. i to *Ant*. 12.265).

שמעון הקרוי התטי Simon called Thatis. It is suggested that 'Thatis' is derived from Aramaic and meaning 'the Zealot' (Marcus, n. j to *Ant*. 12.265); in the Syrian translation it is התרסי, which means 'provider'.

יהודה הקרוי המכבי Yehudah called Maccabaeus. The most widely accepted etymology proposed for this name is from the Hebrew מקבת 'hammer', hence 'Yehudah the Hammerer', describing his prowess. Others suggest the nickname was given to him at birth because of the shape of his head. Still others argue that the letters מכבי, *m.k.b.y.*, are an acronym of the hemistich in Exod. 15:11, מי כמוך באלים י״ (Hachlili 1984:196).

אלעזר הקרוי החורי Eleazar called Horan/Auran. The nickname חורן 'Horan' has been interpreted in several ways. Some scholars maintain that the nickname was given after his death, on account of the חור *hor* 'hole' he opened in the elephant (1 Macc. 6:46), hence 'the Borer'. Others contend that Eleazar, like his brothers, was given his nickname at birth (1 Macc. 2:5, note in the Hebrew translation), meaning his being עורן 'Auran', 'vigorous', 'forceful', 'alert' (Schürer *et al.* 1973:158, n. 49).

יונתן הקרוי החפי Yonatan called Apphus. The interpretation of this nickname goes back to the Hebrew חפש 'the Searcher', or 'the Digger' (*Ant*. 12.266, Marcus in a note there).

Another nickname in the Hasmonaean dynasty is that added to Alexander Jannaeus: "and as a result of his excessive cruelty he was nicknamed Thrakidas (the 'Cossak') by the Jews" (*Ant*. 13.383; Marcus notes that the Thracians were known for great ferocity; cf. also Stern 1960:209).

In the following, nicknames are listed according to place of origin, title, occupation, physical characteristics and defects, honorific or age related titles, disabilities, positive and negative qualities, and endearment. It is likely that some of these are in *status emphaticus* as nicknames (or surname) and were often derogatory.

4.1.1 Place of Origin

The place of origin is the most common nickname in the period, and is also frequent in the biblical period as well as in the Mishna and Talmud periods (Hachlili 1984:200). The nickname usually derives from the name of a place, a tribe, or a sect. It usually appears with ה 'the', and sometimes with מ, מן, ד 'from X' is added to the name. Also found is איש 'man from'. Only selected examples are listed here.

On ossuaries from Jerusalem we have יוסף הגלילי 'Joseph the Galilean' (Frey 1952: no. 1285; הגלילי the Galilean on a papyrus 52 from Murabaat, Benoit *et al.* 1961:169); A family is called אמיה, חנין, פפיס הבשני 'Amiah, Hanan, and Papis from Beth Shean' (Frey 1952: nos. 1372-4; Rahmani 1994: no. 139); on an inscribed bowl from Jericho three generations of a family are mentioned: ישמעאל, שמעון ופלטיא מן ירושלם 'Ishmael, Shimeon, and Pelatya from Jerusalem' (Hachlili 1978:45-7); פילון הקיריני is 'Philon from Cyrenaica' (Bagatti & Milik 1975:81, oss. 10, insc. 74), as is הלל הקיריני 'Hillel from Cyrenaica' (Benoit *et al.* 1961:220), הקרני 'the Qaranaite' or 'the Cyrenian' (Yadin & Naveh 1989:26, no. 424) and אלכסנדרוס קרנית 'Alexander the Cyrenian', inscribed on an ossuary lid from the Kidron valley in Jerusalem (Avigad 1962:10-1; see below for the other interpretation, that is, the namebearer's occupation). ארסתון אפמי 'Ariston of Apamea' is inscribed on ossuary no. 31 from Akeldama, Jerusalem. The interred person bears two names: Ariston, a Greek name possibly meaning that he originated in Apamea in Syria; it seems that יהודה הגיור 'Judah the proselyte', the other name on this ossuary, was his Hebrew name after his conversion (Ilan 1996:66). Another ossuary from Akeldama, no. 17, has a Greek inscription, 'Aza[ria] son of Berous' or possibly of 'Beirut' (Ilan 1996:60-1). On an ossuary from Ammunition Hill, Jerusalem, the inscription reads יהוד בר שבט מין בת אלון 'yehud son of Shevat (or *shevet*, 'rod'?), from Bet Alon'; bet Alon might refer to Bet Alonim, identified as Ramat el-Khalil, near Hebron (Rahmani 1994:146, no. 293).

At Masada, most of these are single nicknames without a personal name:

הגדריאן 'the people of Gadara', 'the Gadarians' (Yadin & Naveh

1989:24, no. 420, 2);

העמקי 'of the Valley' (Yadin & Naveh 1989:28, no. 434), or a village near Acco (Naveh 1992:44);

ציפון 'north' (Yadin & Naveh 1989:28, no. 436).

שמעון בר נוטוס 'Shimeon son of Notos'. 'Notos' is a Greek word meaning 'south' or 'southern' (Yadin & Naveh 1989:40, no. 462), or possibly the name בנימין, Benyamin or a similar name, is implied here.

חניה נותוס 'Hananiah Notos' appears on a Qumran document, 4Q477 (Eshel 1997:51).

Also found are:

הלל הנוסי 'Hillel the Nusian' (?), 'of a place named Nos' (Yadin & Naveh 1989:41, no. 473);

שלום הגלינ]ליתן 'Shalom (or Salome) theGali[lean]' (Yadin & Naveh 1989:22, no. 404).

Josephus mentions several nicknames of place of origin, such as יהוחנן מגוש חלב 'Yehohanan from Gush Halav' (in the Galilee); ניקולאוס מדמשק 'Nikolaus from Damascus' (Herod's philosopher and court historian); מלתקה השומרונית 'Meltaka the Samaritan' (one of Herod's wifes); יהודה איש הגולן 'Yehudah man from the Golan' (*Vita* 189-196; *Ant.* 15.185; 18.4, 23). Josephus also records the names of several sect members: יוחנן האיסי and יהודה האיסי 'Yehudah the Essene' and 'Yohanan the Essene'; שמעון האיסי and מנחם האיסי 'Menahem the Essene' and 'Shimeon the Essene'; and צדוק הפרושי 'Zadok the Pharisee', who was one of the founders of the zealot sect (*Ant.* 15.373-379; 17.346-348; 18.4).

4.1.2 Title

These nicknames indicate the class, status and office of a person. Some were given to the person for his own role but many of the titles were inherited with the office. The most common titles were הכהן 'the priest' and הסופר 'the scribe/secretary'.

הכהן 'the priest'. This nickname was very important, since it was intended to preserve the purity of the priests, but only few of these titles have been found. (On the genealogy of the priests see Josephus, *Vita* 6 and *Apion* 1.7; Klein 1939:30-50; Jeremias 1969:213-4). In Jerusalem tombs, several ossuaries were inscribed with this title: פנחס ועקביה כהנא 'Pinhas and Akaviah the priests'; שלומציון בת שמעון הכהן 'Shlomzion daughter of Shimeon the priest'. We also have בן שמעון הכהן 'the son of Shimeon the priest' (Frey 1952: nos. 1221, 1317, 1411); מנחם מן בנא יכים כהן 'Menahem of the sons of Yachim the priest' (Bagatti & Milik 1975:89 92, oss. 83, pl. 81); and יהוחנה ברת יהוחנן בר תפלוס הכהן הגדול 'Yehohanah daughter of Yehohanan son of Thephilus the high priest' (Barag & Flusser 1986:39).

On an ossuary from Akeldama, Jerusalem a Greek inscription records 'Megiste the priestess', probably meaning wife or daughter of a priest, not a woman with a religious function or an official position (see the discussion by Ilan 1991/2:157-9; 1996:61-2). Another example is חנניןה כהנא רבא עקביא בריה 'A[nani]as the High Priest, Aqavia his son'. This inscription, inscribed on a vessel found in Masada, probably designates priestly shares (Yadin 1965:111; Yadin & Naveh 1989:37-9, no. 461). In Beth She'arim, several inscriptions mention the priestly title יהודה הכהן 'Yehudah the priest'. We also have: שירה בת נחמיה אמה של הכהנת 'Shirah the daughter of Nehemiah the mother of the priestess'; כהנים 'the priests' (Schwabe & Lifshitz 1974: nos. 181, 66, 49; see also Avigad 1976:23, who maintains that it might be a family name, not a title);

סופר 'secretary/scribe'. The title was the person's office and possibly inherited. Some scholars maintain that all officials were thus titled (Hachlili 1984:201, and n. 230). On ossuaries from Jerusalem several inscriptions mention this title:

יהודה הסופר, יהודה בר אלעזר הסופר 'Yehudah the secretary', 'Yehudah son of Eleazar the secretary' on an ossuary from Jerusalem (Frey 1952: no. 1308; Klein 1920:19-20).

יהוסף בר חנניה הספר 'Yehosef, son of Hananya, the scribe' inscribed on an ossuary from Mt. Scopus, Jerusalem (Sussman 1992:94).

אלעזר בר הספר 'Eleazar, son of the scribe'. This inscription at Masada is of doubtful authenticity (Yadin & Naveh 1989:66, no. 667; for the title see Hachlili 1984:201).

Other titles, such as חלקיה שומר האוצר 'Hylkiah the keeper of the treasure' probably the temple treasurer, and יוסף סוכן הבית

'Joseph the house steward', are noted by Josephus (*Ant.* 20.194; 15.185; Alon 1966:51; Jeremias 1969:160-7; Stern 1966:244, n. 56).

Officers in the temple are listed in the Mishna and Talmud, (m. Sheq. 5:1 and y. Sheq. 5, 49a), where they appear with their personal name and title. Among them are גביני הכרוז 'Gabini the herald'; נחוניה חופר השיחין 'Nehuniah the trench-digger'; פנחס המלביש 'Phineas the dresser' – possibly he was in charge of the vestments (Bichler 1966:88, 101). The most important officer in the temple after the high priest was חנינא סגן הכהנים 'Haninah the priests' deputy' (Mishna Sheq. 6:1), 'the temple strategus' (Alon 1966:256; Jeremias 1969:160-167; Schürer *et al.* 1973:371). He was a permanent officer in the temple and a substitute high priest (Bichler 1966:88).

רבי, מורה, in Greek *didaskalos*, 'Rabbi, the teacher', is on an ossuary from Jerusalem (Sukenik 1930:140-1, and n. 6). Various titles were used in the First Temple period and in synagogue inscriptions of the 4th-6th centuries CE (Hachlili 1984:202), such as חזן 'caretaker', פרנס 'warden', גזבר 'treasurer', and ארכון 'head of the community'.

4.1.3 Occupation

Such a nickname is given to a person on account of his occupation, or derives from a profession that was common in the period. Frequently it was inherited and became a family name or nickname.

In an ossuary inscription from Jerusalem two interesting nicknames appear connected to the building of the temple: סימון בנה הכלה 'Simon builder of the sanctuary', probably one of builders or engineers who took part in the construction of Herod's sanctuary (Naveh 1970:34). ניקנור עושה הדלתות 'Nicanor who made the doors', is inscribed on an ossuary from the Nicanor family tomb on Mount Scopus (Avigad 1967:124-5). It is difficult to determine if these nicknames were used by the people during their lifetime or given to them after their death in order to commemorate their pursuits. יחוני החרש 'Yehoni the artisan, craftsman' or possibly 'smith', (or 'deaf, mute') is inscirbed on an ossuary from Dominus Flevit, Jerusalem (Bagatti & Milik 1975:83, inscr. 12, Fig. 22, photo. 80).

A similar nickname appears on an ostracon from Masada, בר חרשא 'son of artisan, craftsman' (or it too could mean 'deaf', see below; Yadin & Naveh 1989:26, no. 421,5).[4] בן הציד (הציד) 'son of the hunter' or 'the painter' is inscribed on an ossuary lid found at Bethphage (Frey 1952:278, no. 1285). צידא is 'the hunter' (Yadin & Naveh 1989:29, no. 440). קצבא is 'the butcher': a nickname or else the jar belonging to a butcher (Yadin & Naveh 1989:43, no. 512). ר' זכריה בן הקצב 'Zachriah son of the butcher' was a priest at the end of the Second Temple period (Margaliot 1945:270-1; Bichler 1966:7, 10). שלמיה נגרא 'Shelamiah the Carpenter' is written in a name list on a fourth century BCE document from Ketef Yeriho (Eshel & Misgav 1988:171; Eshel 1997:42). בן הנחתם 'son of the baker' appears on a Masada ostracon (Yadin & Naveh 1989:28, no. 429 יהודה הנחתום 'Yehudah the baker' is a nickname of a sage (y. Ḥag. 2a). יהונתן קדרה is 'Yehonatan the potter' (or the 'pot'); Naveh (1970:34-5) suggested an Aramaic word for the 'potter'. Yadin (Naveh 1970:35, n. 1) argued that it could be a derogatory nickname, 'the pot' meaning 'pot-bellied'.[5] יהו[ד]ה בר בשמ[א] '[Ju]dah son of the druggist', is inscribed on an ostracon from Masada (Yadin & Naveh 1989:41, no. 471). אלכסנדר קרנית 'Alexsander Qornyt', that is 'Alexsander the druggist', is inscribed on an ossuary lid from the Kidron valley, Jerusalem (Avigad 1962:10-1), possibly reflecting his occupation as the merchant of scent, spice; similar to the sage יהודה בן ישעיה הבשם 'Yehudah son of Yeshiah the druggist' (Margaliot 1945:422-3). אלעזר הקפר 'Eleazar Ha-Qapar' is, according to some scholars, a 'druggist', if the word 'Qapar' is a spice from which drugs were made (Naveh 1978:26). In תרפט הנשבה 'the captive physician' תרפט might have referred to a physician' (Rahmani 1994:16, 97, no. 80). יהוסף קני is 'Yehosef (the) Zealot', or '(the) silversmith' (Yadin & Naveh 1989:41, no. 474), and בר בניה is 'the son of Benaiah' or the 'son of the builder' (Yadin & Naveh 1989:26, no. 421,6; 423)

---

[4]See also לעמא הנסך 'to Ama the craftmen' (Phoenician?), inscribed on a Phoenician tombstone (Hestrin & Israeli 1973: no. 143).

[5]Cross (1969:24*-26*) suggests that some of the 'Yahud' seal impressions from Ramat Rachel, on which the word (פחרא=) פחוא meaning 'the potter' appears, are potters seals.

Many nicknames of occupations and professions, possibly of guilds, are mentioned in the Bible and in rabbinic litrature. Among the 64 inscriptions found in the Jaffa cemetry, only 10 nicknames are added to the interred names. The Beth She'arim cemetery yields only a few nicknames (Hachlili 1984:200-1). On ostraca from Thebai, Egypt (2nd century BCE), several occupations are mentioned: a weaver, a painter, cobblers, fishermen (Tcherikover *et al.* 1964:194, nos. 6, 63, 65, 66-8, 95, 107).

The nicknames attest to the social aspect of the occupations that are common in different periods. In the First Temple period, the nicknames probably allude to the guilds and/or families that these people belonged to. In the Second Temple period, the nicknames are few and possibly indicate these people's real profession. It is difficult to know if these nicknames were inherited. Some of these nicknames, especially in ossuary inscriptions – as, for example, 'Simon builder of the Sanctuary' and 'Nicanor who made the doors' – might have been used as commemorations, although it is possible that they were nicknames used during their bearers' lifetime.

4.1.4 Physical Characteristics and Defects

גלית Goliath. The name was inscribed in Jewish and Greek scripts on four ossuaries in the Goliath Tomb in Jericho (Hachlili 1979:52-3). In all these inscriptions, Goliath is added to the personal name and family relation of the interred individual. The references to this name in the Bible and in rabbinic sources all emphasize Goliath's stature, his most outstanding physical characteristic. The examination of the skeletal remains of four male members of this family indicated they were exceptionally tall (Hachlili 1979: Table 1). Hence, the name Goliath is a nickname describing a physical characteristic that became a family name. It should be noted that it is rare for a Jewish family to bear the name of an historical enemy. Only one other occurrence appears among the families coming back from Babylonian exile, the sons of Sisera (Ezra 2:53; Neh. 7:55).

It is interesting that Josephus mentions a similar nickname, 'Eleazar the Giant' (*Ant.* 18.103): "Among which included a man,

7 cubits tall, a Jew by race, named Eleazar, who on account of his size, was called the Giant". Columella, a Latin author (1st century CE), describes 'a man of the Jewish race who was of greater stature than the tallest German (Stern 1974:426-7, possibly identified with the Eleazar referred to by Josephus).

גאיס נניס 'Gaius the small' is inscribed on an ossuary from Mt. Scopus, Jerusalem. The nickname נניס probably derives from the Greek for 'dwarf' (Rahmani 1994:172, no. 421). The name of a sage, שמעון בן ננס (Sem. 8:7; Zlotnick 1966:138), has the same meaning. On a Greek ossuary inscription from El-Jib the name is 'Little (katana) Salona'; the word katana is a Greek transliteration of קטנה 'little one' in Hebrew (Rahmani 1994:194-5, no. 552). זומלית זערא 'small soup-ladle' is inscribed on an ostracon name list at Masada (Yadin & Naveh 1989:25, no. 420,4; Hachlili 1984:197). Several appelatives designating short stature appear in the Beth She'arim inscriptions, such as 'the short', as in אינא הקטן, יהודה הקטן, יוסף הקטן, דומיניקה הקטנה (Mazar 1973: no. 137; Schwabe & Lifshitz 1974: no. 175; Avigad 1976: nos. 10, 11). The interpretation of these nicknames refers either to short stature, or it should be understood as an endearment for children, or else an appellative chosen by a prominent person to designate modesty. In the Talmud too several Aramaic appelatives designating short stature are mentioned: זעירא, קטינא, מר ינוקא, מר קשישא, מר זוטרא (Margaliot 1945:648-9).

4.1.5 Honorific or Age Related Titles

These are nicknames designated to honor individuals or praise a person's character or action. Examples of such nicknames are recorded by Josephus (*Ant.* 12.157; 18.273). We have names such as: שמעון הצדיק 'Shimeon the Just' and חלקיה הגדול 'Hilkiah the Great' (Hachlili 1984:197, n. 85). אבונה שמעון סבא יהוסף ברה 'our father, Shimeon (the) elder, Yehosef his son' was inscribed on an ossuary from the Kidron valley, Jerusalem. סבא is interpreted as 'elder' or as an honorific title (Rahmani 1994:78). The funerary lament inscription, written in chacoal on a wall in Jason's tomb, includes the appellative סבא meaning 'elder', and it was also used as an appellative for the sages (Avigad 1967:104). שמעון בר סבא

'Shimeon son of the elder' is inscribed on an ossuary from Talpiot, Jerusalem. Sukenik (1945:31) maintains that this Shimeon the elder was a Sanhedrin member. שמעון הזקן 'Shimeon the old' is inscribed above a loculus in a tomb in the Kidron valley area, Jerusalem (Sukenik 1947:357). Also, רבא 'great, large, senior' appears on an ostracon from Masada (Yadin & Naveh 1989:21, no. 391)

Antipatros Gadia (*Ant.* 15.252) might mean Gadia as 'kid', youth (but see Klein 1930:269-70). In יוחנן חטלא 'Yohanan *ḥṭl''*, inscribed on a jar from Qumran, the epithet *ḥṭl'* is difficult to explain. It was interpreted by Yadin (1957:62) as 'Yohanan the Youth'; see also תחנה חטלא on the name list in a fourth century BCE document from Ketef Yeriho (Eshel & Misgav 1988:171, and n. 41; Eshel 1997:42).

4.1.6 Disabilities

Nicknames derived from a physical defect of a person were undoubtedly a personal nickname, as the defects were not inherited. These were especially important in priestly families, as disabled priests could not serve in the temple.

הגדם 'The amputated', 'the one-handed', is possibly in *status emphaticus* as a nickname (Rahmani 1994:92, no. 62). In the Wadi Murabaat inscription a similar nickname is found (Benoit *et al.* 1961:220, 232; Hachlili 1984:197-8; see also Noth 1928:227-8 for similar names in the Bible)

חרש 'deaf, mute' (or 'artisan, craftsman, smith') appears on an ossuary (Bagatti & Milik 1958: 83, no. 12), and on a Masada ostracon we have בר חרשא (Yadin & Naveh 1989:26, no. 421,5).

יהוחנן בן-חגקול (=העקול) 'Yehohanan son of the hanged with knees apart', is inscribed on an ossuary from Givat Hamivtar; this interpretation of the nickname is in debate (Naveh 1970:35; Yadin 1973; but see Rahmani 1994:130, no. 218). Some scholars maintain this is a nickname meaning 'the crooked'. If it is a nickname, it was given to the interred after his death and refers to the manner of Yehohanan's crucifixion.

Josephus (*Vita* 3.4), when recounting his ancestry, describes two forebearers, 'Simon the stammerer' and 'Mattaias the humpback', whose nicknames refer to their physical defects, their disabilities. On another occasion he mentions (*Bell.* 5.474) 'the lame one'.

4.1.7 Negative qualities

Many of these nicknames were designated to insult, when people wished to express their disgust for famous or prominent persons, for example בן כלבא שבוע 'son of the sated dog', בן הרצחן 'son of the murderer' (Klein 1929:339, 347; 1939:35-6; Hachlili 1984:198-9). Clines (1972:282-7) maintains that even calling a person by his patronimic alone is a form of insult.

גרידא 'the dour', is a nickname possibly referring to a hard, dry person, inscribed on an ossuary from Mt. Scopus, Jerusalem (Rahmani 1994:87, no. 44). גרידא 'Gerida', meaning 'rind', 'dour' or 'crust' appears inscribed on a Masada ostracon; and is perhaps a nickname for a rough person (Yadin & Naveh 1989:28, no. 432).

Several odd nicknames, perhaps alluding to obesity or greediness are found. An ossuary is inscribed מרים אתת העגל 'Maryam, wife of the calf', or 'the paunchy', a derogatory nickname possibly derived from עגול 'round' and implying 'paunchy' (Rahmani 1994:249, no. 821). Possibly a similar nickname is inscribed on an ossuary, שפירה בת יהוחנן בן רביך 'Shappira, daughter of Yehohanan, son of Revikh'(?). רביך 'Revikh' is difficult to decipher; however, it might indicate an oil-soaked cake of unleavened dough, thus alluding to obesity. בן כנבון 'a round cake', and בר קרזלה 'son of Qarzela', 'rounded, rolled', are inscribed on Masada ostraca and both are nicknames for fat persons (Yadin & Naveh 1989:28, no. 430; 22, 28; nos. 408, 420:3, 421:7);

בר קסא 'son of Qasa', inscribed on a Masada ostracon, may be a nickname meaning 'son of the wooden stick or chip' (Yadin & Naveh 1989:25, no. 420:6).

יהוסף קני 'Yehosef (the) Zealot', or '(the) silversmith' is inscribed on a Masada ostracon(Yadin & Naveh 1989:41, no. 474).

ציפון, possibly 'soap', 'detergent' appears on a Masada ostracon (Yadin & Naveh 1989:28, no. 436).

4.1.8 Positive qualities

Positive nicknames praise a person's character or action, or commemorate an event or a vow of an individual.

Persons were identified as proselytes in Hebrew by גר, and
in Aramaic by גיורא. These were probably used as nicknames
(Hachlili 1984:198). The term גר occurs on several ossuaries, in
combinations such as יהודטוס בן לאגאניון הגר 'Yeodatos son
of Laganion the proselyte' on an ossuary from Jerusalem; or
מריה הגיורת הדולקת 'Mariah the proselytes from Dolek'?, inscribed
on stone of ossuary or sarcophagus (Frey 1952: nos. 1385, 1390,
who suggests she might have been the one who lighted for Jews
on the Shabbat). Three ossuaries from Dominus Flevit, Jerusalem
are inscribed with שלם הגיורת 'Shalom the proselyte', and the other
two mention 'Yehudah the proslyte' (Bagatti & Milik 1975:84, no.
13; 89, no. 21; 95, no. 31). שמעון בר גיורא 'Shimeon bar Giora'
(Bell. 2.521), meaning 'son of the proselyte', was from a family
of proselytes (Klein 1929:333). ישוע גירא 'Yeshua the proselyte'
occurs on a Masada name list inscribed on an ostracon (Yadin &
Naveh 1989:25, no. 420,7). It seems that the most common name
for proselytes was Yehudah (see above; also Ilan 1991/2:154-5)

On two ossuaries from Mount Scopus, Jerusalem are inscribed
חניה בר יהונתן הנזר 'Hananiah son of Yehonathan the Nazirite',
and שלום אנתת חניה בר הנזר 'Shalom wife of Hananiah son of the
Nazirite', which was an honorific nickname (Avigad 1971:196-8).

Another nickname perhaps belonging to this group is סבורא
'savor'a', on an ossuary from wadi el-Ahmediya in the Jerusalem
area. Avigad (1967:131) maintains that it is a nickname meaning
'sage', 'scholar'.

יואב Joab, inscribed on a Masada ostracon, is an extremely rare
name. It probably applied to a man who was very brave (Yadin
& Naveh 1989:29, no. 439).

The following two nicknames with the appellative 'rock' might
have meant 'strong': לאבניא בר צונמין.. (belonging) to the 'stones',
son of 'rocks', an odd nickname inscribed on a Masada ostracon
(Yadin & Naveh 1989:66, no. 668); and בת קתרא 'the daughter
of Qatra', inscribed on a Masada ostracon, might have meant

'daughter of a rock' (Yadin & Naveh 1989:22, no. 405) – or that she is a daughter of the priestly Qatros family.

אשת טיבו 'the wife of *Ṭybw'* is inscribed on a Masada ostracon; טיבו might be a nickname in Aramaic meaning 'goodness' (Yadin & Naveh 1989:21, no. 400).

Some more examples of similar nicknames that describe positive qualities appear in literary sources (Hachlili 1984:198).

4.1.9 Endearment

Nicknames used as endearments or pet names for children or adults are:

יהועזר אקביא קנמומא 'Yehoezer Akabia/Azabia the cinnamon', inscribed on a child's ossuary from the Goliath tomb in Jericho (Hachlili 1979:55-7). קנמומא 'Cinnamon' is derived from the Hebrew-Aramaic word קנמון (Exod. 30:23; Prov. 7:17; Jer. 6:20; Song 4:14 and more) and influenced by the Greek. Cinnamon is an evergreen tree, and incense or ointment was made from its bark (*Bell.* 4.390; *Ant.* 3.197). It was considered a perfume and was associated with sweet smell. The word should be seen as a term of endearment for the child, Yehoezer Akabia/Azabiah. It probably meant 'sweet', and was added in order to differentiate the child from the other child with the same name interred in another ossuary.

חלת בלזמא 'ossuary of Balzama' is inscribed on an ossuary from Jerusalem(?) (Rahmani 1994:180). Balsam is an aromatic plant and it too should be considered a term of endearment. Cinnamon and balsam appear together as plants of paradise (Lev. R. 31:10; Rahmani 1994:180, 245).

יהודה שפירא 'Yehudah Shappira' is inscribed on two ossuaries from Mt. Olives, Jerusalem (Sukenik 1928:196-7, no. 2) and Dominus Flevit (Bagatti & Milik 1975:84-85, no. 13). On another ossuary appears אבישלום אבא יהוחנן [שפרא] (Frey 1952; no. 1393). שפירא 'the beautiful' is a nickname designated as an endearment for men (Hachlili 1984:199; Rahmani 1994:84, no. 35).

Nicknames, such as those found at Masada (see also Hachlili 1999), and used as patronymics without the addition of a personal name, could be variously explained: as the father's nickname; the interred person's own nickname; or nicknames of young people, as distinct from elderly persons, who also appear with their personal name. Or, they may be names of persons belonging to a professional guild (Klein 1930:260; Hachlili 1984:195, and notes 62-63; Naveh 1992:52).

5 Summary and Conclusions

The reasons behind the choice of names in the Second Temple period were different from those in the First Temple period, when names were given in honour of special events occurring in the family or to the people. By contrast, during the Second Temple period, naming children after an ancestor was prevalent. Most common among the Jews in 5th century BCE Egypt was paponymy, naming a child after his grandfather. From the 1st century BCE on patronymy, naming a son (or daughter) after the father, apparently became increasingly common. Matronymy, naming a son after his mother, was also practised sometimes, but only by men, not women. Patronymy was especially prevalent among prominent Jewish families in Eretz Israel, resulting in a small number of personal names appearing and reappearing for several generations in a single family. This custom had some social implications, such as families identifiable by their recurring personal names – for example, Yehoezer in the Goliath family. It seems to have indicated the strong status of the family and its position in Jewish society in the Second Temple period.

Did patronymics on its own, or *ben* with nickname, or a nickname alone – as are many of the names on the Masada ostraca – signify 'nameless people'? Naveh (1990:111-3) contends that these names were characteristic of persons living in a familiar social circle. These were abbreviated names, but names all the same, and people knew to whom they referred: their family connection, their social standing and milieu, or their status in the family tomb. Possibly, several or many had the same personal name and needed the nickname or the patronymic to differentiate and identify them. At Masada the ostraca shards were very small and contained only single names. Thus, only a person with no name at all, in any form, should be designated 'nameless', like

שמעון ואתת 'Shimeon and (his) wife' (Rahmani 1994: no. 150), where the nameless wife is interred in an ossuary with her husband.

Funerary inscriptions on ossuaries are important, as they probably attest to names of prominent figures as well as of common people. Out of 897 ossuaries included in the catalogue published by Rahmani (1994:11, 13) about 227 are inscribed, with the addition of about 10-15 more discovered recently. 147 names are listed, of which 72 are Jewish, 51 are Greek, 7 are Latin, 4 are Palmyrene, and 1 is Nabataean.

On ossuary inscriptions, more men than women had their names inscribed: the ratio of male to female names is about 3.5 to 1. Frequently a women's name includes the father's, husband's, or son's name. In Ilan's list (1989:189), 43 of the 152 women found in burial inscriptions have at least one additional name of a family male member listed. Sometimes a husband's name would appear alone, even though his nameless wife is buried in the ossuary with him, as with שמעון ואתת 'Shimeon and (his) wife' (Rahmani 1994: no. 150), as noted above.

Most of the tombs attested by inscriptions contained families, usually only with members of three generations. From the tombs' inscriptions it is evident that only the sons and their families were buried with their parents. References to grandparents are rare, but several do occur in ossuary inscriptions (Rahmani 1994: nos. 57, 198, 290, 327, 520). Daughters of the family, on their marriage, were considered members of their husband's family and were most likely buried in their husband's family tomb. Customarily, in funerary inscriptions of women they are referred to as daughter, mother or wife, followed by the name of the family member they are closely related to. However, an exception is found at the Goliath family tomb in Jericho: on the ossuary inscription of Shlamzion, the wife of the Goliath family tomb's founder (Hachlili 1979:57, inscr. 11a-c), her status in the family is reported. She is referred to as the mother of Yehoezer Goliath, whereas her husband's name is not mentioned, as is customary. In another inscription, Mariah is called 'daughter of Nath[an] el'; and the daughter, that is granddaughter, of Shlamzion (Hachlili 1979:57, inscr. 7b). Both these inscriptions reveal the important status of Shlamzion in this family. She probably was the matriarch, and, having outlived her husband by many years, she was the person responsible for raising the children and grandchildren (Hachlili 1979:57-8).

A large number of Second Temple Jews bore the same name, and the need to distinguish them resulted in the addition of nicknames. Frequently the original nickname, or an ancestor's name, was attached to the names of sons, wives, daughters and grandchildren, and so it became a family name.

The use of nicknames was common at the time. These alluded to places of origin, especially when the deceased came from outside Jerusalem in the case of local Jerusalem tombs, or Jericho when they originated in Jerusalem. Nicknames refer to title, record, rank and religious status; occupation alludes to social standing, professionals and artisans. Physical characteristics that occur frequently sometimes derive from terms of abuse. Nicknames of praise or positive traits sometimes originated in deeds that marked events in Jewish life, such as הגר 'the proselyte'. Nicknames of endearment sometimes derived from aromatic plants, such as קנמומא 'cinnamon', a child's nickname in the Goliath family of Jericho (Hachlili 1979:56). Negative traits were also used as nicknames alluding to abusive behaviour and terms of derision. The most common nicknames are those designating place of origin. Abbreviated nicknames, without a personal name, are frequently used at Masada. Among priestly families nicknames of physical characteristics, especially disability, are notable, since it was important to identify disabled priests who were forbidden to serve in the temple. Some of the priestly families that got rich through exploitation of the public retained derogatory nicknames, intended to identify them in the community.

The nicknames, especially the inherited ones, were commonly given to the person at birth, as for example in the case of the Hasmonaean sons. However, names referring to physical characteristics, especially to disabilities, were given when the disabilities became evident. Endearment and derogatory nicknames were designated during a person's lifetime. Some of the endearment nicknames found on ossuaries were most likely used to distinguish

between family members bearing the same name, for instance
קנמומא 'cinnamon' given to one of the two children named
Yehoezer Akabiah/Azabiah in the Goliath family at Jericho (see
above; Hachlili 1979:56). Or שפירא 'Shapira', a nickname given
to one of the two family members named Yehudah (Rahmani
1994:84, no. 35). Or the nickname 'aloe' (interpreted as a place
name or 'lament', 'curse'), serving to differentiate between two
relatives who had the same name, Jesus (Rahmani 1994:107, no.
114). Nicknames of title, profession and office were designated
at the time the individuals bearing them began to practise their
office or vocation, unless the title or office were inherited. It is possible that endearments and occupation nicknames were inscribed
on funerary inscriptions in order to identify and commemorate
the deceased; for instance, social standing is expressed by 'Simon
builder of the Sanctuary' and 'Nicanor who made the doors'.

Family names could also be acquired by virtue of a title, profession, or the repeated use of appellative nicknames, and these
could be inherited by subsequent generations.

The personal names, surnames and nicknames reflect the
organization of life and the Jewish social environment, as well
as the use of writing in daily life in the Second Temple period.
Funerary and other inscriptions found at sites in Eretz Israel also
indicate that the main written language was Aramaic, although
Hebrew and Greek were also in use. The inscriptions also provide
ample evidence of the personal names, family names and nicknames commonly in use in the onomasticon of the period.

Table 1: Frequency of Hebrew Personal Names among Jews in the Second Temple Period

Men's Names

Name	Total*	Quantity of names found in sources						Comparable data		
		Ossuary inscrip.	Masada	Josephus	NT	Wadi Murab.	Bar Kochba	High Priests	HB	Mishna, Talmud
שמעון Shimeon / סימון Simon	167	56	44	29	10	19	9	3	2	39
יהוחנן Yehohanan	118	27	60	14	3	11	3	–	16	25
יהוסף Yehosef	112	39	9	21	6	25	12	3	6	46
יהודה Yehuda, Judas	96	39	20	15	6	8	8	–	7	45
אלעזר 'Eleazar	85	28	10	19	2	19	7	3	7	43
יהושע, ישוע Yehoshua'	60	20	5	13	1	13	8	3	4	14
יהונתן Yehonatan	41	9	1	14	–	16	1	3	9	10
מתתיה Mattatiah	38	16	1	14	2	5	–	3	7	7
חנניה Hananiah/Ananias חנינא Hanina	37	11	6	10	3	6	1	1	12	20
יעקב Ya'acob	22	4	3	5	5	3	2	–	1	12
יהועזר Yehoe'zer	19	13	2	3	–	1	–	1	1	2
זכריה Zacharia	19	4	4	5	2	4	–	–	18	4
מנחם Menahem	18	7	1	2	1	4	2	–	1	10
ישמעאל Ishmael	17	8	1	3	–	3	2	3	6	8
חנן Hanan	15	4	–	6	–	5	–	3	8	8
לוי Levi	13	6	–	4	1	1	1	–	1	3
חזקיה Hizkiah	13	6	3	3	–	1	–	–	5	4

* Total of first six columns of names

Table 1a: Frequency of Hebrew Personal Names in Percent

Men's Names

Name	Total	Percent	Percent of names found in sources					
			Ossuary inscrip.	Masada	Josephus	NT	Wadi Murab.	Bar Kochba
שמעון Shimeon סימן Simon	167	18.8%	18.9%	25.9%	16.1%	23.8%	13.2%	16.1%
יהוחנן Yehohanan	118	13.3%	9.1%	35.3%	7.8%	7.1%	7.6%	5.4%
יהוסף Yehosef	112	12.6%	13.1%	5.3%	11.7%	14.3%	17.4%	21.4%
יהודה Yehuda, Judas	96	10.8%	13.1%	11.8%	8.3%	14.3%	5.6%	14.3%
אלעזר 'Eleazar	85	9.6%	9.4%	5.9%	10.6%	4.8%	13.2%	12.5%
ישוע, ישע Yehoshua'	60	6.7%	6.7%	2.9%	7.2%	2.4%	9.0%	14.3%
יהונתן Yehonatan	41	4.6%	3.0%	0.6%	7.8%		11.1%	1.8%
מתתיה Mattatiah	38	4.3%	5.4%	0.6%	7.8%		3.5%	
חנניה Hananiah/Ananias חנינא Hanina	37	4.2%	3.7%	3.5%	5.6%	7.1%	4.2%	1.8%
יעקב Ya'acob	22	2.5%	1.3%	1.8%	2.8%	11.9%	2.1%	3.6%
יהועזר Yehoe'zer	19	2.1%	4.4%	1.2%	1.7%		0.7%	
זכריה Zacharia	19	2.1%	1.3%	2.4%	2.8%	4.8%	2.8%	
מנחם Menahem	18	1.9%	2.4%	0.6%	1.1%	4.8%	2.8%	3.6%
ישמעאל Ishmael	17	1.9%	2.7%	0.6%	1.7%	2.4%	2.1%	3.6%
חנן Hanan	15	1.7%	1.3%		3.3%		3.5%	
לוי Levi	13	1.5%	2.0%		2.2%	2.4%	0.7%	1.8%
חזקיה Hizkiah	13	1.5%	2.0%	1.8%	1.7%		0.7%	
Total	897	100%	100%	100%	100%	100%	100%	100%

Women's Names

Name	* Total	Quantity of names found in sources						Comparable data	
		Ossuary inscrip.	Masada	Josephus	NT	Wadi Murab.	Bar Kochba	HB	Mishna, Talmud
מרים Mariamme	48	35	3	5	1	4	–	–	1
שלום Salome	40	26	1	6	1	–	6	2	7
שלומציון Shelomzion	18	15	–	2	–	–	1	–	–
מריה Mariah	15	9	1	1	4	–	–	–	–
מרתה Martha	14	13	–	–	1	–	–	–	1
שפירא Shapira	10	8	–	–	1	–	1	–	–
יהוחנה Yehohana	8	5	–	–	1	–	2	–	–

* Total of first six columns of names

Source, Material and Percentages

A Response to Hachlili

Gerard Mussies   (University of Utrecht)

This interesting survey was mainly criticized for the way in which figures and statistics are handled in it. Right from the start the material for Jewish onomastics in the Second Temple Period is called "vast". This is, however, hardly the case. As compared with the overwhelming multitude of Greco-Roman pagan personal names, the Jewish material can at best be labelled as rather modest. That is the very reason why it is so difficult to say to what degree the little that we have can be considered to be representative of the Jewish population as a whole, whose precise numbers, moreover, are a problem in itself. One of Hachlili's conclusions is, however, that the names Maryam, Salome and Shlamzion together were borne in this period by about 50% of the total female population, apparently of Palestine. To corroborate this the appended statistics of the very frequent (male and) female names were projected onto the wall (see pp. 113-5 above), but as such these statistics pertain only to a sub-collection, that of the not so many names of high frequency contained in the Hebrew material, and not to the complete collection of Jewish male and female names. The difficulty connected with them is, therefore, that they omit to account for

a) The many Hebrew-Aramaic names that are of infrequent occurrence in the material, such as Anna, Elizabeth, Susanna, Tabitha (all NT), etc, Absalom (4 times in Josephus), Agabos (NT), Barnabas (NT), Jairos (Josephus/NT), etc.

b) All the Greco-Roman names borne by Jews in this period: Alexandra (3x Josephus), Cleopatra (Josephus), Dorcas (Josephus/NT), Rhode (NT), etc, Andreas (NT), Antiochos (Mishna), Jason (Josephus/NT), Justos (Josephus/NT), etc.

c)   Most names of the Diaspora Jews, for, apparently, *CPJ* and part of *CIJ* have not been included in Hachlili's survey.

Because of a), the statistics offered about the Hebrew corpus are inevitably out of focus and will have to be adjusted. As a result, the percentage of the three female names mentioned will already come to amount to less than half the total of the material, while the omission of b) makes it clear that this percentage can have no bearing at all on "the total population". This latter notion is further complicated by c), because the dividing line between Palestinian and Diaspora Jewry has always been a fluid one, and an unknown number of Passover-visitors, travellers and repatriates is certainly included in the Palestinian material in *CIJ* that we now have. But even if some allowance has been made for such cases and a more or less trustworthy Palestinian corpus established, the question of its representativity must still be posed because it clearly contains curious blanks. Why is it that the narrative sources, Josephus and the NT, do not mention, apart from the HB/OT couple, any other persons named Sarah and Abram, whereas these do occur in the rest of our sources? In the datable papyri from nearby Egypt, for instance, there appear four women and six men bearing these names up to the second century CE, with some more to follow in later times. This may be a side-effect of the circumstance that, in ancient historiography, women are far less often mentioned by name than men, or else it may be due to pure coincidence.

Domesticity and the Spindle

Miriam Peskowitz   (Emory University)

The rabbinic visions for Jewish life that developed after the fall of the Jerusalem Temple contained markedly new formulations of family life. New possibilities and new proprieties were imagined. Many of these new formulations were expressed in the language of property, exchanges of labor and support, and other kinds of economic relations. To the extent that early rabbinic Judaism was persuasive to Jews or, to the extent that it was already embedded in a broader Jewish and Roman culture, these economic innovations touched the intimacy of lives that married women and men spent together. Wives and husbands inhabited houses where foods and drink were continually prepared and consumed, where beds were made, slept in and remade, and where a myriad of tasks were carried out, in close relation and close proximity, repeatedly, day in and day out.

The familiarity of family relations makes it remarkably easy to think that concepts such as 'femininity', 'fatherhood', 'family', and 'domesticity' are natural categories. Their repetition makes it easy to believe that although these concepts change, they have an underlying essence that remains relatively stable. It would seem almost oxymoronic, then, to speak of their histories.

But what happens when we do? Most popular and current renditions of Jewish female domesticity – the relations of women, labor and home – turn at some point to the image of the "worthy woman" from Proverbs 31:10-31 that begins "A woman of valor, who can find her?"[1] In this text from the Hebrew Bible, a married woman transforms wool and flax into high quality and useful

---

[1] *'ēšet ḥayil*; the root *ḥyl* has additional meanings related to battles and warriors, such as strong, firm, and mighty. Against the tendency to feminize according to stereotypes of what femininity is and should be, the LXX translation of Hebrew to Greek is instructive: *gynaikas andreias*, a masculine, manly woman.

clothing for her household, her husband, and herself. In addition
to her unpaid labor of overseeing the management of the household and distributing charity, this woman is economically active.
While her husband performs his civic role at the city gates, she
weaves linen and sells it to merchants. With the profits she
acquires land and plants a vineyard. Her textile work results in
products for the market. Spinning and weaving do not function
to demonstrate her sexual fidelity and wifely devotion to her husband, as they would in later texts. Her work yields wages that
can be used to buy land and increase the holdings of the woman
and her family, and for this, the biblical passage praises her.

Eventually, Proverbs 31 would become central to the gender
consciousness of much later Jewish religious culture. It will be
recited, for example, as part of a weekly Shabbat home service
that pays tribute to wives. However, despite its later popularity,
this particular biblical portrait of domesticity was not central to
the gender culture of early Rabbinic and Roman-period Judaism.
In fact, as I will demonstrate in this paper, rabbinic conceptions
that emerged in the second century contradicted this earlier vision
of domesticity in significant ways.

For example, the Targum, a set of Aramaic bible translations
that date from this period, often gloss and expand the biblical
verses which they translate. But Proverbs 31:10-31 receives surprisingly little elaboration in the Targum, suggesting that the
passage evoked little active interest.[2] This is noteworthy, because
in the Roman period, Jewish writers were not at all uninterested
in domesticity and the formation of women into wives. Only, the
possibilities offered by this particular inherited text were of little
use to them. A look at how conceptions of what wives should
be changed between the writing of the biblical book of Proverbs
and the mishnaic tractate Ketubot explains the lack of interest in
Proverbs 31. It also shows the fallacy of imagining families, labor
and domesticity as natural, essential, or unchanging.

---

[2] I will not overinterpret the lack of elaboration on Targ. Prov. 31; in
general Targ. Prov. contains little of the expansion of biblical text that makes
Targum so interesting as still another textual voice within Judaism of the
Roman and Byzantine periods.

1 Laboring for One's Husband

One reason why the passage from Proverbs was not attractive to rabbinic writers was that this biblical conception of the relations of women, labor and property differed greatly from that of the Rabbis. Proverbs' portrait of an industrious wife ran counter to the new character of the rabbinic wife. The proverbial woman labored by her own command. When her work yielded products and profits and property, she owned and controlled these. She is depicted as having a great degree of autonomy and independence.

In contrast, early rabbinic writings move aspects of the ownership and control of a married woman's labors and work to her husband, and this is the first and crucial distinction. The rabbinic husband will own two things: first, his wife's work – the completed products and the wages she garners. And second, he held authority over his wife's labors, defined as the repetitive daily tasks she would do. As the new rabbinic Judaism emerged, female industry and thrift still matter – as they did in Proverbs. But the control of wifely labor becomes part of the definition of being female and male in rabbinic society. Although it does not have to be, in early rabbinic texts domesticity was made into a key component of the discipline of being a woman and a wife.

Early rabbinic law proposed two categories of labor for Jewish wives. In the first, "labors that a woman does for her husband", wives performed unpaid domestic labors. In the second, a married woman produced commodities or sold her services; in turn, she received wages, money, objects in kind, or other kinds of profit and recompense. The Mishnah considers these profits to be "new property", and a wife's "new property" must be turned over to her husband, to whom it will belong.

I turn to the first, to the issue of unpaid labor, as it is articulated in the household code of Mishnah Ketubot 5:5.[3] From one

---

[3]It has become popular to define m. Ketubot 5:5 as a 'household code', in part since doing so places it among other Roman-period household codes and allows analysis. See Colossians 3:18-4:1; 1 Peter; Pseudo-Phocylides, *Maxims* 175-227; Philo, *Apologia for the Jews* 7.3; Josephus, *Against Apion* 2.189-

perspective, this passage classifies and clarifies household work for married women. But to describe it this way means we assume that a prior connection exists between married women and domesticity, and then ask about the details. What happens when we shift perspective, and question the proposition that women and domesticity are inherently linked? From a perspective that does not assume an essential connection between a married woman and domesticity, it becomes clear that the passage first must imagine the wife as a household worker. This is done both as part of and prior to listing the terms for what her work will mean and naming the husband as the owner of her labors.

Mishnah Ketubot 5:5 enumerates the possibilities for a wife to discharge her labors to any household slaves or servants she brought with her to the marriage. This discussion is followed by several comments, respectively attributed to Rabbis Eliezer and Rabban Shimon ben Gamliel. These comments no longer understand female domesticity in terms of actual labor. Instead, labor is understood in terms of sexuality and leisure – a significant shift from the biblical vision.

The passage Mishnah Ketubot 5:5. translates as follows:

> These are the labors that the wife does for her husband: she grinds, and she bakes and she launders; she cooks, and she nurses her child; she tends the bedding and she works in wool.
>
> If [the wife] brought to [the husband, when they married] one household slave, then she does not grind and she does not bake and she does not launder.

209; Philo, *Decalogue* 165-167; Plutarch, *Mulierum virtutes*; Iamblichus, *Life of Pythagoras* 54-57; Plutarch, *Advice to Bride and Groom* 138b-146a; Callicratidas, *On the Happiness of Households* 105.20-22, and of course, the ever-repeated guide to household management, Aristotle, *Politics* 1.1253b.1-14. In particular, m. Ketubot 5:5 has close parallels in Hierocles, *Oikonomikos*, a second century CE Stoic tractate. In the *Oikonomikos*, the wife's domestic tasks are outlined as spinning wool, making bread, and cooking, followed by a general statement that her work includes everything of a domestic nature; see the edition of Hense and Wachsmuth, vol. 3, 679-701.

[If she brought to him] two [household slaves] she does
not cook and she does not nurse her child.

[If she brought to him] three [household slaves], she
does not tend to the bedding and she does not work
in wool.

[If she brought to him] four [household slaves], she may
sit upon a chair of leisure.

Rabbi Eliezer says: Even if she brought to him a hundred household slaves, he forces her to work in wool,
because leisure brings about sexual temptations and
suspicions.

Rabban Shimon ben Gamliel says: If through a vow
[her husband] forbid his wife from doing work tasks,
he must divorce [her] and give the k^etubbah to her,
because leisure brings lifelessness upon her.[4]

Ancient references to everyday life seem factual and real. However,
in this passage, we are deeply immersed in the realm of rabbinic
fantasies about domesticity. Under the principle of labors that
a wife must do for her husband, the passage lists seven tasks:
grinding grain, baking bread, laundering clothing and other tex-
tiles, cooking, nursing children, tending the bedding, and working
in wool.

Following this, the passage moves immediately to consider how
a wife's economic status might affect domesticity. Her economic
position is established by the number of servants or slaves she
brings with her into the marriage. For households in which wives
have servants or slaves, the passage begins to reverse the association of wives with domestic labor. The labor of servants or slaves
can replace her own. If, through a dowry or inheritance, the wife
brought to the marriage one slave, she does not have to grind,
bake or wash. Two slaves will release her from cooking and nursing children. With three slaves, she can refrain from tending to
the beds and from working in wool. With four servants or slaves, a
married Jewish woman can pursue a life free from domestic labor.

---

[4] All translations are my own.

Through these exchanges, task after task is removed from her set of responsibilities until none remains.

Reading only this far into the passage, it seems as if Mishnah Ketubot 5:5 uses distinctions of economic status to create a variety of wives. Depending on her wealth, the contents of a woman's domesticity might differ.[5] Eventually, if a woman were sufficiently wealthy, her wifery could be constructed on terms in which her husband was not the recipient of her labor. Reading this far, for women with sufficient wealth in servants and/or slaves, being a wife could be separated from the domesticity.

Reading further, however, it becomes clear that the passage's argument moves away from allowing wives to hold various relations to household labor and domesticity. Instead, the passage removes the possibility of the final, liberating exchange. Following the calculus of traded labors, the position attributed to Rabbi Eliezer reneges the possibility that a wealthy wife could trade away her domestic labors. Even with economic privilege, a woman can never entirely remove domestic duties from being a wife. In this view, all married women must be linked to domestic labor.

Furthermore, Eliezer's position links wifely labors with concerns about female sexuality: Even if the wife brought a hundred household slaves to the husband when they married, the husband can force her to work in wool. His reasoning is that leisure brings about sexual temptations and suspicions. Thus, the link between domesticity and wifery must be retained, and the link will be symbolized by woolwork. This passage echoes other contemporary Roman writing, from Livy, to Dionysius of Halicarnassus, to Apuleius. It evokes the familiar notion that labor – and especially woolwork – protects women (and the men who claim them) from the sexual temptations associated with leisure. The symbol

---

[5]Tosefta Ketubot 5:4 begins its comment on this passage by noting that the Mishnah had classified seven labors, but did not assign the rest. t. Ketubot 5:4 concludes its list of labors by noting how the ethos of a place matters. Where wives do not usually do certain kinds of labors, her husband must not force her to do so. Thus, the details of domesticity will vary according to a woman's economic status, and according to the cultural customs of the place where she and her husband reside.

of woolwork reassures husbands that the sexual temptations of their female relatives and wives are tightly under control.

Thus, woolwork becomes the symbol of marital piety for Jewish women. Because of this symbolic association, it becomes the only task that a wife cannot trade away. The earlier part of the passage had envisioned *almost all* married women, from poor to affluent, engaged in woolwork. Eliezer expands this continuum. *All* women, including the most affluent, must work in wool. As a metaphor, woolwork insures sexual loyalties that, like labors, are owed to the husband. If a woman forsakes this labor, she risks also forsaking her sexual morality.

Woolwork signals two things: a wife's resistance to sexual temptations, and her laboring debts to her husband. A wife's household labors belong to her husband. They are placed under his control. A wife's labor is not imagined as a form of religious piety, for example, nor as a sign of her devotion to her family. Instead, a wife's labor more singularly expressed her piety and devotion to her husband. To conclude this reading, Jewish wifery includes domestic labor as a way to protect a husband from his wife's sexual betrayal. And, including domestic labor in the definition of Jewish wifery also protects a husband's privileges to a wife's household labors and to the labors of her body. Releasing any wife – even and especially a wealthy wife – from household work effectively removes these labors from her husband's domain, and deprives him of something he might otherwise have. Eliezer's position refuses to diminish so completely this element of a husband's authority.

Eliezer's position is followed by one attributed to Rabban Shimon ben Gamliel. A husband cannot make a vow that forbids his wife from performing her domestic tasks. If the husband makes this kind of vow, he must divorce his wife and give her the $k^e tubbah$ payment. The reason given is this. Jewish women must not lead lives of leisure, because the result of leisure for women is 'lifelessness'. Female leisure yields lifelessness.

However, if as readers of this text we show some skepticism at the logical ease of this equation, important features become clear. The point that domesticity must always be part of Jewish wifery is made a second time, but in a different way and with another set of ramifications. Gamliel's position effectively prohibits individual husbands and wives from undoing the rabbinic binding of wifery to domesticity. In Roman-period Judaism, vows functioned as a kind of folk religion, in which certain acts or goods were renounced or set aside in exchange for a wish, promise, or other hoped-for result. For example, through a vow, a husband could reorganize the distribution of labor in his household. If he wished, he could release his wife from her domestic labors. In contrast, Gamliel's position prohibits any individual attempts to separate domesticity and wifery. His position will not allow husband-and-wife-couples to imagine and enact family labor on alternate terms.

The rationale given for this prohibition is the protection of women. It is this language of protection that specifically needs our critical attention. In this idea of family labor, wives perform household labors for their own good. Individual husbands must not undermine their wives' domesticity, because domesticity benefits her by preventing a slide into a condition of lifelessness. The logic of protection is a bit tricky and needs to be unraveled. As a whole, Mishnah Ketubot 5:5 places wives into an economy of female domesticity, slavery, servitude and household labors. When viewed more structurally, it becomes clear that the entire economy is organized around the husband, who is present and engaged only as the recipient and owner of labors. To recall, the entire passage explicates the general principle of "labors that the wife performs for her husband" This construction of household life underscores the husband's privileges. Unlike the others, he is not a domestic laborer but the recipient of labors performed by his wife, by servants, or by slaves.

The first named position – Rabbi Eliezer's – had deciphered that economy in sexual terms. Domestic labor is a discipline that composes and displays a wife's sexual fidelity. The second position – Shimon ben Gamliel's – provides a very different explanation. A wife's labor is for her own benefit. It protects her from the perceived negative effects of (something imagined as) leisure. The two positions offer very different perspectives on women, labor and family relations. In Eliezer's position, woolwork controls women's sexuality; according to Shimon ben Gamliel, household labor is necessary because it protects the quality of women's lives.

Thus, Mishnah Ketubot 5:5 concludes with an argument about the protection of women. The language of protection is almost always quite difficult to unravel. Declarations of care, kindness and benevolence mask the fact that the people involved have unequal relations to power. Shimon ben Gamliel's comment envisions a world in which women are imagined to need rabbinic protection.[6] Included in this is the notion that rabbinic law protects women against the whims of their Jewish husbands. From this rabbinic perspective, if an individual Jewish husband releases his wife from domestic labor, this release hastens her downfall into lifelessness. To counter the husband's potential and dangerous vows, Gamliel claims that the demand that wives engage in domestic labor in fact protects the quality of Jewish women's lives.

Of course, on some level, it is impossible for us to judge how a Jewish woman living in Roman Palestine might have evaluated these options. Either choice limits her considerably, and both choices imagine her as controlled by men. It might be the case that a woman would have preferred other kinds of options; we can never know. However, as contemporary readers, when we side either with Gamliel, or with the imagined husband, we are still thinking within, and not against, rabbinic logic. If the comment sees the question of wives' domestic labors as a battle between rabbinic law and Jewish husbands, we need not follow the rabbinic text into the logic of its argument. Reading otherwise, and from other starting assumptions, the following becomes clear. In

---

[6]Variations on the idea of protection appear both in Mishnah and in scholarly accounts of Mishnah. In the latter, arguments about protecting women appear as normative explanation, such that often the ancient rabbinic discourse is not recognized as distinctive at all. By way of illustration see Falk, *Introduction to Jewish Law*, 292: "the following rule [m. Ketubot 5:5] defined the duties of a wife and prevented exaggerated demands on the part of the husband". In its depiction of the uncontrollable man and the vulnerable woman, such a scenario constructs (for them and for us) women as in need of protection by 'good' men (in this case, the Rabbis), who will protect Jewish women from other 'bad' men (including their husbands). It simultaneously forges a distinction between Rabbis and other Jewish men, so that the former are morally heroic and the latter are in need of control.

this scenario neither husbands nor Rabbis protect wives. Shimon
ben Gamliel's position would restrict an individual husband from
undermining the economy that the Mishnah sets up as a crucial
part of marriage. His claim to protect women from husbands and
from lifelessness masks the fact that the passage's real intent is
to protect men and husbands. By focusing, as Mishnah Ketubot
5:5 does, on what women do, the passage effectively hides from
view the very men whom it privileges and whose advantages it
will extend. This position hides the husband who controls and
owns the wife's labors. And it hides from view the Rabbis who
imagine themselves as legislators, but who were, simultaneously,
husbands themselves. Doing so, it makes an economy of discipline
and control seem benevolent, and for a woman's own good.

2   The Work of Her Hands

Discourses of gender are almost always contradictory, internally
riven and at odds. Whereas Mishnah Ketubot 5:5 imagines a
wife's daily life as devoted either to domesticity or to leisure, the
second category for women's labor attends to other possibilities,
in which a wife works and receives wages and earns a profit.

Mishnah Ketubot 5:5 had established women's non-waged
work at home, and constituted these as labors she owed to her
husband. The second category of female labor, to which I now
turn, was the "work of her hands" (*ma‘ᵃśêh yādêhā*). This category includes work through which a wife or daughter brings 'new
property' – money, products, and such – into the family economy.
It was an innovation of early rabbinic Judaism to give the profits
of a woman's labor to her husband or father, and by doing so,
to control women's wages, products, profits and properties so
extensively. This form of economic control affected not just wives,
but all women and girls who were part of families and family
economies.

The general principle was formulated in Mishnah Ketubot 6:1:
"[The] finds of the woman and [the] work of her hands [belong]
to her husband, and [concerning] her inheritance, he [owns] fruits
[of the inheritance] during her lifetime".[7] Anything of value that

---

[7] The passage which remands a wife's new property to her husband segues

a woman gained through her own activity belongs to her husband. That which became hers through means less active than by her own labor (either as dowry, inheritance or gifts, for example) belongs to her, but the husband controls the property and owns the profits.[8] These historic innovations of early rabbinic Judaism remanded the work profits of wives to their husband. The innovation of the legal concept of 'the work of her hands' was paired with another, that of 'maintenance', (or *mĕzônôt*), a husband's responsibility to maintain and support his wife. It is in the passages that link 'the work of her hands' and 'maintenance' that we find ourselves facing once again the symbol of the spindle.

3   The Spindle's Surplus Value

The spindle appears repeatedly. It is the stable symbol of very unstable and changing notions of femininity. The spindle is present at the climax of Mishnah Ketubot 5:5, in which Rabbi Eliezer invokes it as the unremovable marker of female domesticity, the task that cannot be traded away. It recurs in early rabbinic

---

into a discussion of who owns the compensation for more overt violences to her body. The first position is that compensation for indignities to her, and damages for injury to her body, belong to the woman (m. Ketubot 6:1 end). The dissenting position argues that these payments should be split in differing proportions between the woman and her husband, or alternately, that her portion of the damages must be used to purchase land, of which the husband will enjoy the usufruct.

[8]A corollary passage, m. Ketubot 9:4, provides a policing mechanism whereby the husband can put his wife under oath to insure that she accurately reports her earnings to him; also m. Shebuot 7:8. Regarding the status of finds (*mĕṣî'āh*), see m. Baba Metzia 1:3–1:4, 2:1–2.2, m. Giṭṭin 5:8, and m. Makorot 2:8–2:10. The examples used to discuss finds are mundane objects that are either found by chance or collected and gathered. For all objects, tannaitic process is to attempt to locate the owner before taking possession. The father, or *ba'al ha-bayit*, owns things found by his wife, by his minor sons and daughters, and by male and female non-Jewish slaves. Finds by adult sons and daughters, male and female Jewish slaves, and a divorced wife awaiting her marriage settlement belong to the finders. There is no scriptural authority for his control over the finds of the other family members; on slaves and servants, see Leviticus 25:39-43 (on 'Hebrew' slaves) and Leviticus 25:44-46 (on 'Canaanite' slaves).

discussions of the work of her hands, in their discussions of what
to do with a woman's waged labor. The passage Mishnah Ketubot
5:9 discusses the special case of a husband who maintains his wife
through a guardian or agent (i.e., through a third person). Such a
case might result because the husband lives in a different locale,
because he is looking for employment or travels for business, or
because he has several wives and does not live with all of them
at the same time. The details of a husband's responsibility to
maintain his wife are narrated vividly; it is the only place in the
Mishnah that elaborates these details. If a husband supports his
wife through an agent he must provide her with a bed, mattress
and mat, with shoes and clothing, and with assorted amounts
and types of food. In addition to these material goods and foods,
the husband, through his agent, must provide the wife with a silver coin (a silver *mînāh*) for what the passage describes as "her
needs".[9] Introducing this last aspect of maintenance – and still
discussing the specific case of a woman provided for by a guardian
– Mishnah Ketubot 5:9 translates: "He gives her a silver *mînāh*
for her needs, and she eats with him from one Sabbath to the
next".

But the passage yields immediately to an instance of conflict.
What if the husband's agent does not provide his part of the
bargain? What if he reneges on the silver coin? What can the
wife do?

If this happens, according to the same passage, the wife's legal
recourse is to withhold the profits from the work of her hands. The
text continues: "And if he does not give a silver *mînāh*, the work of
her hands is hers". But what is striking is that when the passage

---

[9] Her needs: *šĕrākêhā*. See the expansion of the list of third-party or guardian support in t. Ketubot 5:8-9. The list of materials ends with reference to
the daughter of Naqdimon ben Gurion, a childless widow who, while awaiting
a levirate marriage to her brother-in-law, contests the amount of her maintenance. The text considers the maintenance award more than sufficient (noting
it in the exaggerated terms of five hundred dinarii per day for spices alone,
but see parallel texts), and the tale ends with her downfall into poverty, in
which she must pick barley pieces from waste. The mishnayot about maintaining wives and other dependent women conclude with a sense of rabbinic
mistrust of these women, and caution about the possibility of female greed.

measures the amount of her earned wages that would equal the silver coin, it uses the metaphor and weight of spun yarn:

> What must [the wife] do for him? [Her work] must weigh five *sêlā'im* of warp thread, in Judea, which equals to ten *sêlā'im* in the Galilee. Or, [her work] must weigh ten *sêlā'im* of woof thread in Judea, which equals twenty *sêlā'im* in Galilee.[10]

Despite the many kinds of work that women in Roman Palestine might have done to earn wages or other kinds of profit, the passage measures the work of her hands in terms of quantities of spun yarn. Furthermore, this spun yarn is described in weights and thicknesses necessary for weaving at the loom. The framework of the web is established by the heavier warp yarn, and the thinner woof yarn is woven in between.

By measuring her labor as yarn and not as money, the passage narrows the range of female labors into the more singular icon of woolwork. By describing a woman's profit-bearing labor through a symbol of domesticity, the passage shortens the range of services and labors it will imagine women doing.

How does the early rabbinic spindle work? First, the spindle combines women's domestic and unpaid labor with women's paid labors. It links a woman's unpaid household labor with the waged fruits of her labor that she also owed to her husband. Thus, the spindle flattens out and effaces the major difference between these: namely, that in one of these categories of labor, a woman's work potentially takes place outside of her relation to domesticity and away from her husband's domain. This use of the spindle sees as impossible an economic existence for a married woman who is not controlled by her husband. It cannot imagine or legislate a womanly life in which the husband is not the ultimate recipient of a

---

[10] On the upright looms in use, warp thread hangs vertically. Warp thread is thicker and heavier than the woof thread which is woven in and out, horizontally. The passage explains the relation between the two forms of spun wool as a 1:2 ratio, in which five sela of vertical warp will equal (in weight? in time spent in production?) ten sela of horizonal weft; see Peskowitz, *Spinning Fantasies: Rabbis, Gender and History*, esp. chapter three.

woman's bodily labors. Through the recurring figure of the spindle the work that might place a wife, even temporarily, outside the realm of domesticity is reconfigured as a domestic task.[11]

Writing about these things through the spindle facilitates this kind of discursive and legal control. If a woman's domestic labor is symbolized as woolwork, using this figure to regulate her waged labors makes it more familiar and 'natural' to place these labors on a continuum with her domestic labor. Connecting nonwaged labor to waged, even a wife's waged labor is placed – legally and conceptually – under her husband's control.

For the real and unknowable families of Roman Palestine, the material results of wives' labors probably mattered greatly. The resources and services made available through the interrelated labor of various household members – wives, husbands, children, parents, other relatives, and servants or slaves – contributed to making the household run. In the most immediate sense, the surplus value of a woman's paid labor produced resources that made a positive difference, resources that made life just a bit easier and better for all.

But the rabbinic text does not concern itself with things so prosaic. Consider what is absent from rabbinic possibilities of what wives might do. They express no desires for well-kept houses, or

---

[11] This section links a wife's paid and unpaid labor, and also associates these with elements of control in another way. Textually, her labors are the beginning and end points of a discussion that ranges through the overlapping issues of work, sex, and gender. The discussion of household labors in Mishnah Ketubot 5:5 is connected to the principle of the work of her hands (m. Ketubot 6:1) through a series of mishnayot. The literary pathway from household labors to the control of a wife's new property takes a reader through vignettes of laboring wives; to leisurely wives with sexual temptations; to the possibility that a husband might use a vow to restrict his sexual intercourse with his wife (5:6); to the rebellious wife (môredet) who loses money from her kĕtubbāh (and any forthcoming inheritance) for each week of her rebellion (5:7); and to lists of maintenance (mĕzônôt), food, provisions, clothing, and support that a husband must provide for his wife (5:8–5:9). The path from the household labors (5:5) to sexual intercourse to domestic control of the unruly wife to the husband's material protection of her moves – finally, in m. Ketubot 6:1 – to the principle that all her profits, products and wages belong to him.

for the actual property and resources that a woman's wages add to their families' well being. The surplus value of women's labor was not conceived in terms of actual products and services. Through the spindle's long shadow, the value of economic resources slides into something else, into the spindle's other value: feminine domesticity, loyalty to husbands, and appropriate practices for being a Jewish wife. In Mishnah Ketubot 5:5, even if a wife had slaves or servants to do the actual tasks, and even if the family could afford to buy all the cloth, clothing and other textile products it wanted or needed, still her woolwork is necessary to display her fidelity to her husband. If the woman and her family were wealthy, the material products of her body's labors were economically unnecessary. In this rabbinic fantasy of Jewish wives, however, she still must spin. The spindle declares that a woman's body and her body's labors belong to her husband. This economic ownership is part of what it will mean to be a married woman.

4   Back to Proverbs

There is a radical economic difference between the wife portrayed in Proverbs 31 and the wife developed in early rabbinic literature. The wife in Proverbs had economic agency. She wove her linen cloth and sold it to merchants. With her profits she bought land, and she planted the land with a vineyard. Her initial work at the spindle was transformed into an investment in grapes that would ideally yield continuous profits as new grapes grew, were harvested, sold, or made into wine, year after year. The profits would be her own. Her textile work corresponds with her market activity. She produces, she sells, she makes decisions, she buys, she prospers.

This is what separates the ancient expression of domesticity in Proverbs 31 from the newer rabbinic version. In the Roman period, rabbinic law began to extend the privileges of husbands by giving them greater control over family economy and over their wives. For instance, one legal innovation reconfigured the husband's relation to his wife's "old property", that which she brought with her into the marriage. In this innovation, the husband now controlled this property, and the profits were his through his right to usufruct. This new arrangement of control over the woman's "old property" was accompanied by the legal innovations, discussed here, that granted the husband ownership and control of the wife's "new property", to include everything she found or collected, everything produced by the work of her hands, as well as the profits from inherited property she owned.

These Roman-period innovations clarify the difference between Proverbs 31 and early rabbinic notions of family economy. If the woman of Proverbs 31 had lived instead in the rabbinic imaginary, the profits she made by selling her linen would belong to her husband. The land she bought would be owned by her husband. And the fruit produced in her vineyard would belong to him as well.[12] Proverbs 31 assumes that a wife owns her earnings. In contrast, early rabbinic law remands a wife's earnings to her husband. As compared to this much earlier Israelite text that was a privileged legacy for Jews, the Mishnah defines women and women's work through very different sets of social, sexual, economic and family relations.

5 Concluding Remarks

Interpreters of biblical and rabbinic texts often point to the spindle as a marker of continuity in Israelite and Jewish notions of wives. But this derives from the cultural habit of making the spindle into the symbol of a putative essence of womanhood, an essence that remains the same despite surface differences and changes. But in a critical gesture that upsets the idea that gender or family roles are essential necessities, the dissimilarities will be suddenly highlighted and more easily seen.

---

[12] A philological note: The terminology used by Prov. 31 for female labor is related to that used in early rabbinic texts, but the lack of actual overlap is significant. In Proverbs 31:31, references to female work use these phrases: *ma'ăśêhā* (her work) and *pĕrî yādêhā* (the fruits of her hands). The phrase common in rabbinic writing – *ma'ăśêh yādêhā* – is absent from Proverbs. A version of the phrase does appear in Isaiah 45:11, where it refers to male labor. In the Mishnah and Tosefta the same phrase is used specifically to refer to female labor.

The spindle changes. In Proverbs 31 and biblical texts more generally, the woman's spindle is a general marker of sexual difference. It refers to femininity as masculinity's difference. It marks a boundary that delineates femininity as what men should not be and what men should not do.[13] The difference between the biblical spindle and its later meanings is the following. The biblical spindle symbolizes differences between women and men; it does not include the lessons of sexual containment that the Roman-period spindle conveyed. In Proverbs, woolwork and the spindle are signs of female productive labor. In Mishnah Ketubot 5:5 – and especially in the specific context of Rabbi Eliezer's statement – the products that result from woolwork are economically unnecessary. Productivity in material terms is not what matters. In tractate Ketubot, woolwork is not what facilitates the acquisition of land and vineyards, it is an antidote to what rabbis imagined as always potentially present and dangerous – a wife's sexual desires for someone other than her husband.

This early rabbinic tangle of woolwork, domesticity and female sexuality forms a dramatically different metaphor when compared to Proverbs 31. Unlike the Roman-period text, Proverbs 31 does not always frame its representation of female labor with concerns about sex and promiscuity. Female sexuality and female labor are not joined in the same ways that they will be in Roman and in early rabbinic writing. Proverbs, too, has its fears of unrestrained female sexuality, but it does not incorporate these into its representation of the wife. Tractate Ketubot recasts women's economic participation into a repetitive situation in which husbands control their wives. Labor becomes a wife's display of sexual loyalty and fidelity. In other words and in the passages in question, domestic labor demonstrates a wife's commitment to containment. If the early rabbis were ever concerned that even woolwork and the spindle might not fully control their women; they never committed this fear to writing.

---

[13] 2 Samuel 3:29; for developed discussion of this point see Peskowitz, *Spinning Fantasies*, chapter two.

Unraveling the Rabbis' Web

A Response to Miriam Peskowitz

Lieve Teugels   (University of Utrecht)

This is a reconstruction of the response which I gave to the paper of Prof. Miriam Peskowitz, in her absence. Because of this peculiar situation, the response was addressed to the paper rather than to the speaker. It was in the first place meant to trigger the discussion among the participants of the conference after the reading of both the paper and the response. I will first recapitulate what I saw as the main points of the paper. Then, I will formulate my personal remarks about different aspects of the paper. I will sometimes refer to Peskowitz' book, from which the paper, for the larger part, was taken, to provide a broader context for my remarks.[1]

1 Summary

The spindle – or woolwork – is often considered as a marker of continuity between biblical and rabbinic Judaism. It is conceived as *the* symbol of Jewish womanhood. As such, the concepts 'woolwork' and 'spinning' are often considered as natural categories that represent the eternal essence of female work or domesticity, the essence of the relationship between wife and husband, and even of female being *tout court*. The fact that the spindle is considered a particularly apt symbol of femininity is because it reappears in biblical and rabbinic literature: when female work is described, it is often woolwork.

Also in Greek and Roman literary and iconographic remnants, women are often described and depicted with spindles. A woman with a spindle was a metaphor for a good, productive and chaste woman and wife.[2] In Roman-period Judaism, the ancient Israelite icon of the spindle has met the Greek and Roman metaphors of

---

[1] M. Peskowitz, *Spinning Fantasies: Rabbis, Gender and History*, Berkeley, etc. 1997.

[2] *Op. cit.*, chs. 1–3.

woolwork. And it has developed further into a specific Roman-period *Jewish icon*.[3]

Woolwork was, however, not a mere symbol. On the contrary, textile was one of the main industries of Jewish Palestine in the Roman period.[4] As such it was a very common and ordinary activity, both in the Jewish and the non-Jewish world. Daily work and ordinary activities are also the places where gender is produced.[5] Because woolwork was for the larger part done by women, it could easily be conceived as a 'natural' female task, with inherent 'natural' associations such as productivity, domesticity and chastity, and inherent 'natural' differentiations between women and men. The latter is demonstrated by the fact that, in the Hebrew Bible as well as in rabbinic literature, it is considered 'not done' for a man to engage in woolwork.[6]

Gender is not defined by biology but by society and such concepts as 'femininity' and 'domesticity' are no natural categories; and 'woolwork' is not an unchanging metaphor for 'wifery'. Even though the same words are used, they can have very different contents, with different associations in different periods of time. It is easily forgotten that such images and concepts – especially the very familiar ones – do not have an underlying essence, that their meaning changes, and that they have a traceable history. Even though the same icon is used in the Hebrew Bible and in rabbinic literature, its recurrence does not mean mere continuity, but also a great degree of development.

Thus, the concept of the spindle symbolizes different things in the two texts that were chosen by Miriam Peskowitz as representatives of these two stages of Jewish literature: Proverbs 31 and Mishna Ketubot 5:5 and 9. The kind of domesticity that is symbolized by female woolwork is not the same: In Proverbs, woolwork represents the independence and the spirit of enterprise of the 'strong woman'. In the Mishna, it represents the economical

---

[3] *Op. cit.*, 72, 107 and passim.

[4] *Op. cit.*, 24 and passim.

[5] Peskowitz defines 'gender' as the "knowledge" or "social organization of sexual difference" (*op. cit.*, 8).

[6] *Op. cit.*, chapter 2.

dependence of the wife on her husband, and, moreover, it symbolizes female sexual containment. This 'surplus value' of the spindle is an inheritance from its Greek and Roman imaginations. It is not found in such terms in the Bible. However, the rabbis construed their own version of this icon of female sexuality: whereas in Greek and Latin writings, stories about spinners and weavers are often ambiguous, pointing at the impossibility of a total control of female sexuality, the rabbis do not seem to be aware of this danger. At least, they did not include it in their writings.[7]

'A spindle' and 'a spindle' are not necessarily the same things, just as the concept of female domesticity changes. To consider them as eternal and stable categories is the result of essentialist thinking that steered and legitimized rabbinic thinking about woolwork and female domesticity and that still dominates most rabbinic scholarship.

2 Some Remarks

2.1 The analysis of the rabbinic texts

The analysis of the texts from Mishna Ketubot is, in my opinion, the strongest and most revealing part of the paper. Some eye-opening examples are given of how textual data appear different, when we look at them through different eyes. That is, when we try to shift perspectives and put aside the ideas that precondition us, especially when we are used to reading rabbinic texts. Examples of such presuppositions are that there is an essential link between 'femininity' and 'domesticity', and that the only meaning of the concept 'woman' is the one which is derived from its relationship with an opposing male concept, such as 'husband' or 'father'. An additional fact that is self-evident, but often looked-over by students of rabbinic literature, is that all these texts are written by men, and that even when they deal with women, they deal with the aspects that relate to their husbands or fathers. Other female subjects, that are of no interest to men, are not treated in these rabbinic regulations. Thus, the image transmitted of 'women' in

---

[7] *Op. cit.*, 107.

rabbinic times is always partial and fragmentary. Therefore, there might well have been other, more independent aspects to being female, which are not mentioned in the rabbinic sources.

2.2   The biblical legacy

It is clear that Peskowitz' interest and focus of attention goes to Roman-period Judaism. The same holds for the book of which the paper makes up one chapter: it is a book about the production of gender in Roman-period Judaism. There is, of course, nothing wrong with that. But in contrast with the 'pagan' Greek and Roman life and literature which are well developed in the book, the biblical imagination of the spindle is not developed at all, apart from the very short discussion of Proverbs 31, which we also find in the paper, and an even shorter discussion of 2 Sam. 3:29.[8] Neither is the general 'ancient Israelite' view of female domesticity. When it comes to questioning the 'continuity' between the biblical and the rabbinic symbol of the spindle, both should be developed in order to demonstrate what makes the real difference. This deficiency renders the whole argumentation inveracious because it lacks a strong basis.

It should further be asked whether Proverbs 31 can be considered as the representative – the only one that is discussed in this paper and, together with 2 Sam. 3:29, the only ones that are mentioned in the book – of 'ancient Israelite' or 'biblical' Judaism. There is a danger here of falling into the same pit of 'essentialist' thinking which the author warned us against. Even much less critical scholars have come to the insight that there is no such thing as 'the' biblical concept of women, or of wife-husband relationship. Not only the 'woman of valor' in Proverbs, but also Sara and Rivka, whose husbands pretended that they were their sisters in order to save their own lives, are biblical women. And what about Tamar and Dinah, whose fate is addressed elsewhere in this book? Or, to stay with the book of Proverbs, what about the many warnings against 'dangerous' and 'wicked' strange and foreign women, while nowhere the counterpart of the 'dangerous

---

[8] *Op. cit.*, 72.

seducing foreign man' is attested? Peskowitz intercepts this critique partly by stating that "Proverbs, too, has its fears of unstrained female sexuality, but it does not incorporate these into its representation of the wife". However, this does not explain away that Proverbs cannot be considered as the sole representative of the 'ancient Israelite' image of female domesticity, only because the same metaphor – woolwork – is present in both texts.

2.3 The comparison of a song of praise and a halachic text

If someone sets out to write a 'history of a concept' such as, in this case, the spindle as a symbol of female domesticity, what determines her choice of literary sources? What texts can be put next to each other for comparison? I only refer to literary sources, since in this paper no other material, for example from archeological finds, was mentioned, even though Miriam Peskowitz considers them as very important alternative sources for writing the history of women. As to the literary sources, one might ask whether a song of praise, which Prov. 31:10-31 is, can be compared with an halachic or juridical text without any justification or even reservation about the possibility of comparing two texts which belong to such different literary genres.[9] To be sure, I do not want to deny the possibility of extracting information about the reality in which the author of a song or a poem lived by reading 'between the lines'. Especially in gender-oriented study, this way of reading

---

[9]In the discussion, Dr I. Kottsieper remarked that Prov. 31 might be not so much a 'song of praise', as I labeled it, as a sort of manual for women, to be acceptable to men. Even though I am not entirely convinced by this new *Sitz im Leben* for Proverbs 31, it would only strengthen my argument that the woman in Prov. 31 is far from independently working for her own profit, but mainly working for the needs of her family, her husband and her children. In that case, even seemingly independent economical activities would only be performed with a view to being acceptable as a wife. That is to say, the whole song would have been written by men, to teach women how to please their husbands by their independently taken initiatives, which, however, are in the end only directed toward the well-being of the family and the image of the husband, who can be proud of having such as hard-working, well-behaving wife.

often yields the most interesting results. Nevertheless, it should be asked if a song of praise is the most apt source of information about domestic regulations, especially when compared to such a detailed legalistic source as Mishna Ketubot. Is it possible to say that a subject of a song, such as the woman of Proverbs 31, has 'economic agency'? Even if one agrees that the image of the 'woman of valor' in Proverbs is more emancipated and more appealing to a present-day reader than that of the women who are the subject of Mishna Ketubot, it would not be realistic to conclude from this song that the average woman of the biblical period operated in this way. To do so would be the same as taking Dallas as a representative portrait of an average American life-style, or, perhaps more apt, as deducing from the text of a present-day love song, that this is the way in which most men speak and think about their lovers or wives in daily life. If there were such a thing as early rabbinic poetry, this could perhaps provide the material to compare like with like; but, unfortunately, the rabbis did not seem to be very interested in *belles lettres* as we understand it. However, it would have been possible to consider 'loose' rabbinic remarks about women in less juridical contexts, such as we find spread through the rabbinic Midrashim.

2.4   The interpretation of Proverbs 31

The author's interpretation of Proverbs 31 raises some questions. As a matter of fact, this interpretation is not really developed in the paper (see the second remark): it is taken for granted that Proverbs 31 reveals a positive view towards woman. But what does it mean to be a 'strong woman'? Also in Proverbs, the criteria for being considered a 'strong woman' are male criteria, most probably written down by a man. Most of the things that make her praiseworthy consider her domestic activities – even though these are described as relatively *independent* domestic activities. I say *relatively* independent because all the activities of the woman described here relate to her care for her household: she spins and buys food, looks after her husband and her children, feeds them and clothes them. And not only this, but all her valor is described through the eyes of her husband: he is the one who praises her

(v. 28), she does *him* good (v. 12), he is the one whose heart trusts
in her (v. 11). Therefore it is hard to follow Peskowitz' hypo-
thesis that "*if* the woman of Proverbs 31 had lived instead in the
rabbinic imaginary, the profits she made (...) *would belong to her
husband*". Also in the author of Proverbs' imagination, her profits
belong to her husband. How else should we understand v. 11: "*he
will have no lack of gain*". And at the end, in v. 31, it is said that,
because she is so worthy, *he* should give her a share in the fruit of
her hands (תנו לה מפרי ידיה). What is so different here from Mishna
Ketubot 5:9, where it is said that a woman should be provided
with what she needs, and if necessary, with what she earns from
'the work of her hands' (מעשׂה ידיה)? From this perspective, the
sharp opposition between Proverbs 31 and Mishna Ketubot 5 is
far from evident. In both texts, everything that is said about
the woman, is related to her husband. To be sure, within this
framework of female subordination to her husband, the 'woman
of valor' as represented in Proverbs receives the better part: at
least she is praised because of her good care. But again, this is
what could be expected from a song of praise, and not from a
juridical-halachic text.

2.5 Rome as the scapegoat?

In the paper, as in the book, the rabbinic period is designated,
with good reasons, as 'Roman-period Judaism'. The changing,
more oppressed image of women in rabbinic literature, when compared to the 'biblical image' is due to 'Roman-period innovations'.
When it comes to the representation of women, the rabbis dealt in
their own way with the Roman cultural heritage.[10] Thus, Roman
culture, in which rabbinic Judaism was embedded, is pointed to
as the real cause for the deteriorating image of female work, represented by the spindle, and the socio-economic position of women
in general. This looks like a variant on the well-known opposition, made by many before, between the Greek or Roman world-
views on the one hand and the Jewish world-view on the other
hand. Proverbs 31 would then stand for the good old biblical,

---

[10] *Op. cit.*, 72, 107 and passim.

Semitic times, and rabbinic literature for a Judaism contaminated by Greek or Roman thought. In one way, this is a refreshing view, because Hellenistic or Roman influences in rabbinic literature are too often denied. It is interesting to see how rabbinic literature, which is often taken as the prototype of 'Semitic' thinking and as such as the counterpart of Greek thought, said to be found in early-Christian literature, is presented here as heavily influenced by Roman social thought and gender imagination. On the other hand, it seems somewhat easy to make Rome the scapegoat for the discrimination of Jewish women in post-biblical times, and to identify the biblical image – or rather the image of Proverbs – as the 'authentic' Jewish view, especially since this view is not at all developed.

Part II

Some Cases of Early Christianities: New Testament Images

"Keeping It in the Family"

Culture, Kinship and Identity in 1 Thessalonians and Galatians[1]

Philip F. Esler   (St Mary's College, The University of St Andrews)

1   The Challenge of Cultural Difference

The audience of this essay when it was first delivered had gathered in Amsterdam, a beautiful city in modern (reasonably) Northern Europe to discuss various aspects of Near Eastern, Israelite and Christian family experience in the ancient Mediterranean. To bring out some of the incongruity of that situation I begin now – as I did then – with an anecdote which reflects how the family features in Mediterranean life in ways alien to the North Atlantic cultural zone or its colonial offshoots like Australia, the one from which I hail. A few years ago I was on a plane flying from Edinburgh to London and seated next to a Scots engineer who was making his way back to the Egyptian oil well where he worked. He told me that at his installation there was a handful of Northern European engineers like him and a large force of local workers who took their instructions from an Egyptian overseer. I asked him if most of the workers were relatives of the overseer. He looked at me in surprise and said, "Yes, in fact they are. How did you know that?" But even a passing acquaintance with Mediterranean culture teaches that one aspect of the centrality of the family which characterises it is a determination to share all available goods and benefits, including well-paid jobs on oil wells, among relatives. This is just one aspect of 'keeping it in the family'. Still, the engineer was surprised by my question. He did not expect another North Atlantic person to be aware of such a difference in

---

[1]I gratefully acknowledge the detailed response to an earlier form of this paper provided by Jan Willem van Henten, although he bears no responsbility for the views here expressed.

outlook, to have made some effort, however modest, to bridge the cultural distance between the two worlds.

The subject of the family in early Christianity, or any specific aspect of it, offers itself for investigation from a variety of perspectives and methodologies, each treating the underlying data within a particular theoretical framework and for a particular purpose. Some sense of this diversity can be seen by comparing and contrasting two recent collections of essays which look at the field from a socio-historical point of view, the first edited by Halvor Moxnes[2] and the second edited by Carolyn Osiek and David L. Balch,[3] with recent work considering early Christian families from a theological perspective.[4] My own aim in this essay is to investigate the significance of 'family' in 1 Thessalonians and Galatians in a way which brings to the forefront the issue of cultural difference with which I began. My intention is to employ tools of social analysis as a way of offering a plausible construal of particular historical phenomena. Yet, at the same time, I will make a particular suggestion for how Paul's understanding might impact on our own contemporary experience in a heavily individualistic North Atlantic culture, whether within the confines of Christian community or beyond.

In focusing on 'family' I do not mean to suggest that it would not be appropriate to discuss the Pauline corpus, or early Christianity more generally, in relation to other types of ancient collectivity, such as *collegia*, philosophical schools, or Old Testament images of the people of God, to name just a few. I have sought to

---

[2]H. Moxnes (ed.), *Constructing Early Christian Families: Family as Social Reality and Metaphor*, London & New York 1997.

[3]C. Osiek, D. Balch (eds), *Families in the New Testament World: Households and House Churches*, Louisville, KY 1997. Also see C. Osiek, "The Family in Early Christianity: 'Family Values' Revisited", *CBQ* 58 (1996), 1-24.

[4]See S.C. Barton, *Discipleship and Family Ties in Mark and Matthew* (SNTS MS, 80), Cambridge 1994; S.C. Barton (ed.), *The Family in Theological Perspective*, Edinburgh 1996; J.D.G. Dunn, "The Household Rules of the New Testament", in: S.C. Barton (ed.), *The Family*, 443-63; J. Francis, "Children and Childhood in the New Testament", in: S.C. Barton (ed.), *The Family*, 1996, 65-85.

concentrate on what I see as a strong familial theme in 1 Thessalonians and Galatians both to offer a contribution relevant to the subject of this book (as with the conference from which it derives), and also because I consider that kinship is a particularly noteworthy feature of the group orientation present in these texts.

Moreover, in using the word 'family' I readily acknowledge the wide diversity of family forms, of 'families', across the Mediterranean, then and now. My point is that 'family' – as I will describe it later – is a worthwhile concept to employ at an appropriate level of generality in relation to the ancient Mediterranean, especially given that even its ancient inhabitants recognised its diversity-transcending regionality. Thus, Plato's Socrates said of those who dwelt between the Phasis river (in the east) and the Pillars of Herakles (in the west) that "living around the sea we are like ants or frogs around a pond" (*Phaedo* 109B), while the Romans called the region the *orbis terrarum*, the circle of lands. With justice one modern author remarked: "Ceaseless intercourse back and forth along 'the wet ways' bound together the Mediterranean peoples into one great community life".[5]

1.1 Culture and Identity

It is often interesting to conduct the following simple social experiment on any group of students which includes representatives from Northern Europe and North America on the one hand and Mediterranean countries on the other. One asks each of the students carefully to consider how best to explain to someone else who he or she really is, how to set down his or her distinctiveness as a person, in short, how to describe his or her unique identity. Then one has the students list the results in ten statements in order of priority. Those originating in a North Atlantic cultural context typically begin with something like "I am a compassionate person" or "I am honest" and proceed to other moral or psychological qualities, before moving to aptitudes and interests (in music, sport and so on) and life ambitions. Features differentiating the

---

[5]E.C. Semple, *The Geography of the Mediterranean Region: Its Relation to Ancient History*, London 1932, 12.

students as individuals usually come first. Sometimes, however, they will mention, usually a long way down the list, their family and ethnic background or nationality, or connection with other social groups, like sporting teams. With Mediterranean students the lists tend to be very different. A popular first statement will be "I belong to X family", or "My country is Y", or "I come from town Z", or "I am a member of the W football club". Anything offered in the area of individual qualities, aptitudes or ambitions generally appears toward the end of the list.

Results like these are important for my argument in this essay in two respects. First, they indicate the salience of culture in the process of self-identification. That is, when we are called upon to give an account of who we really are, our answers will be affected by the culture in which we have been raised. Something as fundamental as our sense of self is culturally conditioned. Secondly, the notion of family, while figuring in the lists of both North Atlantic and Mediterranean respondents, is far more central for the latter.

Considerations such as these have long convinced me of the need systematically to take into account the very different cultural context of those important productions of the Mediterranean world, the various biblical texts, of both Testaments. If we do not do so we run the risk of imposing a modern understanding of social reality, ethnocentrically and anachronistically, upon ancient data. It is worth noting, for example, that neither in Greek nor Latin was there even a word which corresponded to our 'family', although *oikos* in Greek and *domus* in Latin referred to the house and the household, in the latter sense encompassing the senior male (or occasionally female), his spouse, sons (and their wives), daughters, other blood relatives and slaves.[6] While I am not suggesting that the ancient Mediterranean was the same as the modern Mediterranean, I consider that, at an appropriate level of abstraction, a concept just mentioned – where we move above

---

[6]H. Moxnes, "What is Family? Problems in Constructing Early Christian Families", in: H. Moxnes (ed.), *Constructing*, 1997, 13-41, at 20-1. For Old Testament expressions in the area of 'family', see J. Rogerson, "The Family and Structures of Grace in the Old Testament", in: S.C. Barton (ed.), *The Family*, 1996, 25-42, esp. 30-1.

the undoubted diversity of the data to consider larger features of cultural morphology – certain phenomena, alien to, or at least atypical of, modern North Atlantic peoples, have persisted in the region for millennia. Yet even if this were not so, familiarising ourselves with the cultural landscape of the modern Mediterranean will offer us a set of social scenarios radically different from the North Atlantic ones to which we are accustomed, thereby allowing us a certain freedom from the bondage of our habitual attitudes to social reality, and thus go some way to reducing the risk of ethnocentricity and anachronism. For this, the extensive research carried out by social anthropologists in the Mediterranean during the last forty years offers us invaluable help in situating New Testament texts, such as 1 Thessalonians and Galatians, within plausible social settings. As we will see, while further exploration into the nature of the identity Paul advocated for his converts in Thessalonika and Galatia will require assistance from another area of social theory, addressing the challenge of the cultural difference between us and the ancient Mediterranean will be indispensable for what follows.

2   Modelling Mediterranean Culture

In 1980 the Dutch social scientist Geert Hofstede published *Culture's Consequences*, based on an analysis of over 100,000 questionnaires completed by employees of a multi-national company (IBM) which then operated in some fifty countries across the world. Hofstede was able to isolate five variables which could be used to characterise national cultures.[7] The most significant variable was the respective significance of the individual and the group, with most cultures in the world (including those in the Mediterranean world) featuring strongly cohesive groups, while only a few cultures, mainly in the North Atlantic countries of Europe or North America, were 'individualistic'. Accordingly,

---

[7]G. Hofstede, *Culture's Consequences: International Differences in Work-Related Values*, Beverly Hills 1980. For a simplified and updated version, see G. Hofstede, *Cultures and Organizations: Software of the Mind: Intercultural Cooperation and Its Importance for Survival*, London 1994.

collectivist cultures tended to be the norm and individualistic ones the exception. Hofstede's other variables were the respective roles of men and women, the manner of dealing with inequality, the degree of tolerance for the unknown and the balance which was struck between long-term and short-term gratification of needs.

Hofstede's findings provide a useful context for the extensive research conducted into the Mediterranean region by social anthropologists in the last forty years, which can be situated as detailed explorations of one of the many group-oriented regions of the world, while yet having a reasonably distinctive ensemble of features. Leading figures in the recent delineation of a character-istic Mediterranean anthropology include Julian Pitt-Rivers,[8] J.G. Peristiany,[9] Pierre Bourdieu[10] and J.K. Campbell. [11] Also impor-tant is the research of George Foster, working among peasants influenced by Mediterranean culture in Mexico.[12] This research was succinctly modelled and applied to the New Testament by Bruce Malina in 1981 (revised edition 1993),[13] and has been use-fully re-assessed by Timothy Laniak.[14] The most recent research

---

[8]J. Pitt-Rivers, "Honour and Social Status", in: J.G. Peristiany (ed.), (1965) *Honour and Shame: The Values of Mediterranean Society*, London 1965, 19-77; Idem, *The People of the Sierra*, Chicago ²1971; Idem, *The Fate of Shechem; or the Politics of Sex: Essays in the Anthropology of the Medi-terranean*, New York 1977.

[9]J.G. Peristiany (ed.), *Honour and Shame*, London 1965; J.G. Peristiany, J. Pitt-Rivers (eds.), *Honor and Grace in Anthropology*, Cambridge 1992.

[10]P. Bourdieu, "The Sentiment of Honour in Kabyle Society", in: J.G. Peristiany (ed.), *Honour and Shame*, London 1965, 191-241.

[11]J.K. Campbell, *Honour, Family, and Patronage: A Study of the Institu-tions and Moral Values in a Greek Mountain Community*, New York 1964.

[12]G.M. Foster, "Peasant Society and the Image of the Limited Good", in: J.M. Potter, M.N. Diaz, G.M. Foster (eds.), *Peasant Society: A Reader*, Boston 1967, 300-23. (This essay first appeared under the same title in *American Anthropologist* 67 [1965]).

[13]B.J. Malina, *The New Testament World: Insights from Cultural Anthro-pology* (Revised edition), Louisville 1993. See also the brief account of this approach in P.F. Esler, *The First Christians in Their Social Worlds: Social-Scientific Approaches to New Testament Interpretation*, London & New York 1994, 19-36.

[14]T.S. Laniak, *Shame and Honor in the Book of Esther* (Society of Biblical Literature Dissertation Series, 165), Atlanta, GA. 1998, 24-31.

conducted into the Mediterranean has led to a more variegated
and nuanced understanding of its culture, [15] especially by pointing
to local variations or by amplifying women's points of view,[16] but
without invalidating the important findings of the work done in
the 1950s to 1970s. Since this area is now reasonably well known,
I will only sketch in some features which will be important in
my investigation of 1 Thessalonians and Galatians. What follows
should be taken as a model, a heuristic tool useful in comparisons
with data, not as a nomothetic statement.[17] At various points
I will refer to primary data, both Israelite and Graeco-Roman,
to indicate the comparability of the ancient Mediterranean world
with the model.

In societies which are group-oriented the main group tends to
be the family, and the Mediterranean fits this pattern. The dominant institution is kinship and although other groups, including village or town, trade association, army unit and so on exist
and can be significant, the basic social distinction in the society
is between kin and non-kin. Among one's kin there are strong
bonds of affection, co-operation and sharing of available resources,
all aspects of the reality of keeping things in the family which
surfaced in the anecdote with which I began this paper, while
toward outsiders (except those regarded as friends) there is an
attitude of suspicion and competition. Campbell has brought out
this dimension very clearly in his research into the Sarakatsani, a
group of transhumant shepherds in Greece, although the phenomenon has been documented by most anthropologists who have

---

[15] See M. Herzfeld, "The Horns of the Mediterraneanist Dilemma", in:
American Ethnologist 11 (1984), 439-54, and Idem, *Anthropology Through
the Looking Glass: Critical Ethnography in the Margins of Europe*, Cambridge
1987.

[16] See L. Abu-Lughod, *Veiled Sentiments: Honor and Poetry in a Bedouin
Society*, Berkeley *et al.* 1986.

[17] For recent discussions of the use of models in biblical interpretation, see
J. Elliott, *Social-Scientific Criticism of the New Testament: An Introduction*,
London 1995, 36-59; P.F. Esler, *Community and Gospel in Luke-Acts: The So-
cial and Political Motivations of Lucan Theology* (SNTS MS, 57), Cambridge
1987, 6-12; P.F. Esler (ed.), *Modelling Early Christianity: Social-Scientific
Studies of the New Testament in Its Context*, London & New York, 1-20.

worked in the region.[18] Distrust of non-kin can be also analysed from a social psychological perspective using Henri Tajfel's social identity theory, to be discussed below, as just one aspect of the way in which an ingroup (here the family) maintains a positive identity for itself by generating a negative picture of outsiders, in this case stereotyping them as untrustworthy and ever on the alert to defame, deceive or otherwise harm one's family or one or more of its members. The notably conflict-ridden quality of life in the Mediterranean has led researchers to describe the region as 'agonistic'.

The main social value in the Mediterranean region is honour, which refers to one's own sense of worth and the public corroboration of that estimate. The opposite of honour is shame, although there can be varying emphases on either side of the honour/shame contrast in different settings.[19] Honour can be held by an individual or by a group, the family in particular. Indeed, "honor is always presumed to exist within one's own family of blood, that is among all those one has as blood relatives".[20] Accretions of honour by one family member add to the honour rating of the whole family; thus when Eliakim is made chief controller of Hezekiah's household in Isa. 22:20-24 it is said that:

> He will be a seat of honour for his father's family ...
> On him will hang the whole glory of the family, even
> to the meanest members – all the paltriest of vessels,
> whether bowl or pot (22:23-24; *The Revised English
> Bible*).

On the other hand, where one family member is shamed, the whole family is shamed. This is one of the main themes in the *Adelphoe* of Terence (first performed in 160 BCE, although based on an older play by Menander). During the course of this play one brother is reported to have addressed the other brother in these words:

---

[18]Campbell, *op. cit.*

[19]See U. Wikan, "Shame and Honour: A Contestable Pair", *Man* 19 (1984), 635-52.

[20]Malina, *op. cit.*, 38.

"Really Aeschines, how can you perpetrate these shameful acts! How can you disgrace our family in this way" (*haec te admittere indigna genere nostro*; 409). The play contains several references to the way in which the actions of one member of a family can bring shame, referred to as *pudor* or *infamia*, on all the rest.[21]

The prototypical case of family shaming occurs when a female member is seduced or raped. This comes about because in Mediterranean society males have the leading role in the public sphere, with all females needing to be under the control and protection of some male – father, brother or husband – and where a daughter, sister or wife is violated by an outsider (otherwise than in a family-arranged marriage) the men in the family have shamefully failed in their responsibilities. In such a case they will seek to avenge the good name of the family, typically by killing the woman concerned (a practice still common in the Near East),[22] or the man (see the revenge by Dinah's brothers on the Shechem and the Hivites in Genesis 34) or both. On the other hand, men consider that they are honour-bound to seduce or rape the women of other families or groups. Thus, in the Book of Judith Holofernes tells his eunuch Bagoas that they would be disgraced if they let a woman like Judith go without seducing her (12:12). This phenomenon is, indeed, only the most dramatic example of the fact that every area of social interaction in the Mediterranean offers an arena for men (and it is usually men who are involved) to compete with one another and to enhance their honour at the expense of someone else.

There is a recognised pattern for such interactions which is referred to as 'challenge-and-response', since they begin with one person challenging another in some way, that is entering his social space, and continue with various forms of response, ranging from

---

[21] See the discussion in P.F. Esler, "Family Imagery and Christian Identity in Gal. 5:13–6:10", in: Moxnes, *op. cit.*, 121-49, at 125-6.

[22] The (UK) *Sunday Telegraph* Magazine carried a long story in its issue of 12th April 1998 dealing with the fact that in Jordan there are many men in prison, often on light sentences, for having murdered daughters or sisters who had sexual intercourse with some male other than within marriage, or had done something else to besmirch the family honour.

a spoken word or an act of physical violence, or else terminate in the person challenged shamefully refusing to respond. Yet a fundamental aspect of the honour that is vested in a family is that it is only with outsiders that one engages in competition over honour. For outside the circle of the family "all persons are presumed to be dishonourable, guilty, if you will, unless proved otherwise. It is with all these others that one must play the game, engage in the contest, put one's honor and one's family honor on the line".[23]

Malina usefully notes that it is possible to distinguish three degrees of dishonour, for individuals and groups, which might be the subject of patterns of challenge-and-response. The first is the extreme and total dishonour produced by murder, adultery or kidnap, which requires vengeance (often of the most severe kind), since revocation is not possible. The second consists of significant deprivation of honour in circumstances where revocation might yet be possible, as with verbal insult or the restoration of stolen items. The third type consists of the ordinary social interactions which necessitate some response, as with dinner invitations (cf. Lk. 14:12), sporting contests, repartee at meals and so on. Although these categories will help us assess the serious problem of intra-familial disputes, before doing so we need to consider the notion of 'limited good'.

Perhaps because of the underlying peasant economy of the region, a context in which it is unlikely that there will be any expansion of agricultural production over time, there is prevalent the notion of limited good, that all goods exist in finite quantities (and are often indivisible in nature) and that the available quantities cannot be increased.[24] This means that someone can only enjoy an accretion of a desirable good at the expense of someone else. Accordingly, at the village level the respectable man aims merely to retain what he holds, not to increase his measure of goods, since this will be regarded with hostility by his neighbours. The one exception to this is honour, since this is a limited good

---

[23] Malina, *op. cit.*, 38.
[24] Foster, *art. cit.*

which one villager will seek to increase at the expense of another, although as long as the interactions are of the third (or minor) type mentioned above village life will continue without serious disruption.

One way to mitigate the constraining effects of limited good is to establish a relationship with a 'patron', who is someone higher up the social scale with access to resources of various kinds which he is able to direct to his 'clients' in return for their loyalty, respect and other help when necessary. Such patron-client relationships are commonplace in the Mediterranean region today and were also very important in the ancient period, most notably in Rome, where the institution was thoroughly institutionalised.[25]

It is important for what follows to note that the phenomenon of limited good is also present within families, since family property and the regard which the parents have for their children exist in finite amounts and an injudicious allocation of either will lead to sibling rivalry and even violence. Even before they were born, after all, Jacob and Esau struggled with one another in the undoubtedly finite space of Rebecca's womb (Gen. 25:22). Usually, older brothers and sisters have pre-eminence over younger siblings and any inversion of this priority will be resisted, as it was by Esau. The extent to which the notion of limited good and the usual precedence of older over younger brothers can provide a context for conflict in a family also comes out very clearly later in the story of Esau and Jacob. For Esau found to his cost that Isaac only had one blessing to confer and Jacob had tricked his father into giving it to him (Genesis 27). Similarly, David's elder brother Eliab not surprisingly interprets David's appearance at the front as presumption (*zadôn*) in 1 Sam. 17:28. Eliab is suggesting that David is someone who wickedly refuses to keep within his station, who fails to adhere to his role as the youngest and most insignificant son. In Genesis 37 Joseph's brothers regard

---

[25]On patron-client relations, see H. Moxnes, "Patron and Client Relations and the New Community in Luke-Acts", in: J.H. Neyrey (ed.), *The Social World of Luke-Acts: Models for Interpretation*, Peabody, MA 1991, 241-68, and A. Wallace-Hadrill (ed.), *Patronage in Ancient Society*, London & New York 1990.

him in a similar way. The many narratives in the Old Testament
such as these which presuppose the existence of the usual ranking
among brothers and yet offer vivid examples of its subversion have
recently been studied by Greenspahn.[26]

Thus, the possibility of strife between brothers constitutes a
countervailing force ever threatening to undermine the customary
unity and honour of all members of a family. Malina points out
that in this culture first-degree dishonour of the type mentioned
above *within* a family, which constitutes an event quite out of the
ordinary, is actually regarded as sacrilegious. The worst assault
on family honour thus occurs when child kills parent or brother
kills brother. Killing a parent or brother is not just homicide but
patricide or fratricide respectively.[27]

Yet sibling rivalry leading to fratricide is an old theme in the
Mediterranean, as far as the Bible is concerned going back as
far as Cain and Abel in Genesis 4. Here the first-born son Cain
encounters a God who for unexplained reasons favours the offering of his younger brother Abel. As with all goods in this context,
Yahweh's favour, like a parent's love, is finite and Abel receives it
to the detriment of Cain. Not surprisingly, Cain becomes angry
at this and kills his brother. That horror over fratricide as sacrilegious was widespread in the ancient Mediterranean is indicated
by the centrality of this subject in the *Seven Against Thebes* of
Aeschylus, in which the chorus comments as follows on the mutual
slaying of Polyneices and Eteocles:

> When men die by a kinsman's hand,
> When brother is murdered by brother,
> And the dust of the earth drinks in
> The crimson blood that blackens and dries,
> Who then can provide cleansing?
> Who can wash it away?   (735-739; trans. Vellacott)[28]

---

[26] F.E. Greenspahn, *When Brothers Dwell Together: The Preeminence of Younger Siblings in the Hebrew Bible*, New York & Oxford 1994.

[27] Malina, *op. cit.*, 46-7.

[28] P. Vellacott, *Aeschylus: Prometheus Bound, The Suppliants, Seven Against Thebes and The Persians*, London 1961, 110.

The problem of how brother should treat brother was the subject of the interesting first-century CE treatise *Peri Philadelphias* by Plutarch. This work, helpfully discussed by Betz,[29] contains an invaluable collection of Graeco-Roman stock morality on brotherly love. The tensions between the family as linked by honour (479A, D and F; 482A) and the unfortunate propensity of brothers to quarrel with one another come out clearly, especially when Plutarch bemoans the fact that brotherly love is actually rarer than brotherly hatred (478C). I will return to this text later in connection with 1 Thessalonians and Galatians.[30]

3 Social Identity Theory

The features of Mediterranean culture just considered relate to the primary level of socialisation of people across the Mediterranean, ancient and modern. Yet in both 1 Thessalonians and Galatians Paul is addressing an audience of a particular type within this larger context, namely, *ekklêsiai* (1 Thess. 1:1; Gal. 1:2), communities or congregations of Christ-followers, who were in various ways in a state of tension with other people and groups in the surrounding environment, either gentiles (in Thessalonika) or Israelites and gentiles (in Galatia). The status of Christ-followers as members of a particular type of ingroup encountering various outgroups suggests that another area of social-scientific theory, additional to the cultural anthropology employed so far, might be useful to further explicate the situation of Paul's addresses in these two letters. I wish to propose here an area of theory which, as far as I know, made its debut in a developed form in the New Testament field in a paper I delivered in 1994.[31] This is the social

---

[29] H.D. Betz (ed.), *Plutarch's Ethical Writings and Early Christian Literature*, Leiden 1978.

[30] See the discussions in R. Aasgaard, "Brotherhood in Plutarch and Paul: Its Role and Character", in: Moxnes, *op. cit.*, 166-82, and P.F. Esler, *art. cit.*, 127-8.

[31] P.F. Esler, "Social Identity, Group Conflict and the Matthean Beatitudes: A New Reading of Matt. 5:3-12", a plenary paper at the British New Conference in Nottingham, 16 September 1994 (in debate with Dr Francis Watson of Kings College, London, now Professor of New Testament at the University

identity theory pioneered by Henri Tajfel while he was professor of social psychology at the University of Bristol, England from 1967 to 1982 and subsequently developed by his Bristol students into what is still a flourishing field.[32]

Social identity theory adopts a distinctive position in relation to the continuing issue of the relationship of the individual and the group. It rejects the classic North American position, dating to Allport in 1924,[33] that a group must be treated as dissolved into the individuals who composed it (which meant that the group had no conceptual status apart from those individuals) and insists that the crucial question for a genuinely *social* psychological approach to the subject is how, that is, through what psychological processes, society at large or a particular group manages to install itself in the minds and hearts of individuals and to affect their behaviour.[34] The basal result of these processes is to offer members a distinctive identity, an understanding of who they – in some profound sense – really are. As far as this essay is concerned, at a very general level such an approach involves enquiring how Paul goes about having the groups of Christ-followers in Thessalonika and Galatia acquire a sense of identity which draws upon attitudes toward kin and non-kin in their social environment.

Tajfel's foundational insight in this area (in an article published in 1972)[35] was that groups needed to establish a positively valued distinctiveness from other groups in order to provide their members with a positive social identity. The members of ingroups learned who they were in large part by developing a sense of the ways in which they were differentiated from outgroups. The

---

of Aberdeen).

[32] For a biographical sketch of Tajfel and a full bibliography of his publications, together with an important collection of essays by scholars working in the field at present, see P. Robinson (ed.), *Social Groups and Identities: Developing the Legacy of Henri Tajfel*, Oxford 1996. I have employed social identity theory extensively in my work *Galatians*, London & New York 1998.

[33] F. Allport, *Social Psychology*, Boston 1924.

[34] M.A. Hogg, D. Abrams, *Social Identifications: A Social Psychology of Intergroup Relations and Group Processes*, London & New York 1988, 12-16.

[35] H. Tajfel, "La catégorisation sociale", in: S. Moscovici (ed.), *Introduction à la Psychologie Sociale*, vol. 1. Paris 1972, 272-302.

ultimate empirical stimulus for this view lay in research which indicated that merely categorising people as belonging to one group or another led to social comparison with other groups which, in turn, resulted in notable forms of group behaviour, with members favouring one another while discriminating against members of outgroups.

Tajfel interpreted this process as essentially concerned with the establishment of 'social identity', which refers to that part of our sense of self which derives from belonging to groups. He defined social identity as "that *part* of an individual's knowledge of his membership of a social group (or groups) together with the value and emotional significance attached to that membership"[36] He developed this view by noting that belonging to a group had three dimensions:

1. 'the cognitive dimension', which refers to the simple recognition of belonging;

2. 'the evaluative dimension', which covers the positive or negative connotations of belonging; and

3. 'the emotional dimension', which refers to the attitudes, such as love and hate, which members hold towards insiders and outsiders.

This is not to say that our self-concept does not also include aspects which are personal to ourselves and not derived from belonging to groups. Nevertheless, as we observed earlier in this essay, the Mediterranean is one of the majority of cultures in the world which are group-oriented, so that we would expect that here group belonging will be more salient in its contribution to our sense of self than it is in the individualistic cultures of the North Atlantic. The simple experiment which can be carried out with groups of students, as described above, provides some confirmation of the usefulness of this insight. In any event, in 1 Thessalonians and Galatians, unlike the position in 1 Corinthians, we do

---

[36]H. Tajfel, *Differentiation between Social Groups: Studies in the Social Psychology of Intergroup Relations*, London *et al.* 1978, 63.

not even know the name of anyone in the congregations, let alone other information about individual members, so that any interpretation which was interested in the question of individuality would not find much data with which to work.

Applied to 1 Thessalonians and Galatians, Tajfel's theory necessitates examining how Paul has sought to maintain the distinctive identity of his congregations, in each of the cognitive, evaluative and emotional dimensions, in relation to gentile and Israelite outgroups.

According to Tajfel there is a dialectical relationship between social setting and group belonging. There are two sides to this relationship. First, the number and variety of social situations which the individual will perceive as being relevant to his or her group membership will increase in relation to the three dimensions of belonging described above: the clarity of the sense of belonging to the group, the extent of positive or negative evaluations attached to membership and the emotional investment in the fact of belonging and in such evaluations. Secondly, some social situations, persecution especially, will force members to act in terms of their group identification.

Central to the way Tajfel conceives social identity are group norms.[37] A norm in this context is a scale of values which defines a variety of acceptable and unacceptable attitudes and behaviours by members of the group. Norms co-ordinate and regulate behaviour and cover issues such as ideologies, traditions, dress and mores. They assist members to act appropriately in new and ambiguous situations. Thus, norms maintain and enhance the identity of the group. They include the phenomena which New Testament critics refer to as 'ethics', while setting them within a new framework of group identity. Quite often the norms of groups which are at odds in some way with powerful outgroups represent an inversion of such values. The hippy culture of the 1960s is a good example.[38]

---

[37] R. Brown, *Group Processes: Dynamics Within and Between Groups*, Oxford 1988, 42-8.
[38] Brown, *op. cit.*, 251.

Social identity theory describes an ensemble of ways in which a group which feels itself to be at some disadvantage in relation to other groups in its environment – so that there are obstacles to its providing its members with a positive social identity – might venture upon intergroup comparison, even if that comparison eventually leads to conflict. I have dealt with this aspect of the theory in detail elsewhere recently,[39] so I will be brief here. The basic distinction is between situations in which exit from a group is possible and those in which it is impossible or extremely difficult. In the first case ('social mobility'), the problem will be potential defection from the ingroup by individuals, or even mass defection of the members. Paul is facing something like this problem in Galatia as his gentile converts are under pressure to enter the Israelite outgroup by undergoing circumcision and accepting the Mosaic law. In the second case ('social change'), the members must seek to effect a positive re-evaluation of the ingroup in relation to hitherto dominant outgroups. It is possible to interpret Paul's approach to ingroup members in Thessalonika and Galatia in terms of this strategy. If change in the actual relationship between ingroup and outgroup is impossible, the ingroup might (by processes of 'social creativity') compare itself with the outgroup on a new dimension, or bring about redefinition of an existing comparison or even seek to compare itself with a different outgroup. On the other hand, if it is possible to challenge the actual relationship of the groups, the ingroup might improve its access to status and resources to the detriment of the outgroup. This is called 'social competition'.

One extremely common feature of social comparison is the tendency for one group to stereotype outgroups. Within social identity theory, stereotypes are:

> generalizations about people based on category membership. They are beliefs that all members of a particular group have the same qualities, which circumscribe the group and differentiate it from other groups. A specific group member is assumed to be, or is treated

---

[39] P.F. Esler, *Galatians*, London & New York 1998, 49-55.

as, essentially identical to other members of the group.[40]

Stereotypes are often associated with evaluation and there is a noticeable tendency to attach positive stereotypes to one's ingroup and negative stereotypes to outgroups.[41] There are many examples of both kinds of process in Galatians, some of which I will discuss below.

Having now broadly described features of Mediterranean culture relevant to this paper and set out some of the main characteristics of social identity theory, I am able to proceed to investigate whether, and if so how, the nature and importance of family in Paul's general cultural setting is taken up in his communications to the groups of Christ-followers in Thessalonika and Galatia, in particular in the type of identity he may recommend to them.

4   Culture, Kinship and Identity in 1Thessalonians

A central focus of Tajfel's theory is the extent to which human beings derive a sense of identity from belonging to a group and develop ways of differentiating their ingroup from negatively regarded outgroups. This type of social categorisation is more pervasive in a group-oriented society such as characterised all parts of the ancient Mediterranean world than it is in our individualistic North Atlantic culture. Paul's concern with a particular ingroup in 1 Thessalonians emerges as early as the first verse of the letter, in the salutation: "Paul and Silvanus and Timothy to the congregation (ekklêsia) of the Thessalonians in God the Father and the Lord Jesus Christ, grace and peace to you!" Here we find – closely integrated – both a strong sense of the existence of an ingroup of a particular kind, namely, one that is characterised by its relationship to God the Father and Jesus Christ, and also the inevitably desirable nature of belonging to it, given these connections. To employ Tajfel's terminology, Paul is articulating

---

[40]M.A. Hogg, D. Abrams, *Social Identifications*, 65 (see n. 34).

[41]For a detailed discussion of stereotypes, see H. Tajfel, "Social Stereotypes and Social Groups", in: H. Tajfel, *Human Groups and Social Categories: Studies in Social Psychology*, Cambridge 1981.

for his readers/listeners a pronounced cognitive dimension, a sense of belonging to the group, and also a very favourable evaluative one, since the emotional rewards of membership must have been high. Moreover, Paul expressly acknowledges that his mission to the Thessalonians was born in the midst of great conflict, of *agôn*, no doubt with outgroups (1 Thess. 2:2). This statement confirms both the 'agonistic' nature of the surrounding culture discussed above and also the relevance of Tajfel's theory, given its focus on how the social identity of members of one group is developed in conflict-oriented differentiation from other groups.

At various places in the letter Paul underlines this fundamental division between ingroup and outgroups, between us and them. This distinction straddles past, present and future.

As to the past, his addressees were previously immersed in the world of pagan idolatry but have now left it behind to serve the living and true God (1 Thess. 1:9). This indicates that they had been gentiles prior to joining the *ekklêsia*, since such language would be quite inappropriate, indeed grossly insulting, if the ingroup comprised Israelites as well as gentiles.[42] This is quite a different picture from that presented by Luke in Acts 17:1-9, where Paul's converts are made up of Israelites, gentile God-fearers and wealthy women.[43] As already noted, Tajfel brings out clearly the

---

[42] I am increasingly persuaded of the inappropriateness of using the words 'Jew' or 'Jewish' in relation to first century CE phenomena, both because of the extent to which these words carry too many connotations of the subsequent experience of the people (from the development of the Mishnah to the Holocaust) and because they miss the strongly geographical sense of *Ioudaios*, denoting someone who looked to Judaea and its temple, whether living in Judaea or the Diaspora, as a mark of Israelite identity, as far as both Israelites and non-Israelites were concerned (see P.F. Esler, *Galatians*, 4 and the literature there cited). 'Israelite' at least has the advantage of being a word used by the people themselves which does not carry inappropriate connotations in translation.

[43] In spite of efforts in various quarters to reconcile the information provided by Paul himself with what we find in Acts, the most likely solution is that Luke has described the early days of the Thessalonian congregation in a manner which accords with his distinctive picture of the Pauline mission field (see P.F. Esler, *Community and Gospel in Luke-Acts: The Social and Political Motivations of Lucan Theology*, Cambridge 1987, 36-45), not with

extent to which oppression of a group strengthens its members'
sense of belonging, and in this letter we find Paul expressly util-
ising such ill-treatment of Christ-followers in Judaea as a prototypical experience for the ingroup in Thessalonika: "For you,
brothers, have become imitators of the congregations of God in
Judea in Christ Jesus, because you also suffered the same things
from your countrymen as they did at the hands of the Judeans"
(2:14).[44] A little later he adds that they are presently suffering acts
of oppression (*thlipseis*), presumably at the hands of these same
Thessalonians (3:3). As already noted, one aspect of the dialectical relationship between social setting and group belonging is that
some situations, such as the oppression mentioned here, will force
members to act in terms of their group membership. Accordingly,
we would expect that Paul's references to what the Thessalonians
have suffered and are suffering summon before them experiences
which have strengthened their involvement with, and commitment
to, the *ekklêsia*.

The most plausible basis for the tension between the Christ-
following ingroup and gentile outgroups in Thessalonika was that
Paul's converts had abandoned their traditional gods in favour of
the monotheistic brand of faith he was preaching (1 Thess. 1:9).[45]
Within the everyday reality of paganism in this part of the empire, this was likely to cause trouble. Kinship, politics, economics
and religion were inextricably interrelated (Malina 1993: 30-31).
Pagan rites were foci of economic and social interaction, playing
a key role in maintaining the local political and economic system.
Christ-followers who held themselves aloof from these celebrations

---

the facts of the beginnings of the Christ-movement in Thessalonika. For the
difficulties of relating Acts 17:1-9 with what Paul himself says, also see D.
Lührmann, "The Beginnings of the Church in Thessalonica", in: D.L. Balch,
E. Ferguson, W.A. Meeks (eds.), *Greeks, Romans, and Christians: Essays in
Honor of Abraham J. Malherbe*, Minneapolis 1990, 237-49.

[44] The vexed question of whether 1 Thess. 2:14-16 are genuine or comprise
a later interpolation (as first proposed by Baur) cannot be entered into here.

[45] There are helpful treatments of conflict in the social situation of the
Thessalonians in J.M.G. Barclay, "Thessalonica and Corinth: Social Contrasts in Pauline Christianity", *JSNT* 47 (1992), 49-74 and Idem, "Conflict
in Thessalonica", *CBQ* 53 (1993), 512-30.

were likely to sustain the charge of misanthropy (MacMullen 1981: 40). More dangerous was the charge of atheism, since the elite believed that the *hoi polloi* needed to take part in the local worship to ensure political stability (MacMullen 1981: 2-3; Barclay 1993: 515). Israelites also abstained from the local cults, but their practices and beliefs were known to be ancient and they were generally tolerated in diaspora cities.

The interesting possibility, raised by Jewett (1993),[46] that Paul's Thessalonians were all members of the non-elite, socially insignificant tenement-dwellers,[47] without representatives from the local elite as seems to have been the case in Corinth, would have meant that they lacked patrons sufficiently high up the social scale to afford them some measure of protection against local harassment.

The focus in 1 Thessalonians on future events provides an important means of differentiating the positively valued ingroup from negatively valued outsiders. The destiny of an ingroup can certainly function in this way, even though Tajfel himself did not devote much attention to this issue, nor to the area of social change, as recent commentators influenced by him, such as Condor[48] and Reicher[49] have observed. Condor, in fact, makes an observation which brings out the fairly close connection between her rightful insistence on the importance of diachronicity for social identity and Paul's message in 1 Thessalonians, given the congregation's evident concern for members dying before the *parousia* (1 Thess. 4:13-18): "the (future oriented) actions of collectivities are often directed towards an imaginary distal future beyond the

---

[46]R. Jewett, "Tenement Churches and Communal Meals in the Early Church: The Implications of a Form-Critical Analysis of 2 Thessalonians 3:10", *Biblical Research* 38 (1993), 23-42.

[47]This feature of Jewett's argument, *art. cit.*, may be separated from his far less likely views on the previous connection of Paul's addressees with the cult of Cabirus.

[48]S. Condor, "Social Identity and Time", in: P. Robinson (ed.), *Social Groups and Identities: Developing the Legacy of Henri Tajfel*, Oxford 1996, 285-315.

[49]S. Reicher, "Social Identity and Social Change: Rethinking the Context of Social Psychology", in: Robinson, *op. cit.*, 317-336.

lifetimes of existing category members".[50] In 1 Thessalonians, this
relationship between social identity and the future of the group
emerges clearly in the belief that Jesus, God's son whom Paul
and his addressees are awaiting from heaven, will save them from
the wrath that is to come (1:10), unlike other people who (it
is implied) will not be so fortunate. Paul tells his audience who
they are in relation to what they might experience by praying that
they will stand before God in holiness with blameless hearts when
Jesus comes with all his holy ones (3:13). Most notably, however,
he vividly dramatises his vision of their future destiny in strikingly
Israelite terms[51] by describing how those who are still alive when
the Lord comes and the trumpet sounds will join those who have
died. Those who have died will rise first and then the living will
be snatched into the clouds to meet the Lord in the air; thus they
will always be with him (4:15-17). The object of all this is that
they might live with him (5:10). It is remarkable that Paul should
have persuaded the ex-gentiles who comprised the congregation
in Thessalonika to subscribe to a such a strongly Israelite myth[52]
of the future. We will see, however, that there were some areas of
his presentation where Paul did not appeal to Israelite ideas and
later in this essay I will consider why such is the case.

But it is the differentiation of ingroup and outgroups in 1
Thessalonians *in the present* that I wish to focus upon here, since
this is where kinship language is prominent. I will begin with
some general illustrations of such differentiation. Paul reinforces
the reference to the congregation of the Thessalonians in 1:1 with
a variety of other expressions distinguishing his addressees from
outgroups. They are "loved by God" (1:4). Most graphically, they
are "all sons of light, sons of day", not belonging to the night or
to darkness (5:5). People who are not members of the ingroup are

---

[50]Condor, *art. cit.*, 306-7.

[51]For Paul's use of Israelite apocalyptic imagery here, see J.M.G. Barclay.
"Thessalonica and Corinth", 50-52.

[52]For a useful general discussion of myth, see I.G. Barbour, *Myths, Models
and Paradigms: A Comparative Study in Science and Religion*, New York *et
al.*, 1976. I have considered the nature of myths of the future in: P.F. Esler,
*The First Christians in Their Social Worlds: Social-Scientic Approaches to
New Testament Interpretation*, London & New York, 98-101.

simply "those outside" (4:12). We have seen how important norms are to the creation and maintenance of a particular social identity, and Paul explicitly raises such issues in the letter, especially in Chapter 4 where he begins by announcing his interest in this area by use of the word *peripatein* in connection with how the Thessalonians are to please God (4:1) and then proceeds to offer detailed advice, which matters I will return below. Material of a similar kind appears as well in Chapter 5, which also requires further comment below.

In his introduction to a collection of essays on family in the early Christ-movement, Halvor Moxnes brings out the fundamental distinction between kinship and fictive kinship, between reality and metaphor in this area.[53] Many of the members of Paul's *ekklêsiai* were not presumably related, and yet he continually deploys the language of kinship from the surrounding culture in relation to them. On the other hand, references to the fatherhood of God were probably intended by Paul as statements of literal reality in a spiritual sense, admittedly within a particular cultural framework for the meaning of 'father'. To understand his point in using, literally or metaphorically, various sorts of kinship language we need to bear in mind both the distinctive features of Mediterranean family life set out above and also the various ways in which he utilises such features in seeking to develop and maintain a positive group identity for his converts in distinction to negatively valued outgroups.

Kinship language begins in the first verse of 1 Thessalonians with the reference to the *ekklêsia* which belongs to God the *Father*. Paul refers to God as father shortly below, in 1 Thess. 1:3, and then twice more later in the letter, at 1 Thess. 3:11 and 13. On each of these three occasions Paul employs the expression "our God and father" (*ho Theos kai patêr hêmôn*) which underlines the fact that 'father' is not simply a title (an impression one might derive from the usage a 1 Thess. 1:1) or a means of describing his relationship to Jesus (as in Rom. 15:6; 2 Cor. 1:3 and 1:31), but that God's fatherhood is an essential feature of how

---

[53]Moxnes, *op. cit.*, 1-2.

Paul's addressees encounter him. Most significant in this regard is the Endtime vignette in 1 Thess. 3:13 where Paul prays that at the *parousia* his converts will stand holy and faultless before "our God and father". In a context which could have been a trigger for other aspects of the future activity of God and his Son, such as judgment, Paul offers an image of the faithful assembling before *their father*. We must bear in mind here that the experience of fatherhood which Paul is invoking in 3:13 is that current in an ancient Mediterranean, in particular Graeco-Roman, culture, and not that of the modern North Atlantic cultural zone. This necessitates our making a conscious effort to envisage what this might have meant to the Thessalonian Christ-followers in a group-oriented setting where fatherhood and family life had a different meaning than they do for us. Above all, perhaps, the need to preserve family honour should be treated as of major importance.

It is interesting to observe that specific references to God as "*our* Father", although certainly part of Paul's thought elsewhere (and probably a feature of the preaching of the historical Jesus), are not very common in Paul's epistles. In Romans there is one instance at 1:7, together with a reference to the Spirit which allows *us* to cry "Abba! Father!" at 8:15. There is one instance in 1 Corinthians (1:3). In 2 Corinthians we have a reference to "God our father" in 1:2 and the possible allusion to 2 Sam. 7:14 at 6:18 where God says "I will be a father to you and you will be my sons and daughters", where 'daughters' has been added to the (putative) source. Galatians contains the phrase 'God our father' in 1:4 and the statement that, because his addressees are sons, God sends the Spirit of his son into *our* hearts crying "Abba! Father!" at 4:2. The words 'God our father' occur twice in Philippians (1:2 and 4:20) and once in Philemon (3). Given this data, the three occurrences of 'our God and father' in 1 Thessalonians, especially the two in the substance of the letter (3:11, 13), are quite significant. Accordingly, the abundant kinship language which Paul employs in the letter, which I will now discuss, finds its ultimate legitimation in the reality of God's fatherhood, which is here accorded a notable prominence.

It should be noted, however, that Paul never in 1 Thessalonians explicitly refers to his addressees as 'sons' (*huioi*) or 'children' (*tekna*) of, or in relation to, God, even though one might think that such a relationship is implied and he uses such expressions elsewhere in his writings (cf. Rom. 8:16, 21; 9:8 [*tekna Theou*]; Phil. 2:15; Gal. 4:2). Yet he is happy to refer to the Thessalonians as sons of light and sons of day (1 Thess. 5:5). Perhaps Paul is concerned here not to blur the status of Jesus as 'his (sc. God's) son (*huios*)' expressly recognised in the letter at 1:10.[54] Calling his addressees "sons" too might suggest that their position is parallel with that of Jesus, a conclusion Paul apparently resists in 1 Thessalonians.

Paul also employs father-child imagery in 1 Thess. 2:11, when he states that he dealt with each one of them "just as a father does his child" (*hôs patêr tekna heautou*), appealing to them, encouraging them and urging them to live worthily of God who calls them into his kingdom and glory. Shortly before this, in 1 Thess. 2:7, he employs household, if not strictly kinship, imagery in a very similar way by saying that he treated them "as a nurse cares for her children" (*hôs êan trophos thalpê ta heautês tekna*). Although these are similes, whereas his references to the fatherhood of God in this letter no doubt convey his view on the nature of reality, they are similes which indicate how readily he was inclined to liken his addressees to related siblings being cared for by an individual, either father or nurse.

The main area of (fictive) kinship language in the letter, however, consists of the frequent use of 'brothers' (*adelphoi*). On fourteen occasions he directly addresses his audience as *adelphoi*.[55] There are also references to the Thessalonian members of the Christ-movement as brothers at 4:6 (an important instance discussed below), 5:26 and 27. He describes Timothy as his "brother and co-worker" at 3:2 and mentions how his addressees have assisted "all the brothers throughout Macedonia" (4:10). The extent of such fictive sibling language in such a short letter is very impressive and it is unfortunate that a version such as the

---

[54]I am indebted to my St. Mary's colleague Ronald A. Piper for suggesting, from his own work on John's Gospel, this kind of sensitivity in relation to 'Son' and 'sons'.

[55]At 1 Thess. 1:4; 2:1, 9, 14, 17; 3:7; 4:1, 10, 13; 5:1, 4, 12, 14, 25.

Revised English Bible completely obscures this point for the
reader by translating *adelphoi* as either "friend" or "fellow-
Christians", as opposed to the Jerusalem Bible which is content with "brothers" or the Authorised Version which opts for
"brethren", a word which includes women as well as men. While
the extent to which women were regarded as full members of the
movement in Thessalonika is uncertain, the chances are greater
that they were not prominent, as Fatum has suggested.[56]

No doubt Paul's insistence upon the fatherhood of God, possibly aided by his own protective fatherhood, serves as one form
of legitimation for such language. Yet it is difficult to avoid the
view that he also engages in this usage to encourage those to
whom he wrote the letter to treat one another like kin. In the
group-oriented culture of Thessalonika this meant sharing and
protecting one another's goods, including their joint honour, and
not competing with one another in the manner typical of unrelated males. In the language of Tajfel's theory, Paul was seeking to develop a group identity drawing on the most prominent
model of harmonious intragroup relationships in the ambient culture. Explicit confirmation for this view comes in 1 Thess. 4:9,
when he tells the Thessalonians that "You do not need anyone
to write to you concerning brotherly love (*philadelphia*), because
you yourselves have been taught by God to love (*agapan*) one
another".

Although we have already mentioned Plutarch's treatise on
philadelphia, the word is actually rare in early texts of the Christ
movement.[57] Paul only uses *philadelphia* once elsewhere (Rom.
12:10), and there are only a few instances elsewhere in the New
Testament.[58] Betz notes that there is no obvious explanation why

---

[56] L. Fatum, "Brotherhood in Christ: A Gender Hermeneutical Reading of
1 Thessalonians", in: Moxnes, *op. cit.*, 183-97, at 192-4.

[57] J.S. Kloppenborg, "PHILADELPHIA, THEODIDAKTOS and the Dioscuri:
Rhetorical Engagement in 1 Thessalonians 4.9-12", *NTS* 39 (1993), 265-89.

[58] Heb. 13:1; 1 Pet. 1:22; 2 Pet. 1:7 (twice). The adjective *philadelphos*
occurs at 1 Pet. 3:8. There are only three instances in the Septuagint, at 4
Macc. 13:23, 26; 14:1, while *philadelphos* also appears, at 2 Macc. 15:14; 4
Macc. 13:21; 15:10.

this term was considered proper in the Christian context, since it was apparently just considered part of *agape* and there was no further need to explain it.[59] Yet in a context in which Paul was intent on maintaining the appropriateness of kinship patterns from the surrounding culture to his Thessalonian congregation, the use of a word at home in Greek perceptions of the family had a lot to recommend it.

There are other sections of the letter, in particular 1 Thess. 4:1-12 and 5:12-22 where it is arguable that some of the elements of *philadelphia* emerge in concrete terms. Critics often classify these passages as 'paraenesis', on the basis that the 'ethics' of New Testament texts are susceptible to scrutiny as a differentiated subject in this field. While it is indisputable that Paul does remind his addressees of certain rules (*paraggeliai*; 4:2), the adoption of Tajfel's theory in this particular ancient Mediterranean context suggests that we re-situate the discussion within a framework where Paul's insistence on behavioural norms falls within the larger purpose of recommending to the Thessalonian Christ-followers a positive group identity. In other words, Paul may want to tell them how they should behave, but only in the course of installing in their consciousness the larger and more important reality of who they are.

While Paul uses the word *peripateô* to create an *inclusio* in 4:1-12, by placing it (twice) at the beginning of the passage (4:1) and once at the end (4:12), we are justified in translating it broadly, "be of a particular identity", an identity which certainly includes moral norms, rather than the narrower "behave in a particular way". Such an approach is prompted by the way in which Paul delineates ingroup from outgroup in the passage. He does not simply lay down prescriptive ethical rules, but reminds them who they are and should be through group differentiation. He addresses them as people whom God has called to holiness (*hagiasmos*; 4:3, 7) and to whom he has given his Holy Spirit (4:8), and who are characterised by *philadelphia* (4:9), all in sharp contrast to those

---

[59]H.D. Betz (ed.), *Plutarch's Ethical Writings and Early Christian Literature*, Leiden 1978, 232.

who they are not, namely, people caught up in sexual misconduct (*porneia*; 4:3) and impurity (*akatharsia*; 4:7), "gentiles who do not know God" (4:5), or, simply, "those outside" (*hoi exô*; 4:12).

Lying close to the heart of the identity Paul is recommending to the Thessalonians is the model of harmonious relations among a respectable family in the surrounding culture. While the reference to their brotherly love at 4:9 is the most obvious example, the word *adelphos* occurs four times in the passage (4:1, 6, 10 [twice]). Particularly instructive is 1 Thess. 4:6, where Paul asserts that it is God's will that (in the matter under discussion) none of them should "transgress against (*hyperbainein*) and gain an advantage over (*pleonektein*) his brother". Leaving aside the notorious difficulties in determining precisely the problems Paul is addressing here, especially as far as the meaning of 'vessel' (*skeuos*) in 1 Thess. 4:4 is concerned,[60] it is plain that he is seeking his converts to eschew attitudes to one another common among unrelated males in this culture and to treat one another as *brothers* should, especially by not invading one another's social space. Thus Paul is endorsing a fictive kinship within the *ekklêsia* which is imbued with the ideal characteristics of actual kinship in Mediterranean culture. Similarly, Paul's final invocation in this section to his readers/listeners in 1 Thess. 4:10b-12 draws upon the image of a respectable non-elite family in a world of limited good, which lives quietly, engages in hard manual labour, presents a united and harmonious front to the outside world and looks after its own. In short, Paul wants them to keep things in the family.

Essentially the same case can be made for 1 Thess. 5:12-22. Paul is both advocating a particular identity for his Thessalonian Christ-followers and bringing out some of its specific features,

---

[60]The three main possibilities for *skeuos* are: (a) one's wife, advocated by C. Maurer, "*skeuos*", in: *TDNT*, vol. 7, 358-67, at 365-7; (b) one's body, supported by D. Lührmann, "The Beginnings of the Church in Thessalonica", in: Balch, Ferguson, Meeks, *op. cit.*, 237-49, at 245-7; and (c) one's penis, advocated by K.P. Donfried "The Cults of Thessalonica and the Thessalonian Correspondence", *NTS* 31 (1985), 336-56, at 342 as a reference to the strong phallic symbolism in the cults of Dionysus, Cabirus and Samothrace prevalent in Thessalonika, so that with *ktaomai* it means "to gain control over one's penis, or over the body with respect to sexual matters".

including certain behavioural norms. His repeated address to them as brothers (5:12, 14) is matched by a number of other indications that he has family relationships in mind as the appropriate model. This is most clearly seen in his direction in 1 Thess. 5:15 that they do not pay back evil for evil but always do good to one another and the group as a whole (*pantes*), in relation to which we must remember that exacting revenge for insults suffered at the hands of non-kin was socially acceptable, indeed necessary, for honourable males. Paul exhorts them to love those who have authority among them on account of their work and to be at peace with one another (5:12-13). They must warn the idlers, encourage those who lack courage, help the weak, be patient with everyone (5:14). Paul is calling on them to drop their customary attitudes and adopt norms of behaviour appropriate among real brothers. Yet that these directions find their place within a larger reality, that of identity, is underlined by his also reminding his addressees of non-ethical *desiderata* of their existence, that they should always be joyful, pray continually, give thanks for everything, while being careful not to quench the Spirit or suppress prophecy (5:16-17).

5 Culture, Kinship and Identity in Galatians

Paul's problem among the *ekklēsiai* of Galatia is very different from the situation in Thessalonika. I will now quickly summarise how I see the position, which I have dealt with at length elsewhere in recent years, especially in my 1998 monograph on Galatians.[61] Some time before Paul despatched the letter, he had founded congregations of converts in Galatia which consisted of gentiles and Israelites. This meant he had established an ingroup which faced two powerful outgroups, namely, local gentiles engaged in their usual practices of idolatry and local Israelites. An essential feature of Paul's Galatian congregations was that the Israelite and gentile members engaged in table-fellowship in which they shared, that is, passed from hand to hand, the one loaf and the one cup of the eucharist (cf. 1 Cor. 10:16-17). Such a practice was gravely offensive to everyday Israelite opinion at this time, presumably

---

[61] Esler, *op. cit.*, and also see Idem, *The First Christians*, 52-69.

because of the risk of idolatry if one of the gentiles surreptitiously rendered the wine a libation offering to a pagan god.[62] Accordingly, pressure was brought to bear on the Israelites who were thus dining with the gentiles within Paul's congregations to end the scandal of this practice by having the gentiles undertake circumcision (6:12-13), thereby leaving his ingroup to join the Israelite outgroup. The ultimate source of this pressure being deployed upon Israelite members of the Christ-following congregations was either local Israelites unconnected with the congregations, or outsiders, probably Israelite Christ-followers from Jerusalem who had previously caused much the same trouble for Paul in Antioch (Gal. 2:11-14), or a mixture of both. To Paul this represents a lamentable alteration of the Gospel he preached (1:6-9), made even worse by the fact that some of his gentiles have begun to move in an Israelite direction, even if they have not yet been circumcised (4:10).

The situation in Galatia can be usefully analysed using Tajfel's social identity theory.[63] Paul's gentile converts are being exposed to a powerful and attractive Israelite group identity that is largely summed up in the notion of 'righteousness', which I consider to mean on his opponents' lips something like 'the blessed and morally exalted status of being a faithful Israelite'. In response to this challenge Paul seeks to promote the positive identity of his congregations and to devalue that of the Israelite outgroup using strategies which can be interpreted in terms of Tajfel's 'social creativity' and 'social change', and the associated process of stereotyping, discussed above. As far as righteousness is concerned, for example, Paul audaciously seeks to disconnect it from its Israelite home and attach its core notion of privileged identity to his own congregations.[64]

Turning now to the specific focus of this essay, it is apparent

---

[62] Esler, *Galatians*, 93-116.

[63] *Ibid.*, and also see P.F. Esler, "Group Boundaries and Intergroup Conflict in Galatians: A New Reading of Gal. 5:13–6:10", in: M. Brett (ed.), *Ethnicity and the Bible*, Leiden 1996, 215-40, and "Family Imagery and Christian Identity in Gal. 5.13-6.10", in: Moxnes, *op. cit.*, 121-49.

[64] Esler, *Galatians*, 141-77.

that family imagery figures prominently in Galatians in the establishment of a positive group identity. This is most evident in Gal.
5:13–6:10, but before readers of Galatians reach that passage,
which I will discuss below, they will have already encountered five
major areas of such imagery. Firstly, the members of the congregations experience God as father (1:1-3); they are all sons of God
through faith in Christ Jesus (3:26), whom they donned through
baptism (3:27); through Jesus they become God's adopted sons
and cry "Abba! Father!" (4:1-7). Secondly, through Christ, who
is the seed of Abraham (3:16), they too are sons (3:7) and seed
of Abraham (3:29). Thirdly, Paul also portrays the Galatian converts as his children (*tekna*: 4:19-20). Fourthly, they are children
of the promise made to Sarah (4:21-31); she is their mother (4:31).
Finally, there is the repeated designation of his addressees as
'brothers' (*adelphoi*: 1:2, 11; 3:15; 4:12, 28, 31; 5:11, 13; 6:1, 18).

In using this imagery to establish a positive social identity for
his converts, Paul is both tapping into the high regard for one's
family typical of the Mediterranean region and also seeking to re-
define kinship with illustrious ancestors like Abraham and Sarah.
For Paul to assert that such ancestry legitimately belonged to his
mixed gentile-Israelite congregations – and not to ethnic Israelites
– testifies both to the boldness of his rhetoric and also to the
evident appeal such lineage held.

Each of the five areas of kinship (the fatherhood of God)
or fictive kinship (the remaining areas) contribute to the three
dimensions of group-belonging identified by Tajfel. The fact of
knowing that Paul's Christ-followers were each part of a family, in particular one which traced its line back to Abraham and
Sarah, strengthened their sense of belonging to the group (cognitive dimension) in ways which could only result in a very positive
attitude to it (evaluative dimension), while stimulating feelings
of affection and amity for fellow members and of hostility toward
outgroups (emotional dimension).

Of particular interest, however, is the passage Gal. 5:13–6:10
which culminates in exhortation, "let us do good to everyone,
especially to the house-members of the faith (*oikeioi tês pisteôs*)".
The very existence in the letter of this passage, with its strong

interest in matters internal to the congregations and often characterised as 'ethical', has been a source of controversy in New
Testament scholarship and has led to suggestions that it is an
interpolation,[65] that it was by Paul but unrelated to the letter as
a whole,[66] that it indicated that Paul had a second problem to face
in Galatia quite different from that caused by the circumcisers,[67]
or that it is actually integrated into the letter.[68]

My own approach to this passage stresses its integration into
the letter on the basis that there is an intrinsic connection between
the external issue, the need to stay within the boundaries of
the congregation and not leave the ingroup to join the Israelite
outgroup, and the internal conditions of the congregation.[69] As
Anthony Cohen, the professor of social anthropology at the University of Edinburgh has noted, "Having crossed a boundary,
we have to think ourselves into our transformed identity which
is far more subtle, far more individualised than its predication
on status".[70] The identity which Paul develops, as suitable for
his congregations in Gal. 5:13–6:10 and as sharply differentiated
from both Israelite and gentile outgroups, draws heavily upon

---

[65] J.C. O'Neill, *The Recovery of Paul's Letter to the Galatians*, London
1972.

[66] M. Dibelius, *A Commentary on the Epistle of James*, ed. H. Greeven
(Hermeneia Commentary), trans. M.A. Williams, Philadelphia 1976, 1-11
(where he discusses the emergence of an early Christian paraenesis arguably
not at the heart of Paul's thought) and his *From Tradition to Gospel*, trans.
B.L. Woolf, London 1934, 238-9, where he suggests Gal. 5:13–6:10 reflects
such paraenesis.

[67] See W. Lütgert, *Gesetz und Geist: Eine Untersuchung zur Vorgeschichte
des Galaterbriefes*, Gütersloh 1919, and J.H. Ropes, *The Singular Problem of
the Epistle to the Galatians*, Cambridge, MA. 1929.

[68] See H.D. Betz, *Galatians: A Commentary on Paul's Letter to the Church-
es in Galatia* (Hermeneia Commentary), Philadelphia 1979; G. Howard, *Paul:
Crisis in Galatia: A Study in Early Christian Theology*, Cambridge 1979; and
J.M.C. Barclay, *Obeying the Truth: A Study of Paul's Ethics in Galatians*,
Edinburgh 1988.

[69] Esler, *Galatians*, 205-34.

[70] A.P. Cohen, "Boundaries of Consciousness, Consciousness of Boundaries", plenary paper delivered at the conference on *The Anthropology of Ethnicity: A Critical View*, The University of Amsterdam, 15th-18th December
1993, 10.

general Mediterranean notions of kinship and more specific aspects derived from Israelite tradition. I will now briefly explore some features of Paul's strategy.

Gal. 5:13-15 encapsulates much of his approach:

> 13. For you were called for freedom, brothers; only not freedom which is an opportunity for the flesh, but be enslaved to one another through love. 14. For the whole law is fulfilled in the one statement: "You will love your neighbour as yourself". 15. But if you bite and devour one another, see that you are not consumed by one another.

Paul is reminding them that freedom and love are characteristics of the ingroup, while the outgroups represent the realm of the flesh: which induces the sort of behaviour appropriate to wild beasts referred to in 5:15. The significance of kinship imagery emerges here in a number of factors: first, the reference to 'brothers' in 5:14; secondly, the fact that Paul has just previously connected freedom with their alleged descent from Sarah (4:21-5:1); thirdly, the notion of mutual service and love which is more at home in a familial context than anywhere else in this culture; and, fourthly, the savage, mutual aggression castigated in 5:15 which epitomises precisely the sort of behaviour that, although characteristic of the world at large, should never occur among siblings. Plutarch, indeed, mentions the hostility of animals towards one another in search of food as an example of the sort of behaviour brothers should avoid (*Peri Philadelphias*, 486b).

These themes are explored in more detail in 5:16-26. In 5:15-16 Paul lays out the fundamental nature of the opposition between the two zones of spirit and flesh characterising ingroup on the one hand and outgroups on the other. There is a marked degree of stereotypification here, but social identity theory leads us to expect that such a phenomenon characterises group comparison as intensive as this, especially in a culture which ascribes to the notion that all goods are limited and, very commonly, indivisible. At 5:16 Paul employs the word *peripateô* in an injunction accurately translated (in line with our suggestion for the meaning of this word in 1 Thess. 2:12; 4:1, 12) as "adopt an identity governed by the Spirit", since he is referring to a reality which is larger than ethical norms (although they are included within its ambit).

The heart of 5:16-26 consists of the two lists in 5:19-21 and 22-23, the first of "works of the flesh" and the second of the "fruit of the Spirit". Of fifteen itemised works of the flesh, at least nine are forms of behaviour which have the tendency to tear the community apart, because of strife between either individuals or factions: sorcery (*pharmakeia*), hostilities (*echthrai*), actual conflict (*eris*), jealousy (*zêlos*), outbursts of rage (*thymoi*), selfish manipulation (*eritheiai*), dissensions (*dichostasiai*), factions (*haireseis*) and outbursts of envy (*phthonoi*). These are all examples of the competitive conflict Paul had mentioned in 5:15. Although not explicitly mentioned here, this sort of behaviour is completely at odds with what was expected within families, where siblings were expected to work together to maintain the harmony of family and preserve its honour in the eyes of the outside world.

On the other hand, the elements which comprise the fruit of the Spirit in Gal. 5:22-23 evoke the proper identity of congregations of Christ-followers. Paul sets out norms which, by signalling how the Galatians should behave in new and ambiguous situations, form one part of a larger ensemble of social features which tell them who they really are. It is clear that these norms are only one part of the social identity Paul is attempting to fashion for his readers/listeners both because of their function within the broad contrast he establishes between the worlds of Spirit and flesh and because of the presence of joy and peace in the list. Joy and peace are not ethical norms but emblems of identity.

The themes we have been encountering reappear in summary form in Gal. 5:25-26. In 5:25 Paul suggests that "if we live by Spirit, let us also *keep in line* (*stoichein*) by Spirit". This last expression evokes an image of a group which has all of its members in the right place, which is necessary for harmonious life in the community. He then proceeds to warn them of precisely the opposite of this: "Let us not engage in empty boasting, challenging (*prokaloumenoi*) one another, envying one another". Paul here presents, as the antithesis of the right identity, a picture of

Mediterranean men, ever alert to engage in the pattern of challenge-and-response, envying those who are more fortunate than themselves and boasting even when their achievements do not warrant self-promotion.

The last section of the passage, Gal. 6:1-10, is framed with the language of fictive kinship, since it begins with another address to brothers (6:1) and concludes with mention of the house-members of the faith (6:10). In 6:1-6 he advises on ways of encouraging behaviour appropriate to the congregations and their identity. His opening recommendation, in Gal. 6:2, is to bring erring members into line by peer pressure, something Plutarch suggested for brothers (*Peri Philadelphias*, 483a-b), in a spirit of gentleness, which is a gift of the Spirit (Gal. 5:21), but also what one would expect among family members.[71] Bearing one another's burdens (6:2) is also characteristic of families, as the most common site of mutual assistance and co-operation. Gal. 6:3 represents counsel against making unfounded claims to honour and 6:4-5 is a critique of comparing oneself with others in the typical agonistic fashion of the local social setting. In 6:6 Paul urges the one who is being taught the word to share all good things with the one who is teaching. This is another sign of 'siblings' keeping things in the family. Plutarch, similarly, held the view that brothers had a good relationship with one another if they had in common their father's property, friends and slaves (*Peri Philadelphias*, 478c).

After a stern warning to his addressees to take responsibility for their actions, given the divinely ordained consequences of living in the realm of flesh and not Spirit (6:7-9), Paul comes at last to 6:10: "So then, as we have an opportune time, let us do good to everyone, especially to the house-members of the faith (*oikeioi tês pisteôs*)". This last expression makes explicit what has been implied since 5:13, that his Galatian converts are members of one *oikos*, household, comprising relatives and, perhaps, slaves and this reality should condition their group identity, especially in the area of behavioural norms. In first-century Mediterranean culture the household represents the most natural metaphor

---

[71] F. Hauck, S. Schulz, "*praus, prautês*", *TDNT*, vol. 6, 645-51, at 646.

to express the unique identity of the Galatian believers in Christ as they seek to live in accordance with the love which the Spirit brings. The metaphor of the household expands upon the earlier adumbration of their identity in terms of kinship with God, Abraham and Paul himself. There may be a particular point to the metaphor of *oikos* if the congregations in Galatia, like those elsewhere, actually met in households owned and still used by wealthier members. This would mean that there was a close link, of the sort I have explored elsewhere, between domestic architecture and group identity.[72]

6   Conclusion: Keeping It in the Family

We are now in a position to draw together some of the threads from the investigation of the theme of family in 1 Thessalonians and Galatians and to make a proposal for how this kind of research, given the cultural and chronological gap between Paul and ourselves, might yet have an impact in our contemporary world.

6.1   A Comparison of 1 Thessalonians and Galatians

A comparison of 1 Thessalonians and Galatians brings out strong areas of similarity and other areas of difference. In both letters Paul is concerned to generate a particular type of positive group identity for his Christ-followers which is notably differentiated from that of negatively evaluated outgroups. In both cases this identity draws on an understanding of kinship in the local context as offering a desirable model for the solidarity, harmony and intimacy which he wished to characterise his congregations.

These considerations lead me to question the thesis of Schäfer,[73] at least as far as 1 Thessalonians and Galatians are

---

[72]P.F. Esler, "'House Members of the Faith': Domestic Architecture and Early Christian Identity", *Cosmos* 12 (1996), 223-39. Also see the various essays in C. Osiek, D. Balch (eds.), *Families in the New Testament World: Households and House Churches*, Louisville, KY 1997, on the subject of house and household among early Christ-followers.

[73]K. Schäfer, *Gemeinde als "Bruderschaft": Ein Beitrag zum Kirchenverständnis des Paulus* (Europäische Hochschulschriften, 23/333), Bern 1989.

concerned, that in Paul brotherhood, seen as 'egalitarian' fellow-ship, is contrasted with the patriarchal model of family relations evident in Graeco-Roman households, so that Paul is setting up his congregations as antitypes of the family in the ancient Medi-terranean world, as a form of *Kontrastgesellschaft*.[74] My problem with this view is that although Paul does advocate a counter-cultural position, he does so not by distinguishing brotherhood from *oikos* but by insisting again and again that unrelated males in this culture who are members of the *ekklêsia* should treat one another as brothers. In both 1 Thessalonians, where Paul advo-cates *philadelphia* as a model for his converts, and Galatians, where members of the Christ-movement are both brothers *and oikeioi*, we find persuasive evidence against Schäfer's thesis.

Yet the two letters present a major difference in the way Paul develops the point. In 1 Thessalonians, with its exclusively gentile audience and no signs of Israelite pressure on the congregation, Paul does not attempt to enlist fictive descent from Israelite ancestors like Abraham and Sarah as he does in Galatians. The explanation for this is that in Galatia Paul had to react to oppo-nents who were intent on imposing Israelite practices and beliefs on his gentile converts and who were able to present *Ioudaismos* in a very attractive light as dependent on ancestors as glorious as Abraham and as providing the path to the glittering prize of righteousness. A large part of Paul's endeavour in Galatians is to detach these goods from Israel and lodge them very firmly among his *ekklêsiai*. At the same time the powerful nature of the case being directed at his gentile converts propels him to emphasise strongly the distinctiveness of the ingroup and this results in the types of stereotyped portrayal of the outgroup featured in Tajfel's theory. The best example of this is his creation of such a sharp antithesis between Spirit and flesh as emblematic of the ingroup and outgroups. All of this results in a much richer array of identity-creating language in Galatians than in 1 Thessalonians.

---

[74]This view is also critiqued by K.O. Sandnes, "Equality Within Patri-archal Structures: Some New Testament Perspectives on the Christian Fel-lowship as a Brother- Or Sisterhood and a Family", in: Moxnes, *op. cit.*, 150-65.

6.2   Bridging the Cultural Gap: The Significance of Interculturalism

A recent collection of essays edited by Stephen Barton testifies to the current interest in reaching a theological understanding of family and also to the continuing debate,[75] well illustrated in Barton's own essay in the volume,[76] as to whether and, if so, how the Bible might play some role in this discussion. Barton himself sees systematic theology as necessary in giving biblical understandings of family a contemporary edge, since otherwise 'truth' becomes a matter of "somehow 'living within the story' rather than of the application of critical reason to the claims about God and reality which the biblical text conveys".[77]

Without denying systematic theology its proper place, I wish to suggest that there is more to the importance of "living within the story" than Barton allows.[78] This, after all, is the primary experience for most adherents of a religion, since the probing of the ontological status of its truth claims, which Barton seems to privilege, is usually only the preserve of a tiny minority of the membership. This is not to say that the existence and status of such claims are unimportant to the general membership, only that they do not keep them at the forefront of their attention. Similarly, perhaps, most of us enjoy the *experience* of driving our car from place to place, aware that it has an engine under the bonnet but happy to leave a closer familiarity to the experts, and then only when things go wrong! Barton's claims for systematic theology in this area represent an emphasis inappropriate for the majority of those who will be interested in these texts. On the other hand, the type of biblical interpretation conducted in this essay, historical research alive to the fundamental cultural divide

---

[75] S.C Barton (ed.), *The Family in Theological Perspective*, Edinburgh 1996.

[76] *Ibid.*, "Biblical Hermeneutics and the Family", 3-23.

[77] *Ibid.*, 15.

[78] For my views on the relevance of the thought of George Lindbeck in this area, see my introduction in P.F. Esler (ed.), *Modelling Early Christianity: Social-Scientific Studies of the New Testament in Its Context*, London & New York 1995, 14-20.

between our ancestors in faith like Paul and his congregations on the one side and ourselves on the other, arguably has the potential to enrich the Christian story for believers, and also for all men and women of goodwill who will be content to find in the Bible valuable insight if not logically coercive truth.

Is this possible? To many commentators, after all, historically-oriented New Testament research which emphasises the cultural distance between ourselves and the earliest Christ-followers relegates the texts to a hopelessly distant past. But this common sentiment fails to take into account the recent development of the study of interculturalism, to which W.B. Gudykunst and Y.Y. Kim provide a good introduction.[79] The insight underlying this field of research is quite straightforward. Imagine that we travel to a culture very different from our own, learn the language and immerse ourselves in the local setting for a lengthy period. In due course, all going well, we become acculturated and perhaps reach the stage where we interpret the social realities of our existence in much the same way as the locals. Now imagine that we then return to our initial culture. For a transitional period we will be strongly aware of living with our feet in two worlds; we will be able to interpret and assess each culture with respect to the other and become aware of a much wider range of social possibilities in consequence. In short, we will have become intercultural. This is likely to be an enriching experience, since we will have acquired a range of understanding and sensitivity generally unavailable to our monocultural friends in either place. Moreover, the greater the cultural difference the greater the degree of enrichment.

To interpret the Bible, in this case, the data on how Paul seeks to legitimate, that is, to explain and justify, the social identity of his congregations in Thessalonika and Galatia, in a manner predicated on the cultural distance between him and us, offers benefits similar in kind if not equal in intensity to the phenomenon of contemporary interculturalism. In particular, the group-oriented nature of Paul's enterprise comes into provocative conjunction

---

[79]W.B. Gudykunst, Y.Y. Kim, *Communicating with Strangers: An Approach to Intercultural Communication*, New York *et al.* [2]1992.

with the very individualistic way in which those of us with Northern European or North American cultural backgrounds organise our lives, both inside and outside ecclesial settings. In sum, we reach a point where the recognition of the socially constructed nature of different ways of "keeping it in the family" becomes a potent stimulus to imagining for ourselves alternative modes of being in the world now, and alternative futures.[80]

---

[80]I set out the promise of an intercultural approach to Galatians in P.F. Esler, *Galatians*, 235-9.

The Family is Not All That Matters

A Response to Esler

Jan Willem van Henten   (University of Amsterdam)

1   Esler's Argument

Let me first summarise Philip Esler's main points as I read them. After a brief discussion of cultural difference as eye opener, the aim of Esler's paper is formulated as an investigation of the significance of 'family' in 1 Thessalonians and Galatians. Starting from the assumption of the "longue durée" of Mediterranean cultural features Philip Esler argues – rightly in my opinion – that social anthropological research is helpful in the attempt to situate NT texts in plausible social settings. He refers especially to the synthesis of this research and its application to Early Christian literature by Bruce Malina in his *The New Testament World: Insights from Cultural Anthropology* (1981[1]; 1993[2]), but several other publications by Malina seem to be relevant as well. This anthropological framework implies that:

1. Kinship is the dominant institution in the ancient Mediterranean world;

2. the basic social distinction is that between kin and non-kin; and

3. the main social value is honour, with shame as its opposite.

Esler adds a fourth structural element to the paradigm, namely the notion of limited good that is also important in the context of the family. Next he discusses Henri Tajfel's social identity theory and explains its relevance for the interpretation of NT writings. This theory focuses on the establishment of group identity and group norms and attitudes toward kin and non-kin connected with it. Tajfel distinguishes between three dimensions of social

identity (cognitive, evaluative and emotional), and between three
social processes (social mobility, social change and social competition). The second part of the paper offers a discussion of kinship
and family language in 1 Thessalonians and Galatians, building
on the theoretical framework indicated. In both letters Paul is
using fictive kinship language in order to differentiate between
in-group and out-groups. In his discussion of the more important
passages Philip Esler argues that in both letters Paul was seeking
to develop a group identity based on the most prominent model of
relationships in the ambient culture: the family. In this way Paul
would have used the high regard for the family in ancient Mediterranean culture in order to tell the Thessalonian and Galatian
followers of Christ who they were and how they had to behave: in
accordance with the values of solidarity, harmony and intimacy
of the family. In one phrase: "keeping it in the family".

2   Theoretical Framework

I do think that anthropological studies of the Mediterranean world
improve our insights into Early Christian and post-biblical Jewish
writings and their contexts, but I am hesitant about a tendency
to discuss these writings in connection with one rather mono-
lithic and static paradigm or even force data to fit into such a
model. A paradigm should be dealt with in a heuristic fashion, so
that the particularities of individual texts and their settings can
come to the fore. Therefore, I prefer to use the plural 'families'
instead of the singular, also because my own work into Jewish and
non-Jewish non-literary sources has made me aware of the plural-
istic character of ancient Mediterranean society, notwithstanding
important common cultural features. Philip Esler acknowledges
this observation in the printed version of his paper. Nevertheless, he emphasises the 'constants' time and again. The variation
in the constructions of images of families is on the theoretical
level discussed by, among others, Jon Bernardes.[1] With respect to
ancient Mediterranean culture I will give some examples to make
my point.

---

[1] J. Bernardes, *Family Studies: An Introduction*, London & New York 1997.

Philip Esler rightly suggests that domestic architecture and group – often family – identity were closely linked together. As becomes more and more well-known, the picture of housing in the ancient world is rather variegated. Carolyn Osiek and David Balch summarise discussions about houses and the way they were used by families and others and point in this connection to the considerable difference between the Roman *atrium*-house, with its significant openness to non-kin and a lot of space for public and business affairs, and Greek houses with a *peristylon* but no *atrium* and a separate part of the house indicated as the women's quarters (*gynaikonitis*).[2] A second example concerns Jewish families. A discussion of Jewish housing and family life in the first century CE by Prof. Shemuel Safrai, from the Hebrew University, made me rebellious a few years ago and write an article, together with Stefan Joubert, with the title "Two A-Typical Jewish Families".[3] Safrai suggests that a Jewish family usually lived in a middle-sized or small town, shared a courtyard with other families, and lived in a house with at least two stories. The impression of a rather uniform and ideal picture of Jewish families in this period is strengthened time and again by sentences like one concerning the baking of bread, which was supposed to be a weekly task for the whole family: "The biblical picture of 'the children gathering wood, the fathers kindling the fire, and the women kneading the dough' (Jer. 7:18) remained the custom in the first century as well." (p. 740).[4] Not only is the reference to Jer. 7:18 ironical, since the passage concerns idolatry: making cakes for the queen of heaven and drinking offerings for other gods than the Lord; but also it can aptly be demonstrated from literary and non-literary

---

[2]C. Osiek, D. Balch, *Families in the New Testament World: Households and House Churches*, Louisville 1997, 6-10; 24-31.

[3]S. Safrai, "Home and Family", in: S. Safrai, M. Stern, *The Jewish People in the First Century: Historical Geography, Political History, Social, Cultural and Religious Life and Institutions* (CRINT, 1/2), Assen & Philadelphia 1987, 728-92; J.W. van Henten, S. Joubert, "Two A-Typical Jewish Families in the Greco-Roman period", *Neotestamentica* 30 (1996), 121-40.

[4]Cf. Safrai, "Home and Family", 732; also 745: "The presence of many lamps in Jewish homes is probably related to the practice of studying Torah at night, which was current among many strata of the Jewish population".

sources alike that the lives and representations of Jewish families
in the Greco-Roman period varied considerably.

Things become even more complicated if we realise that Paul
usually points at fictive and not at real kinship in his letters. We
know from other NT passages that Jesus seems to have radically
relativized kinship relations (Mk 13:12-3; Mt. 10:21-2, 35-6; Lk.
12:52-3). This is not so obvious for Paul, but Jesus and Paul
alike have referred to fictive kinship relationships.[5] First, this fact
raises the question how we can characterise the in-groups of Jesus'
followers or Paul's implied readers. Can we understand them as
fictive or alternative families, or should we reckon with the use
of family language for the construction of the identity of another
kind of group. I intend to come back to this question later, but
at this point I already would like to stress that I do not agree
with Malina's statement, referred to with approval by Esler, that
"honor is always presumed to exist within one's own family of
blood...".[6] Athletes and politicians were honoured and rewarded
by their native cities, soldiers sacrificed themselves in order to
save their people or the emperor and were highly praised for that
posthumously, not to speak of Jewish or Christian martyrs who
were venerated as heroes of the people.[7]

My final remarks may imply that by looking for the process
of establishing social identity in Early Christian contexts we may
have to take into consideration theories that do not take kinship
relations as point of departure. In the margin of my own research
I have come across one or two, but I am not sure whether they can
stand up against Tajfel's theory. I mention only one briefly here,
the sociological concept of a "reference group", i.e. an exemplary
group which functions as a model for a larger in-group and exem-
plifies important values and attitudes, which the members of the

---

[5] H. Moxnes (ed.), *Constructing Early Christian Families: Family as Social
Reality and Metaphor*, London & New York 1997, also referred to by Esler.

[6] B.J. Malina, *The New Testament World: Insights from Cultural Anthropology*, Louisville [2]1993, 38.

[7] For further references: J.W. van Henten, *The Maccabean Martyrs as Saviours of the Jewish People: A study of 2 and 4 Maccabees* (JSJ Sup, 57),
Leiden 1997.

in-group would have liked to share.[8] This concept can be applied
to kinship and non-kinship situations alike and easily connected
to the ancient concept of *paradeigma/exemplum*, i.e. exemplary
persons. B. Fiore has argued convincingly that several of the NT
letters made use of this concept in paranetic passages.[9]

3   Family Imagery in 1 Thessalonians and Galatians

I agree on Philip Esler's basic point that family language is used
by Paul to establish social identity of the implied readers in
1 Thess. and Gal. I am not sure whether I agree with all the
details of his reading (e.g. his interpretation of 1 Thess. 2:14
and *peripatein* as "being of a particular identity"), but that is of
minor importance now. The principal questions for me are: 1) How
exactly is the family imagery used and to what identity does it
lead in both writings? 2) Is the family language alone formative
for the establishment of social identity? And if not, how is this
language related to other imagery used by Paul as instruments in
the formulation of the identity of Jesus followers in Thessalonika
and Galatia?

This is hardly the place to elaborate the first question seriously. Esler offers a discussion of the relevant passages that may
persuade most of you. But somehow I feel uneasy about the simple
formulation of his results by the catching phrase "keeping it in
the family". I note only in the margin that in his discussion of
Galatians the second out-group, the local Gentiles, hardly plays
a role. I would like to spend the last part of my response on
the second question. In my opinion there are at least three other
models, together with their respective semantic fields, that have

---

[8] About this concept, see R.K. Merton, *Social Theory and Social Structure*,
New York 1968, 279-440; H.H. Hyman, "Reference Groups", *International
Encyclopedia of the Social Sciences*, vol. 13, 353-61; H.H. Hyman, E. Singer,
Readings in Reference Group Theory and Research, New York 1968. Negative
reference groups are being discussed by T.M. Newcomb, *Social Psychology*,
New York 1960, 226-7; 260.

[9] B. Fiore, *The Function of Personal Example in the Socratic and Pastoral
Epistles* (AnBib, 105), Rome 1986.

functioned in Early Christian literature as points of departure for
the formulation of socio-cultural identities of Christian groups.
All three of them have also functioned in Jewish contexts in the
Greco-Roman period. The first one is that of Christians as a holy
community and a priesthood for the Lord, as can be found in
the book of Revelation (Rev. 1:6; 5:10; 20:6).[10] The second one,
that of Christians as a group of special philosophers (a *hairesis*),
appears somewhat later in Early Christian literature,[11] but has
elaborate Jewish parallels in writings from the first century CE
onwards (Philo, *Probus*; Josephus; 4 Maccabees).[12] Finally, there
is the concept of the Christians as a unique people, analogous to
Israel as the chosen people of the Lord, and unfortunately in anti-
Jewish texts from the second century CE onwards also as successor
of Israel. This idea is already explicitly formulated in the *First
Letter of Clement to the Corinthians*, as I have argued elsewhere.[13]
A quick survey of the texts seems to imply that the semantic fields
of these models for the construction of socio-cultural identity, if I
may call them as such, sometimes overlap. An interesting example
would be Philo's depiction of the Essenes in his *Quod omnis probus
liber sit* as a group of unique Jewish philosophers, as opposed to
non-Jewish philosophers. They live a celibate life, but exemplify
several ideal norms of family life including the virtue of brotherly
love. The best example of such an overlap I know of is 4 Maccabees, a Jewish martyr text from about 100 CE, where we find a
combination of ethnic, priestly, philosophical and family identity
patterns. These findings lead me back to some of the passages discussed by Esler, like Gal. 4, refering not only to brothers but also

---

[10] E. Schüssler Fiorenza, *Priester für Gott: Studien zum Herrschafts- und
Priestermotiv in der Apokalypse* (NTA, NF 7), Münster 1972.

[11] A.-M. Malingrey, *"Philosophia": Étude d'un group de mots dans la
littérature grecque, des Présocratiques au IVe siècle après J.-C.* (Études et
commentaires, 40), Paris 1961.

[12] Van Henten, *Maccabean Martyrs*, ch. 7 with references.

[13] J.W. van Henten, "The Martyrs as Heroes of the Christian People: Some
Remarks on the Continuity between Jewish and Christian Martyrology, with
Pagan Analogies", in: M. Lamberigts, P. van Deun (eds.), *Martyrium in Multidisciplinary Perspective: Memorial Louis Reekmans* (BETL, 117), Leuven
1995, 303-22.

to the patriarch and matriarch of the Jewish people, Abraham and Sarah. In short: Is the family all that matters?

The Women in John

On Gender and Gender Bending

Sjef van Tilborg (Catholic University of Nijmegen)

1 The Problem

The way women are presented in the Johannine Gospel evokes a kind of fascination. Most female characters show a remarkable mixture of dependence and independence. In a certain way they are subject to the social code of the time: women in service to men; women in typical female roles when they serve at table; women as wailing persons, as persons who feel responsible for the dead body of Jesus. But at the same time the Johannine women act also in a very independent way: Jesus' mother who takes the initiative in the story of Cana and keeps it; the Samaritan woman who has five or six husbands; Martha and Mary as Jesus' disciples who are involved in the development of Johannine theology; Mary of Magdala who seems to function completely on her own.

This ambiguity is always seen anew in exegesis, but up to now it has been difficult to combine these two elements. Dependent on the exegete's preference, the accent is put on one aspect or the other, but the data are not brought together. In this study I want to find out how far the concept of 'gender bending' can be used as a literary device to show more precisely how this mixture has come about and how, thereby, the stories can be understood in a more coherent way.

2 Character as a Reader's Construct

We must start with the question of whether, in a literary work, one can speak of characters at all.[1] The question is even more

---

[1] In this I am encouraged by a number of articles in the 1993 issue of *Semeia* on characterization. See esp. F.W. Burnett, "Characterization and Reader Construction of Characters in the Gospels", 2-23, D.R. Beck, "The Narrative Function of Anonymity in Fourth Gospel Characterization", 145-

urgent for a literary work from antiquity which does not possess
the fascination of a 19th and 20th century novel, in which the
development of the characters is often the *raison-d'être* of the
story or is proposed as such. The question is still more urgent
in the context of exegetical discourse, certainly in the context
of main stream New Testament exegesis, in which every kind of
applied psychology is set aside as psychologizing, with the argument that New Testament authors are not interested in the
psychology of their characters. But even within literary-scholarly
discourse it is not always selfevident that one can speak about
characters. The question is whether the character does not
dissolve into an accidental mixture of codes.

In a way the discussion is about the opposition: text or person.
Already in 1983 Culpepper wrote: "Contemporary approaches to
characters in narrative literature fall roughly into two camps depending on whether characters are seen primarily as autonomous
beings with traits and even personalities or as plot functionaries
with certain commissions or tasks to be fulfilled".[2]

For the first opinion he refers to S. Chatman,[3] who pleads for
as much openness as possible "to treat characters as autonomous
beings, not as mere plot functions". Therefore, he assumes that
a confrontation of the reader with the external world will lead to
more information – as, for example, a trip to Dublin "which helps
us to understand the special quality of paralysis attributed to its
denizens by Joyce"![4]

76, and M.M. Thompson, " 'God's Voice You Have Never Heard, God's Form
You Have Never Seen': The Characterization of God in the Gospel of John",
177-202.

[2] R.A. Culpepper, *Anatomy of the Fourth Gospel: A Study in Literary
Design*, Philadelphia 1983, 102.

[3] S. Chatman, *Story and Discourse: Narrative Structure in Fiction and
Film*, Ithaca & London 1978, 119-21.

[4] According to Chatman one can learn a lot more making such a trip to
Dublin: "We will learn about the distinctively Irish way of being trapped –
the religious overtones, the close family ties, the sense of guilt, the sentimental
admixtures that make the prison comfortable... and so on". Chatman becomes really candid when he adds, "I have never been to Ireland, but I know
that the peculiar sort of 'strutting' that Eveline's father does would be clearer

It is always a reader's construction, but readers should be as open-minded as possible to get the most out of the confrontation with the characters in the story.

Because most of the characters in John appear only for a short time and it is, therefore, difficult "to form an impression of them as 'autonomous beings'", Culpepper prefers the second opinion: "Most of the characters (in John) appear on the literary stage only long enough to fulfil their role in the evangelist's representation of Jesus and the responses to him. As a result, one is almost forced to consider the characters in terms of their commissions, plot functions, and representational value".[5]

In Culpepper's opinion this is a formalistic and structuralist approach to the text, but that is only true to a certain extent. The terms used – 'commissions', 'plot functions' and 'representational value' – need to be filled in and construed by a specific reader. The question then is whether readers are ready to agree with these reductions as they experience them. Can the Samaritan woman be completely subsumed in the plot of Jesus' Samaritan mission? Is Mary of Magdala's character identical with the commission she receives from Jesus to tell the disciples that Jesus is risen and has appeared to her? It cannot be really true that the character 'Martha' coincides simply with her confession that Jesus is the Christ and the Son of God.

The strongest resistance to this way of reading the texts can be found in Schüssler Fiorenza's book, *Jesus: Miriam's Child, Sophia's Prophet*:

> More recently, the literary dimension of the form- and redaction-critical paradigm has been discovered. Literary studies continue to work within this research paradigm as they explore how individual stories or the overall narrative constructions of the Gospels depict Jesus as a literary character in relation to the women characters of the Gospels. They show, for instance, how the androcentric narratives of the Gospels restrict

---

if I had" (Chatman, *op. cit.*, 120).
[5]Culpepper, *Anatomy of the Fourth Gospel*, 102.

discipleship to male characters while they accord fol-
lowership to the women characters. They underline
that the kyriocentric text centers on Jesus and makes
female figures either dependent on or peripheral to this
central male character. By adopting linguistic masculine determinism, they reinscribe both kyriarchal and
anti-Jewish relations".[6]

By merging the character into the text there is a danger that
all characters, and certainly those who play a role only in the
sub-plots – a position which is given especially to women and
which has made Culpepper call them 'minor characters' – will be
drowned in the literary work of art and simply be lost in it.

Therefore, there is good reason for Shlomith Rimmon-Kenan,
in her 1992 edition of *Narrative Fiction*,[7] to insist on a firm relation
between the reader of a text and characterization. Her solution
or, at least, her proposal starts from the possibility of allowing
the characters to play a role on two levels of the reading process.

On *the level of the text-continuum* the readers see direct and
indirect indications of character and construct nodes in the verbal
design with changing attention for character and plots.

On *the level of the story* the characters are – by definition –
non (or pre-)verbal abstractions, constructs. "Character, as one
construct within the abstracted story, can be described in terms
of a network of character-traits. These traits, however, may or
may not appear as such in the text. How, then, is the construct
arrived at? By assembling various character-indicators distributed
along the text-continuum and, when necessary, inferring the traits
from them". (p. 59). And though these constructs are not human
beings in the literal sense of the word, they are partly modelled on

---

[6] E. Schüssler Fiorenza, *Jesus: Miriam's Child, Sophia's Prophet: Critical
Issues in Feminist Christology*, London 1995, 84; see also L. Schottroff, "Important Aspects of the Gospel for the Future", in: F.F. Segovia (ed.), *"What
is John?": Readers and Readings of the Fourth Gospel*, Atlanta 1996, 209;
she points to the need to confront John's texts with a broad social-historical
inquiry in the social context.

[7] S. Rimmon-Kenan, *Narrative Fiction: Contemporary Poetics*, London &
New York 1992.

the reader's conception of people and in this they are person-like (p. 33).

Developing from there, I first want to propose a provisional classification and select the stories accordingly. I will follow the broad division which Adele Berlin proposed for the characters in biblical narrative:[8] *the full-fledged character* with a multitude of traits, *the type* which is built around a single quality or trait, and *the agent* which serves as a simple functionary and which is not characterized at all. I believe that the Johannine Gospel shows examples of all three classes, but that only the full-fledged characters are important for our investigation.

I will not deal, therefore, with the women who are mentioned in 19:25. It is simply an enumeration and its meaning is not very clear; and it is only stated that they "stand under the cross", even though that seems somehow relevant. Neither will I deal with the woman who is mentioned in 18:16-17: the young doorkeeper in the court of the High Priest. Although she does not play an unimportant role in the final plot of the story – through her it is made clear that 'the other disciple' is well-known in the house of the High Priest, and in her presumed innocence she makes Peter speak his first betrayal – it looks as if she completely merges into her role. She is a functionary or a type, at the most.

We have a somewhat more complicated situation in the two scenes in which Jesus' mother appears. It is remarkable that she is not mentioned by name (unless one presupposes in 19:25 that only two women are mentioned: Jesus' mother is Mary, the daughter of Clopas, and her sister is Mary of Magdala, but the problem is then that there are two Mary's in one family). Anyhow, in 19:26-27 she is used narratively as a type – which in exegesis has brought about the various typologies. She plays a more personal role in the Cana story, even though her own son 'reduces' her to 'just a woman': *"O woman, what have you to do with me?"* (2:4). This does not prevent her from acting actively as the mother of the protagonist: "Do whatever he tells you". The question remains open whether

---

[8] A. Berlin, *Poetics and Interpretation of Biblical Narrative*, Sheffield 1983, 23.

Jesus' mother acts as a full-fledged character.[9]

With regard to the four women who are left, we need to have no *a priori* hesitations. The Samaritan woman, Martha and Mary, Lazarus' sisters and Mary of Magdala are, therefore, for me the characters to be discussed.[10]

3 The Female Characters and the Main Plot

Summarizing what we said so far: I want to use a double focus in the evaluative description of characters in general, and thus also of the female characters in John in particular. On the one hand, we must try to characterize the characters, to describe them in their own identity, while, on the other hand, we need to explore their own relations with the main plot. This implies a reading on the level of the text-continuum as well as on the level of the story-construct. We have full-fledged characters if they score positively on both levels. Repeating myself, this reading is always about readers' constructions with all its ideological implications. To arrive at a characterization I must fill up the empty spaces which are not directly expressed in the text. Within the limited framework I have, this can only partially be explicated.

Let me start with the story of the Samaritan woman. She, obviously, belongs to the opening phase of the story. After the

---

[9]See for a similar exclusion Sandra M. Schneiders, "Women in the Fourth Gospel and the Role of Women in the Contemporary Church", in: M. Stibbe (ed.), *The Gospel of John as Literature: An Anthology of Twentieth Century Perspectives*, Leiden 1993, 127-29.

[10]Apart from monographs about the various texts – John 4 especially receives ample attention – I can point to the following historical series of studies: R.E. Brown, "Roles of the Women in the Fourth Gospel", *TS* 36 (1975), 688-99; S.M. Schneiders, "Women in the Fourth Gospel and the Role of Women in the Contemporary Church", *BibThBull* 12/2 (1982), 35-45 (published again in Stibbe, *The Gospel of John as Literature* [see note 9]); E. Schüssler Fiorenza, *In Memory of Her: A Feminist Theological Reconstruction of Christian Origins*, New-York 1983, 323-35; T.K. Seim, "Roles of the Women in the Gospel of John", in: L. Hartman, B. Olsson (eds.), *Aspects on the Johannine Literature*, Uppsala 1986, 56-73; M. Scott, *Sophia and the Johannine Jesus*, Sheffield 1992, 174-240; Sj. van Tilborg, *Imaginative Love in John*, Leiden 1993, 169-208; J. McKinlay, *Gendering Wisdom the Host: Biblical Invitations to Eat and Drink*, Sheffield 1996, 178-237.

tumultuous events in Jerusalem – the cleansing of the Temple and the first misunderstanding between Jesus and the Judeans, the tough discussion between Jesus and Nicodemus, the determination of the respective positions of Jesus and John the Baptist – the Samaritan woman takes the initiative to create a contact between Jesus, the Judeans and the Samaritan inhabitants of Sychar. Since Cana, this is the first happy event: Jesus and his disciples enjoy the hospitality of the Samaritans for two days.

This development in the plot is directly related to the way the Samaritan woman acts. She is a special woman who is capable of serious discussion and who does not get lost in it. Much has been written about the misunderstanding in which she gets involved, together with many other characters in the story. Different from Nicodemus, she handles it much more positively. Where Nicodemus ends by saying "How can this be?" (3:9), her final answer is: "Sir, give me this water, that I may not thirst, nor come here to draw water" (4:15). And even though the misunderstanding is not completely solved, it is an answer which I think not to be completely devoid of humour: it somehow relativizes the previous solemn statements of Jesus.

I think I can see a similar inner security in the second topic of discussion: her husband and the men in her life (4:16-18). She is not shameless in her answer but neither is she ashamed. It is a woman who, marked by life, still lives from an inner freedom; it is a way of acting which she has already demonstrated by entering into a conversation with a strange man at the well.

And she knows how to speak. Bringing in the theological problem of Samaria versus Judea (4:19-20) is the high point for her; and she understands what a discussion is for: to achieve new insights as discussion-partner. That is what happens to her, but it also happens to Jesus who for the first time arrives at a self-revelation: ἐγώ εἰμι (4:26).[11]

---

[11]See also the series of questions, for example, in J. McKinlay, *Gendering Wisdom the Host*, 187: "Is this (i.e. the sentence at the start of the discussion about the relationship between Judea and Samaria) slightly tongue in cheek? Is she indeed a slippery woman out to catch one unawares, even verbally? There is a hint of ambivalence about this woman".

The discussion brings her to change her behaviour. She leaves her bucket behind and by her message to the inhabitants of the city, the fruit of the discussion with Jesus, she acts as a unique mediator between Jesus and the city. It is through this extraordinary behaviour that the story gets a new twist. It may be clear that, both on the textual level and on the story level, the Samaritan woman as a character scores high enough.

It takes some time before we find new women. Martha and Mary both belong in the Lazarus story. They take the initiative and in so doing they get involved in the main plot. They warn Jesus about Lazarus's illness (11:3). And even though Jesus reacts in a strange way, narratively speaking it leads him out of a deadlock in the story. He has retired to the place where the story began – the place where John used to baptise (10:40 and 1:28). And even though things are looking up – many come to him and believe in him – it is at most a moment of rest after a deep crisis: the crisis in Capernaum, the crisis among the disciples, the crisis with his relatives, a crisis about the death in Jerusalem with the serious threats and lack of faith. Only when the sisters reach Jesus with their message does it become clear how the story will evolve.

On the level of the text, we see several things too. Martha is the theologian in the story. She is also a very active person: she is the first to go and meet Jesus, she informs her sister, she warns Jesus that the body is smelly, she serves Jesus at table during the meal (12:12).[12] More important is what her words evoke. She tells Jesus about his influence on God: anything which he may ask God will be given (11:22 – witness Jesus' prayer at the tomb: "I knew that thou hearest me always" [11:42]). She makes her sister go to Jesus – and this brings out Jesus' sorrow about the death of his friend (11:28, 33). But what is really special is her confession of faith (11:27). In the immediate story-level this does not seem to be important for the plot – till the narrator ends the story and

---

[12]Some exegetes point to the fact that the special word διακονέω is used here: see R.E. Brown, *Roles of Women*, 690; S. Schneiders, *Women in the Fourth Gospel*, 137; M. Scott, *Sophia and the Johannine Jesus*, 212. The problem remains that this term is also used in John 2:9, but there any liturgical connotation seems to be absent.

says that this confession is what the Gospel is about (20:31).

Mary, on the other hand, is the more affective of the two. She knows how to deal with death and with the dead. The supposition is that she goes to the tomb to weep (11:31); it is through her that Jesus weeps publicly (11:33). Discursively (11:2) and narratively (12:1-8) it is said of her that she is the one who anointed Jesus' feet and dried them with her hair, an act which Jesus interprets as an act of mourning. Of her own accord Mary brings up Jesus' death. And even if she does not, thereby, determine the plot of the story – it is not her action which causes Jesus' death – she colours it in a special way.

Mary of Magdala, finally, belongs in the closing phase of the story. She is one of the women who are present at Jesus' death. She is the first who brings the disciples together again after his death. Her visit to the tomb mobilizes Peter and the other disciple whom Jesus loved. Because of her action the beloved disciple can see the empty tomb and come to faith. Later Jesus will praise him for that without, however, mentioning Mary (20:29). For the progress of the story it is more important that Mary insists: she remains at the empty tomb and (therefore?) she is the first who is granted seeing Jesus after his death. The importance of this apparition of Jesus for the development of the main plot does not need to be emphasized for the readers of John. Mary Magdalene is the first who has seen the risen Jesus and also the first who has announced it precisely as *apostola apostolorum*, a topic which does not find many adherents in the exegetical discourse on Paul.[13]

I am not sure what the relation is between her role in the main plot and the characterization of her character. After finding Jesus' body gone, she is initially active in mobilizing the leaders of the group. Her sorrow comes later. It is mentioned three times (20:11, 13, 15), and twice she herself links this weeping to the disappearance of Jesus' body (20:13, 15). It is sorrow for a disturbed burial

---

[13]For the name *apostola apostolorum*, see R.E. Brown, *The Community of the Beloved Disciple: The Life, Loves, and Hates of an Individual Church in New Testament Times*, London 1979, 190. For the exegetical discussion between the presentation of John and that of Paul regarding the first apparition, see E. Schüssler Fiorenza, *Jesus: Miriam's Child, Sophia's Prophet*, 119-28.

and, therefore, it is supposed to indicate how closely involved with
Jesus she feels; she does not want anything untoward to happen
to him even after his death. It is the same affective involvement
which is clear in Jesus' much discussed words: "Do not touch me",
or, "Stop touching me" (20:17). For Mary Jesus is Rabbouni, but
her discipleship is a deeply affective one.[14]

The fact that the text is apparently indeterminate brings me
to a last question. Is one allowed to think or even to say: the
implied author indicates to the reader that Mary was allowed to
be the first to see the risen Jesus because her love was greater
than any other disciple's love? Or is it better to think that it
is implicitly stated that this vision was also for Mary a kind of
grace, a gift offered freely without there being a causal merit in
her action?

4   The Female Content of the Stories

This article tries to answer the question whether, in the stories
about women in John, there is a kind of gender-bending, an intended mixture of male and female traits which evokes in the
bystander (reader) a confusion about gender.

Let me start by stating what is rather self-evident for most
readers. There is, first of all, the way typical female roles are presented: the Samaritan woman who goes to the well to get water,
Martha who serves at table, Mary who is the mourning woman at
the death of her brother and Mary Magdalene who has a special
attention for the tomb. But that is not all. There is, furthermore,
a rather special phenomenon. There are also several other text

---

[14] E. Schüssler Fiorenza writes in *In Memory of Her*, "Mary is characterized
not so much as the 'great lover' of Jesus who is upset about his death for
personal reasons, but rather as representative of the disciple's situation after
the departure of Jesus" (p. 333). I do not believe there is an opposition
between the two: Mary of Magdala is a representative of discipleship, *because*
she is a 'great lover' (Schüssler Fiorenza points to three other aspects in the
text which make Mary a representative). This necessary relation between
being a disciple and love for Jesus is most clear in 21:15-19, the story where
Peter is asked three times by Jesus whether he loves him. In her love for
Jesus, Mary is a better disciple than Peter!

signals which underline the female character.

In the story of the Samaritan woman, this is conveyed by the repetition of the word γυνή (woman). It is used 13 times to indicate the woman, and it is used twice together with the feminine word *Samaritis* (in 4:9). The parallel story of the man born blind makes clear that this abundant use of the word 'woman' is somehow relevant. The man born blind is also an anonymous character; the text is more or less of the same length and it is also told in the form of dialogues. But the man born blind is called ἄνθρωπος (man) only three times.

This liberal use of γυνή in John 4 is not the only thing. Several times it is used in such a context that precisely the femaleness is accentuated. The woman begins the discussion with the remark that she is a woman and Jesus a man (4:9); Jesus brings up the men in her life and the special position she thus has as a woman (4:17-18); Jesus addresses her as γύναι (woman) at the opening of the Samaria-Judea discussion; the disciples are surprised that Jesus speaks with a woman (4:27); and some exegetes believe that the reaction of the Samaritans to the woman's talk (in 4:42) drags down the woman as woman.[15]

In the other stories with women the emphasis on the female is not so explicit. Obviously, these are already gendered through the female names. Yet in a number of places remarkable and sometimes extraordinary expressions are used.

The Lazarus story opens with a very remarkable expression: "Now a certain man was ill, Lazarus from Bethany, the village of Mary and Martha, her sister" (11:1). It is strange to indicate a village by the name of a person, it is even more so if the names are women's names. This emphasis on the sisters is maintained throughout the rest of the story by the repetition of the word

---

[15]With many others I believe that in this verse there is no opposition between 'we-men' and 'you-woman', but the verse makes rather a difference between being a direct witness and hearing the message from a witness, i.e. the difference between hearing something directly or hearing it mediated through a witness; but recently L. Schottroff reiterated in *Important Aspects of the Gospel*, 209: "It is more difficult to eliminate the dark spot represented by the way in which Jesus' Samaritan followers despised this woman (4:42)".

sister(s). The word is used five times and sometimes – or so it seems – without any good reason, except in order to keep the reader conscious of the female character of the story as in 11:5, "Now Jesus loved Martha and *her sister* and Lazarus", and in 11:39, "*The sister of the dead man*, Martha, said to him..."

In the story of Mary Magdalene we can point to the double use of *guvnai*. The two angels as well as Jesus ask her, "Woman, why are you weeping?" (20:13 and 15). There is also the special use of the name 'Mary' in the scene of recognition (20:16). It is unique in the Gospel. I think it is the shortest sentence which the narrator gives Jesus to say, and, as is clear from the reception of this scene, there is real affective power in it. One can at most compare the scene with Jesus asking Peter for the third time, whether Peter loves him, "Simon, son of John, do you love me?" (21:17), but at the same time it shows the real difference.[16]

There is still more to be said. This female character of the stories with women is reinforced, if we read them in relation to a number of male stories. When individual men play a leading role, a sort of crisis ensues and the men must prove that they can overcome the crisis. If we look at the classical ἀρετή-doctrine, this means that it is demanded of the men to be ἀνδρειοί, to possess the virtue of courage: a courageous attitude towards nobility, power, wealth, tyranny, death and toil.

This is extremely true for the main plot which many exegetes consider to be a story of crisis, crisis in the double meaning of the Greek word: as a situation which demands judgment and as a situation which is chaotic: the crisis between Jesus and his relatives, the crisis between Jesus and his disciples, the crisis between Jesus and the Judeans, and the crisis between Jesus and the world. I will not deal with this in detail here, because I believe that there is a good deal of agreement among exegetes about it.

For our argument it is important to see that this (male)

---

[16]For a reading of the whole passage from a feminist perspective, see S.M. Schneiders, "John 20:11-18: The Encounter of the Easter Jesus with Mary Magdalene – A Transformative Feminist Reading", in: F.F. Segovia (ed.), *"What is John?" Readers and Readings of the Fourth Gospel*, Atlanta 1996, 155-68.

necessity of correctly handling a crisis also returns time and again on the smaller narrative sub-level:

- in the story of the healing of the paralytic who must defend himself against the reproach of the Judeans that Jesus healed on the Sabbath and who, in the end, comes to a confession of Jesus, although expressed in a slightly hidden way (5:9-15);[17]

- in the story of the man born blind and in a judicial setting which, ultimately, brings the man to his impressive confession of Jesus (9:1-42);

- in the story of Lazarus who, because of his friendship with Jesus and the resurrection which therefore happens to him, is threatened with death, together with Jesus, by the High Priests (12:9-10);

- in the story of Nicodemus it is more dispersed. Various exegetes judge this story differently but, in fact, he defends Jesus in the meeting of the High Priests and Pharisees and that brings their derision down on him (7:51-52). At Jesus' burial he appears once more, acting positively in favour of Jesus and resists once again – in public now – the Sanhedrin (19:39-42);

- in the story about Peter there is a total absence of ἀνδρεία. When a young doorkeeper only says that Peter

---

[17]The translation (meaning) of the word ἀναγγέλλω in 5:15 determines what the man does in relation to Jesus: is he an informer, a reporter or a confessor? See the confusion in Bauer, *Wörterbuch*. Under the lemma ἀναγγέλλω n. 2/ he writes: "allg. Eröffnen, melden, verkündigen, lehren"; the examples provided are always translated with the mentioned positive words, except John 5:15 about which is written: "J 5,15 Anzeigen an d. Behörde". In John 4:25; 16:13, 14, 15, the word has always the positive meaning of 'verkündigen'; why not in John 5:15? In his most recent commentary, F.J. Moloney, *The Gospel of John*, Collegeville, Minnesota, 1998, 166;167;169, and 173 does not consider this linguistic argument of the alternative reading of the word (together with the positive implications for the charactarisation of the anonymous man).

belongs to the disciples of Jesus he denies it; and it gets worse when he is asked by the slaves and servants whether it is so and when an eyewitness recognises him (18:17, 25-27). This threefold denial will evoke the threefold question by Jesus about his love for Jesus, but it will also bring him the prediction that he will die on the cross as the ultimate proof of his of ἀνδρεία (21:15-19).

− I ask myself whether the closing *logia* about the death of the beloved disciple (21:21-23) should not be understood against the 'problem' of a lack of of ἀνδρεία.

Even though some details of this list are open to discussion, I believe that the list as a whole is an impressive series and can stand comparison with the stories about the women where exactly this accent on courage is lacking: courage is not demanded of women in the same degree as of men, although the appearance of the women under the cross shows that women, too, find themselves potentially in dangerous situations. Even so, according to the story, this does not cause further difficulty for them.

In the classical doctrine on 'virtues', one finds next to ἀνδρεία which primarily belongs to men, σωφροσύνη as a quality belonging primarily to women: 'temperance' as the avoidance of adultery; the avoidance of desires, sensual pleasures, luxury, and finery; the control of the emotions and the way of conducting oneself in accordance with one's social position.[18] If this had been in some way a topic in the stories with women, the circle would be closed and stories of men and of women would be clearly distinguishable. But this is not the case. One cannot say convincingly

---

[18]The classical doctrine on virtues is much more complicated and is also quite different in the different authors who have written about it. 1) More or less common is the idea that every human being is called to practice all virtues. But 2) men and women have different natural inclinations and in this sense men are more inclined to 'courage' and women more to 'temperance'. 3) The virtues often have a different meaning depending on whether they are practised by men or women. The best known example among exegetes will be the γυνή ἀνδρεία from Proverbs 31:1-29. The main emphasis of the ἀνδρεία of this woman is found in the special way she cares for the home.

– thank goodness, I would say – that the women in John are σώφρονες. They do what women are supposed to do: they go and fetch water at the well (the Samaritan woman); they look for help from a powerful (male) protector (Martha and Mary); they serve the guests at table (Martha); they take care of the tomb (Mary of Magdala). All that has little to do with σωφρόσυνη.

On the other hand, they do break out of this framework but, according to the point of view of the narrator, that does not make them ἀσελγοί/ἀκολαστοί: adulteresses, lovers of luxury, improper in the way they show their emotions or improper in their behaviour. The Samaritan woman enters into a discussion with a man when alone with him at the well and she has had an eventful life, but the story relates this matter-of-factly and does not make a judgment. Martha enters into a theological discussion with a passing man, who is surrounded by a group of people, but the narrator agrees with the content. Mary anoints Jesus' feet and loosens her hair to dry them in the presence of several men, the act of a slave girl which is way below her status as a free woman (see Peter's protest when Jesus acts as a slave in 13:8), but Jesus praises her for it. Mary of Magdala alarms the men early in the morning and she shows her emotions by crying and touching Jesus publicly, but she is rewarded for it and is given an important task.

Some of these actions – speaking with a man alone, acting below one's status, showing emotions which are not proper in the given situation – verge on intemperance, if they are not already beyond it.[19] Because σωφρόσυνη does not seem to be an issue in these stories, this female behaviour is not seen as failure, different from the story about Peter. Peter, being a man, should have been courageous and he is, therefore, corrected by Jesus rather harshly.

Where the male stories certainly speak about a form of ἀνδρεία, the women-stories do not give the impression that one should think of σωφρόσυνη. There is not an easy opposition, and yet John is known for that: day and night, light and darkness,

---

[19]I have serious doubts about that in the story of Mary at the meal: does Jesus correct her or not? It is possible to read the text as a correction. In that case one has to understand Jesus' comment in 12:7 as a re-interpretation which makes the anointing of his feet more acceptable (for male readers?).

truth and lie, life and death. But men and women are not thus opposed to each other.

The situation is even more complicated. Within the classical discourse, the distinction between men and women is, more or less continuously, seen as a distinction between τα ἔξω and τα ἔνδον, the responsibility for the outside realities of life, the politics (the πόλις) and the responsibility for the inside realities of life, the domestics (the οἶκος). Men are responsible for the well being of the state, women for the well being of the home. Marilyn Katz has recently shown that the interpretation of this opposition is heavily influenced by the 19th century bourgeois division of labour in which the man was considered to be responsible for commerce and politics and the woman was supposed to stay at home and take care of the children, the home, and the family.[20] New historical research has shown that the opposition *polis-oikos* in antiquity is far more complicated and more nuanced.[21] If I may say something about first century Ephesus, although the *oikos*-ideology is strongly present – everybody is somehow embedded in some *oikos* or other – this does not prevent certain women from being given a lot of political responsibility as governors of the city, as builders of large constructions, as organisers of all kinds of urban activities and as managers of socio-religious organisations. Women are involved in the well-being of the city on many different levels.

If we look at the Johannine texts from this perspective, a special world is shown. Apparently, no woman is embedded in an *oikos* as one would normally expect: man, woman, children,

---

[20]M.A. Katz, "Ideology and 'the status of women' in ancient Greece", in: R. Hawley, B. Levick (eds.), *Women in Antiquity: New Assessments*, London & New York 1995, 21-43; see also J. Blok, "Sexual Asymmetry: A Historiographical Essay", in: J. Blok, P. Mason (eds.), *Sexual Asymmetry: Studies in Ancient Society*, Amsterdam 1987, 1-52; B.J. Brooten, "Early Christian Women and their Cultural Context: Issues of Method in Historical Reconstruction", in: A. Yarbro Collins (ed.), *Feminist Perspectives on Biblical Scholarship*, Chico 1985, 65-91.

[21]Let us look once more to the *mulier fortis* from Proverbs 31: the man sits at the gate of the city and the woman stays at home, but she does not just take care of the children: she deals with the traders from all over the world; she chooses and buys a field; she teaches lessons of wisdom.

friends, slaves, possessions. It seems that none of the women is
married or has children. Of the Samaritan woman this is said three
times explicitly: "The woman answered him: 'I have no husband'.
Jesus said to her, 'You are right in saying, "I have no husband"
... and he whom you now have is not your husband; and this
you said truly'" (4:17-18). But that is apparently true also for
Martha and Mary who live with their brother, for Jesus' mother,
and for Mary of Magdala. Martha and Mary do what they can to
maintain their own *oikos* (11:3 combined with 11:21 and 11:32),
and Jesus' mother is given by Jesus a male *tutor mulieris* in the
person of the beloved disciple (19:26-27). But this does not result
in normal *oikoi*.

However, something similar happens with the men. The
Johannine text tells about the existence of a normal *oikos*: the
family of the royal official (4:53), Jesus' father and mother (6:42),
the parents of the man born blind (9:18ff), the *oikos* of Caiaphas
(18:13 family, palace, slaves and servants), but apart from the
story of the royal official and 6:42, this is only background information. The *oikos* itself does not really play a role. I believe that
this is due to an important part of the main plot: that Jesus himself is involved in building his own special *oikos*, the protection of
the house of his father (2:16-17) and its expansion by gathering
the scattered children of God (11:52 and 13–17 passim).

The *polis*-side is also complicated. In a way, it is largely an
empty field. The people are indicated as inhabitants of a city:
Andrew (1:40) and Philip (1:43) from Bethsaida, Andrew's and
Peter's city (1:44), Lazarus from Bethany, Martha's and Mary's
village (11:1), Joseph from Arimathea (19:38), Nathanael from
Cana in Galilee (21:2); but the text does not make it clear whether
they have any political responsibilities in those places. Again, the
main plot plays an important role here. Jesus of Nazareth is not a
settled man. He travels and stays, here, then there, for a shorter
or longer period. He gathers disciples who travel with him away
from their own city or village. That does not mean that politics
do not have a central place. In the persons of Pilate and of the
High Priests it plays an important role but then in opposition
to Jesus: the central power only wants Jesus to disappear. This

political involvement of the authorities is part of the main plot
and is connected with the various sub-plots of the conflicts with
local authorities, in which some of the male figures get involved.
Because the women are not confronted with these problems, they
remain, in this sense, outside the *polis*.

On the politically somewhat lower level of 'inner' versus
'outer', the situation is more nuanced. The women do typical female things which fit in with the well-known list of the 'inner':
drawing water, serving at table, mourning. But the women also
act easily in the 'outer' situation: the Samaritan woman gathers
the whole city; Martha publicly enters into discussion with Jesus;
Mary Magdalene brings Peter and the beloved disciple from the
inside of the house into the outside; in the garden she speaks with
the man she believes to be the gardener, and she announces to
the (male) disciples what she has seen and heard. I do not think
one can say that the women take over typically male roles,[22] but
one can say that they take hold of positions which normally are in
the male domain, that they enlarge the range of their activities.

We see something similar in Jesus' behaviour but then in reverse. He acts outwardly as we just said, but linked with this many
things are told of him which have to do with 'the inner' part of
the *oikos*: he changes water into wine, he makes sure there is
water, he restores the *oikos* of the royal official, he makes sure
there is bread, he is the light of the world, he restores the *oikos*
of Martha, Mary and Lazarus; and very specially, he acts in the
group of the disciples as their slave. Therefore, Jesus too enlarges
the range of his activities by taking positions which traditionally
belong to women. These positions are naturally part of his mission and the charge given to him to rebuild the *oikos* of his father
in the cosmos. But the fact that Jesus takes care of the water (he
is the water and he gives the water), of the bread (he is the bread
and he gives the bread) and of the light (he is the light and he
enlightens) *and* that he, at the same time, defends his own *oikos*
against the outside world makes it clear that for him too – as with
the women – the role functions of men and women are no longer

---

[22] An exception is, maybe, Mary of Magdala's apostolate, more so because
she does that on Jesus' command.

(completely) determined by the cultural pattern. Each character acts out the role in its own mixture of male and female roles and positions.

A final observation. It is the lasting merit of feminist and feminist-oriented exegesis that they opened our eyes to the 'high' position of women in the Johannine Gospel. The representational value of the women is not different from that of the men. They are for the reader role models which can be followed: even though Mary, Martha, and Mary of Magdala are probably not members of the group of male disciples – although Mary of Magdala travels with them and is, at least at decisive moments, present in Jerusalem, the other women seem to be home-bound – the women are like the men publicly accepted as Jesus' disciples. They follow the same training as the men: through discussions, dialogues and misunderstandings, and touched by Jesus' love, returning that love. (The beloved disciple and the love which Jesus asks of Peter make it clear that the mutual love-relationship is not only typical for the women but is valid also for the men.) Martha's confession of faith can be compared to that of Peter (6:68-69) and is, narratively, even of a higher order; the Samaritan woman is, in her own way, an apostle to the people of her city, and Mary of Magdala is a favourite apostle who is the first to see Jesus after his resurrection and to announce the good news of that resurrection, roles which in the Gospel are given to the male disciples only as a task for the future.

This 'discovery' of feminist exegetes ran parallel to the 'discovery' of the special position of some women in contemporary literature: the existence of female philosophers,[23] female leaders in religion,[24] in city finances and government.[25] These studies

---

[23] See for example M.E. Waithe, *A History of Women Philosophers*, vol. 1-3, Dordrecht 1987. Volume 1 deals with classical history.

[24] Regarding Jewish women, see B. Brooten, *Women Leaders in the Ancient Synagogue: Inscriptional Evidence and Background Issues*, Chico 1982 and L.J. Archer, *Her Price is Beyond Rubies: The Jewish Woman in Graeco-Roman Palestine*, Sheffield 1990.

[25] S. Pomeroy stands at the origin of this new approach: *Goddesses, Whores, Wives, and Slaves: Women in Classical Antiquity*, New York & London 1975, esp. 120-48; see also for example M.R. Lefkowitz, M.B. Fant, *Women's Life in Greece and Rome*, London 1982; R. van Bremen, "Women and Wealth", in: A. Cameron, A. Kuhrt (eds.), *Images of Women in Antiquity*, London & Canberra, 1983, 207-42; G. Mayer, *Die jüdische Frau in der hellenistisch-römischen Antike*, Stuttgart 1987; for a recent discussion see R. Hawley, B.

showed that, in the first two or three centuries, women (in any case the more wealthy women, but sometimes one can prove that it happened also in 'lower' circles) have taken up positions which before were exclusively reserved for men. In a way, this is really confusing because the women, thereby, become more equal to men. Even though this is quantitatively as well as qualitatively only partially true, it nevertheless implies that a culture in this way develops towards the insight that human beings cannot be distinguished because of gender but only on the basis of their own character, which leads them to act in their own different ways. The theoretical culmination point of this aspiration can doubtlessly be found in Musonius's *oikos* treatises in which, more clearly than anywhere else, a plea for the fundamental equality of men and women is voiced.[26]

The Johannine Gospel participates in its own, and as we have said in a not fully wholehearted way, in what possibly could be called an emancipation of women. The problem is that the Gospel also participates in another cultural movement. In the more encompassing text, women are apparently put down again: when Jesus speaks with his disciples during the leave of the Samaritan woman, her input in the mission is expressed in a way which we can call at best anonymous (4:36-38). When Jesus stands before Lazarus' tomb, Martha is confronted by him with such a critical question that her importance in the first discussion is practically taken away (11:40); in Jesus' last beatitude (20:29), the beloved disciple who has not seen and yet has believed is given preference over Mary of Magdala. In the confusion which the gender-bending evoked, the ultimate choice has apparently

Levick (eds.), *Women in Antiquity: New Assessments*, London & New York 1995.

[26]See for the texts A. Jagu, *Musonius Rufus: Entretiens et fragments: Introduction, traduction et commentaire*, Hildesheim & New York 1979. Regarding the man-woman relations, see A.C. van Geytenbeek, *Musonius Rufus and Greek Diatribe*, Assen 1962, 51-77. Musonius probably plays no role in the exegetical discourse, because there were no easily accessible translations in German and English. For the German translation see now the Artemis edition, *Ausgewählte Schriften: Griechisch-Deutsch. Epiktet, Teles, Musonius*, Zürich 1994. As far as I am informed, the only English translation is in C.E. Lutz, *Musonius Rufus, 'The Roman Socrates'*, New Haven 1947.

been for the familiar patterns. And although this 'solution' is understandable within the omnipresence of the patriarchal culture, it does not mean that one simply has to accept it.

The Johannine Women and the Social Code of their Time

A Response

Reimund Bieringer   (Catholic University of Leuven)

In 1975 Raymond E. Brown published his seminal article on "Roles of Women in the Fourth Gospel" in *Theological Studies*. In a text-immanent approach Brown tried to convince his readers that "John included women as 'first-class' disciples".[1] Brown inferred from this textual reality to its socio-historical background: "The unique place given to women in the Fourth Gospel reflects the history, the theology, and the values of the Johannine community".[2]

This fundamental view is shared by Sandra Schneiders in her 1982 study. Building further on Brown's analysis, she contributed a wealth of new observations. In John she discovered women who:

> played a variety of unconventional roles which the Fourth Evangelist presents as approved by Jesus and the community despite the grumblings of some men. These women do not appear dependent on husbands or other male legitimators, nor as seeking permission for their activities from male officials. They evince remarkable originality in their relationships with Jesus and extraordinary initiative in their activities within the community. They are privileged recipients of three of Jesus' most important self-revelations: his messiahship, that he is the resurrection and the life, and that his glorification is complete and its salvific effects given to his disciples.[3]

---

[1] R.E. Brown, "Roles of Women in the Fourth Gospel", *TS* 36 (1975), 688-99, reprinted as Appendix II in R.E. Brown, *The Community of the Beloved Disciple*, New York 1979, 183-98, 197.

[2] Brown, "Roles", 183.

In 1987 Turid Karlsen Seim made a fresh attempt to demonstrate that a full understanding of women's roles in John is possible only if one takes into account their femaleness. She detected "an egalitarian interest in the leadership of the Johannine community. Authority, witness and proclamation were shared responsibilities including both women and men".[4]

While these three studies focussed on the role of women as disciples, in his 1993 book *Imaginative Love in John* Sjef van Tilborg concentrates on the way "Jesus' ἀγάπη is realised ... in the meetings with men and women".[5] His goal is to work out "a significant difference in the relations of Jesus with men and with women".[6] After a detailed analysis, in which van Tilborg makes use of Hellenistic literature, esp. romance literature, he concludes, "The relation between Jesus and the women in the Johannine Gospel is quite special and, as should be clear by now, it is also somewhat ambiguous. In the beginning of the various stories Jesus is inviting and open ... He also receives a lot".[7] But, "At decisive moments Jesus retreats from this relationship to women: he finds refuge in his relation with the male disciples ...; he retires into himself ... and, in the closing stories, he goes back to this relation with the beloved disciple".[8]

The present paper of van Tilborg is undoubtedly indebted to his 1993 study, but has a different focus. In place of Jesus' relationship with women, he has now broadened his perspective to the "way women are presented in the Johannine Gospel" in comparison with "the social code of the time".[9] This perspective is new

---

[3]S.M. Schneiders, "Women in the Fourth Gospel and the Role of Women in the Contemporary Church", *BTB* 12 (1982), 35-45, 44.

[4]T. Karlsen Seim, "Roles of Women in the Gospel of John", in: L. Hartman, B. Olsson (eds.), *Aspects on the Johannine Literature* (CB.NT, 18), Uppsala 1987, 56-73, 67.

[5]S. van Tilborg, *Imaginative Love in John* (Biblical Interpretation Series, 2), Leiden 1993, 169.

[6]Van Tilborg, *Imaginative Love*, 169.

[7]Van Tilborg, *Imaginative Love*, 207.

[8]Van Tilborg, *Imaginative Love*, 208.

[9]S. van Tilborg, "The Women in John: On Gender and Gender-Bending", 192.

in its broadness, because it is not narrowed down by either the
purpose of showing that women are in fact disciples in John nor
by the question of how Jesus relates to women. Van Tilborg takes
the question of women in John in the broadest possible sense.
In order to achieve this, his point of comparison is twofold: first,
the presentation of men in the Gospel; and second, how John's
presentation of both women and men compares to the social code
of the time. This broad perspective liberates van Tilborg from certain constraints of earlier studies on women in John, for it enables
him to realize that the women in John are not only presented in
an unconventional light, but also show traits of a rather conven-
tional nature. In his own words, "Most female characters show a
remarkable mixture of dependence and independence".[10] As we
shall see, this broad perspective leads to another fresh insight,
namely the fact that a feminist reading of John cannot content
itself with an analysis of the female characters in the story. The
way the male characters are presented may contribute equally to
the quest.

The stated objective of van Tilborg's paper is to explain the
origin of the mixture of dependence and independence, of con-
ventional and unconventional traits of the female characters in
John. The paper offers the following explanation: In John a certain amount of gender-bending is happening. "Gender-bending"
is defined as "an intended mixture of male and female traits, which
evoke in the bystander (reader) a confusion about gender".[11]
According to van Tilborg, not only the reader but also the
author, the fourth evangelist, got confused by this mixture of
male and female roles and traits and as a result reverted back
to familiar patriarchal patterns. Here we note a parallel between
the Johannine Jesus in van Tilborg's 1993 book and the evangelist
in his present paper. In the 1993 book Jesus is presented as first
being inviting and open to women, but then as retreating and
taking refuge with the male disciples. Similarly in van Tilborg's
present paper the evangelist first freely mixes male and female
roles in contrast to cultural patterns, but then gets confused

---

[10]Van Tilborg, "Women", 192.
[11]Van Tilborg, "Women", 201.

and takes refuge in familiar patriarchal patterns. As we saw, the present paper asks a clear question and offers a clear answer. But how did van Tilborg get from the question to the answer? I detect three major parts in the body of the paper:

- the characterization and the plot;

- the virtues: courage and temperance; and

- the spheres of life: οἶκος and πόλις.

It is by seeing the women (and men) in John in these three major systems of reference that van Tilborg tries to reach the answer to his question.

1. Characterization and Plot

The point which van Tilborg reiterates here is not new in the discussion of women in John, namely their decisive roles for the main plot. Women take the initiative and move the plot on in decisive ways. The Samaritan woman acts as a unique mediator between Jesus and the community. Mary and Martha take the initiative by calling Jesus to the sick-bed of his friend Lazarus and, thus, lead Jesus out of a deadlock. Mary of Magdala is the first to see the risen Lord and to announce it to others.

2. The Virtues: Courage and Temperance

Van Tilborg focuses on three Hellenistic texts, that deal with the issue of male and female virtues, which he uses as a point of comparison with John. With regard to John, van Tilborg concludes that men must prove their courage by the ability to overcome crises. Women, however, are not expected to exercise temperance in John's Gospel. They even behave in ways that might be seen as intemperate. Surprisingly, however, the gospel does not present this as a failure. Thus women are presented as breaking out of the traditional framework of female behavior.

3. The Spheres of Life: οἶκος and πόλις

We summarize the findings of van Tilborg as follows:

a) In John women and men are presented in expected, traditional ways.

b) John is silent about certain expected traditional traits of women (the virtue of temperance) and about certain roles of men (active involvement in the πόλις).

c) Women and men (above all Jesus) are presented in ways which would normally be ascribed to the other sex, respectively.

After this positive appreciation of the paper I would now like to raise some critical points, following the same lines of thought of the paper. So, once again:

1. Characterization and Plot
In order to successfully deal with this point, it seems necessary to take a stand as to what is the main plot of John. I was unable to detect what van Tilborg considers the plot of the gospel to be. If the main plot of the entire gospel was established (see e.g. R.A. Culpepper or F.F. Segovia),[12] it would be easier to show how each story with a woman as a main character contributes to this plot. It is also very surprising that van Tilborg does not devote any attention to "the mother of Jesus", even though in 2:1-11 and 19:25-27 her contribution to the main plot is considerable. "Characterization and Plot" is also the only one of the three sections where a comparison with the male aspect is missing. It would be essential to show how the contributions of male and female characters to the main plot compare or differ.

2. The Virtues: Courage and Temperance
I am not convinced that van Tilborg's findings with regard to the classical texts he presents to us are really applicable to John. The discussion concerning the virtues of Johannine characters seems

---

[12]R.A. Culpepper, *Anatomy of the Fourth Gospel: A Study in Literary Design*, Philadelphia 1983, 77-98, esp. 86-98; F.F. Segovia, "The Journey(s) of the Word of God: A Reading of the Plot of the Fourth Gospel", *Semeia* 53 (1991), 23-54.

far-fetched. This raises the issue of criteria for the acceptance of parallels. Is it enough to find a parallel word or sequence of actions in another text in order to consider it a parallel, and to transfer meaning from this text to another text that is presumed to be a parallel? Does the gospel really expect the male characters to prove their courage? Even in the denial of Peter, courage does not seem to be the main concern of the evangelist but, rather, lack of love is the real issue (see John 21:15-17).

Van Tilborg states: "In the classical doctrine on 'virtues', one finds next to ἀνδρεία which primarily belongs to men, σωφρο- σύνη as a quality belonging primarily to women".[13] According to Karen J. Torjesen, however, courage, justice and self-control (σωφροσύνη) are male virtues while silence, chastity and obedi- ence are female virtues.[14] Moreover, van Tilborg's attempt to demonstrate that the women in John are not σώφρονες is less than convincing which, on the other hand, does not mean that John wanted to present women as temperate. I am rather con- vinced that John was not concerned with presenting his characters in the framework of classical virtues. Therefore van Tilborg runs the risk of imposing on John categories that are the gospel is not interested in.

3. The Spheres of Life: οἶκος and πόλις

In this area I find van Tilborg's observations very stimulating. However, I would like to raise the question whether John's use of οἶκος is correctly understood when seen in line with the Hellen- istic and Roman οἶκος ideology. This question seems all the more appropriate as πόλις does not seem to play a significant role in John. This raises the more fundamental question of whether the world of the fourth gospel was so thoroughly penetrated by the Hellenistic culture that we have to expect such a basic reality as

---

[13]Van Tilborg, "Women", 205.

[14]K.J. Torjesen, *When Women Were Priests: Women's Leadership in the Early Church and the Scandal of Their Subordination in the Rise of Chris- tianity*, San Francisco 1993, 115-8. She points to Helen North, *Sophrosune, Self-Knowledge and Self-Restraint in Greek Literature*, Ithaca, NY 1966, esp. 86-7.

οἶκος ideology to be present; or whether there are important areas of life in which the gospel escapes or resists the Hellenistic influence. In any case, it does not seem advisable to presume without questioning that John's uses of οἶκος cannot but express the Hellenistic οἶκος ideology.

By way of conclusion, I would also like to point out that many of van Tilborg's ways of reasoning can only be convincing when applied to a text that has the ambition to present a full picture of the world it belongs to. Taking into consideration the fact that the selection of general life realities present in a gospel is rather accidental, and the amount of material too limited to be representative, I am convinced that many arguments are not fully convincing. For instance, van Tilborg's observation that no woman in John is married or has children would only have value if the gospel was specifically about married life, if it belonged to a genre that could be expected to give a complete picture of the life of its referential world, or if it was voluminous enough to be expected to be a reasonably complete representation of the world in which it came to be. As it is, however, the gospel only gives a glimpse into the life of a community; and it is likely that the gospel takes the fact that women are married and have children for granted. Taking all this into consideration, I am not convinced that there is enough evidence to claim that John practiced gender-bending in his presentation of female and male characters.

Bibliography

Aasgaard, R., "Brotherhood in Plutarch and Paul: Its Role and Character", in H. Moxnes (ed.), *Constructing Early Christian Families: Family as Social Reality and Metaphor*, London: Routledge, 1997, 166-82.

Abel, F.M., *Les Livres des Maccabees*, Paris: Gabalda, 1949.

Abu-Lughod, L., *Veiled Sentiments: Honor and Poetry in a Bedouin Society*, Berkeley: University of California Press, 1986.

Aharoni, Y., "Expedition B – The Cave of Horror", *IEJ* 12 (1962), 186-99.

Albeck, H., *The Mishnah*, vol. 2, Jerusalem and Tel Aviv 1988 (Hebrew).

Allport, F., *Social Psychology*, Boston: Houghton Mifflin, 1924.

Alon, G., *Studies in Jewish History in the Times of the Second Temple, the Mishna and the Talmud*, vol. 1, Tel Aviv 1977 (Hebrew).

Anderson, G., "The Garden of Eden and Sexuality in Early Judaism", in H. Eilberg-Schwartz (ed.), *People of the Body: Jews and Judaism from an Embodied Perspective*, Albany: State University of New York Press, 1992.

Archer, L.J., *Her Price is Beyond Rubies: The Jewish Woman in Graeco-Roman Palestine*, Sheffield: Sheffield Academic Press, 1990.

Avigad, N., *Ancient Monuments in the Kidron Valley*, Jerusalem: Bialik Institute, 1954 (Hebrew).

---, *Beth She'arim*, vol. 3, Jerusalem: Israel Exploration Society, 1976.

---, "The Burial Vault of a Nazarite Family on Mount Scopus", *IEJ* 21 (1971), 185-200.

---, "A Depository of Inscribed Ossuaries in the Kidron Valley", *IEJ* 12 (1962), 1-12.

---, *Discovering Jerusalem*, Nashville: Nelson, 1983.

---, "Jewish Rock-Cut Tombs in Jerusalem and the Judean Hill Country", *Eretz Israel* 8 (1967), 119-142 (Hebrew).

Avni, G. and Z. Greenhut (eds.), *The Akeldama Tombs: Three Burial Caves in the Kidron Valley* (Israel Antiquities Authority

Reports, 1), Jerusalem: Israel Antiquities Authority, 1996.

Bagatti, B. and J.T. Milik, *Gli scavi de Dominus Flevit*, Jerusalem: Franciscan Publishing House, 1975.

Balch, D., *Let Wives be Submissive: The Domestic Code in 1 Peter*, Atlanta, GA: Scholars Press, 1981.

Bar Efrat, S., *Narrative Art in the Bible* (JSOT Sup, 17), Sheffield: Sheffield Academic Press, 1989.

Barag, D. and D. Flusser, "The Ossuary of Yehohanah Granddaughter of the High Priest Theophilus", *IEJ* 36 (1986), 39-44.

Barbour, I.G., *Myths, Models and Paradigms: A Comparative Study in Science and Religion*, New York: Harper & Row, 1976.

Barclay, J.M.C., "Conflict in Thessalonica", *CBQ* 53 (1993), 512-30.

---, *Obeying the Truth: A Study of Paul's Ethics in Galatians*, Edinburgh: T & T Clark, 1988.

---, "Thessalonica and Corinth: Social Contrasts in Pauline Christianity", *JSNT* 47 (1992), 49-74.

Baron, F.S.W., *A Social and Religious History of the Jews*, 2nd edition, 16 vols, New York: Columbia University Press, 1952-76.

Barton, S.C., *Discipleship and Family Ties in Mark and Matthew* (SNTS MS, 80), Cambridge: Cambridge University Press, 1994.

---, (ed.), *The Family in Theological Perspective*, Edinburgh: T & T Clark, 1996.

Bechtel, L.M., "What if Dinah is not Raped? (Genesis 34)", *JSOT* 62 (1994), 19-36.

Beck, D.R., "The Narrative Function of Anonymity in Fourth Gospel Characterization", *Semeia* 63 (1993), 145-76.

Bendor, S., *The Social Structure of Ancient Israel: The Institution of the Family (Beit 'ab) from the Settlement to the End of the Monarchy*, Jerusalem: Simor, 1996 (originally a PhD dissertation in Hebrew, Hebrew University).

Benoit, P. *et al.*, *Les Grottes de Murabbaat* (DJD, 2), Oxford 1961.

Berlin, A., *Poetics and Interpretation of Biblical Narrative*, Sheffield: Sheffield Academic Press, 1983.

Bernardes, J., *Family Studies: An Introduction*, London: Routledge, 1997.

Betz, H.D., *Galatians: A Commentary on Paul's Letter to the Churches in Galatia* (Hermeneia), Philadelphia: Fortress Press, 1979.

---, (ed.), *Plutarch's Ethical Writings and Early Christian Literature*, Leiden: Brill, 1978.

Bichler, A., *The Priests and their Tasks*, Jerusalem 1967 (Hebrew).

Blok, J., "Sexual Asymmetry: A Historiographical Essay", in J. Blok and P. Mason (eds.), *Sexual Asymmetry: Studies in Ancient Society*, Amsterdam: Gieben, 1987, 1-52.

Blum, E., *Die Komposition der Vätergeschichte* (WMANT, 57), Neukirchen-Vluyn: Neukirchener Verlag, 1984.

Bourdieu, P., "The Sentiment of Honour in Kabyle Society", in J.G. Peristiany (ed.), *Honour and Shame: The Values of Mediterranean Society*, London: Weidenfeld and Nicolson, 1966, 191-241.

Brenner, A., "Das Hohelied: Polyphonie der Liebe", in L. Schottroff and M.-Th. Wacker (eds.), *Kompendium Feministische Bibelauslegung*, Gütersloh: Kaiser/Gütersloher Verlagshaus, 1998.

---, *The Intercourse of Knowledge: On Gendering Desire and 'Sexuality' in the Hebrew Bible*, Leiden: Brill, 1997.

Brettler, M.Z., *God is King: Understanding an Israelite Metaphor*, Sheffield: Sheffield Academic Press, 1989.

Brewer, D.I., "Deuteronomy 24:1-4 and the Origin of the Jewish Divorce Certificate", *JJS* 49 (1998), 230-43.

Brooten, B.J., "Early Christian Women and their Cultural Context: Issues of Method in Historical Reconstruction", in A. Yarbro Collins (ed.), *Feminist Perspectives on Biblical Scholarship*, Chico: Scholars Press, 1985, 65-91.

---, *Women Leaders in the Ancient Synagogue: Inscriptional Evidence and Background Issues*, Chico: Scholars Press, 1982.

Brown, R., *Group Processes: Dynamics Within and Between Groups*, Oxford: Blackwell, 1988.

Brown, R.E., *The Community of the Beloved Disciple: The Life, Loves, and Hates of an Individual Church in New Testament Times*, London: Chapman, 1979.

---, "Roles of Women in the Fourth Gospel", *TS* 36 (1975), 688-99 (reprinted as Appendix II in Brown, *The Community of the Beloved Disciple*, 183-98).

Buchanan-Grey, G., "Children Named after Ancestors in the Aramaic Papyri from Elephantine and Assuan", in K. Marti (ed.), *Studien zur semitischen Philologie und Religionsgeschichte: Julius Wellhausen zum siebzigsten Geburtstag am 17. mai 1914 gewidmet von Freunden und Schülern*, Giessen: Töpelmann, 1914, 163-76.

---, *Studies in Hebrew Proper Names*, London 1896.

Burnett, F.W., "Characterization and Reader Construction of Characters in the Gospels", *Semeia* 63 (1993), 2-23.

Burrichter, R., "Die Klage der Leidenden wird stumm gemacht: Eine biblisch-literarische Reflexion zum Thema Vergewaltigung und Zerstörung der Identität", in C. Schaumberger, *Weil wir nicht vergessen wollen...: ... zu einer Feministischen Theologie im deutschen Kontext* (Anfragen: Diskussionen Feministischer Theologie, 1), Münster: Morgana Frauenbuchverlag, 1987.

Campbell, J.K., *Honour, Family, and Patronage: A Study of the Institutions and Moral Values in a Greek Mountain Community*, Oxford: Clarendon Press, 1964.

Carmi, T. (ed.), *The Penguin Book of Hebrew Verse*, London: Allen Lane, 1981.

Cathcart, K.J. and R.P. Gordon (eds.), *The Targum of the Minor Prophets* (The Aramaic Bible, 14), Wilmington: Glazier, 1989.

Charlesworth, J. (ed.), *The Old Testament Pseudepigrapha*, 2 vols, Garden City, NY: Doubleday, 1983.

Chatman, S., *Story and Discourse: Narrative Structure in Fiction and Film*, Ithaca, NY: Cornell University Press, 1978.

Chesnutt, R.D., *From Death to Life: Conversion in Joseph and Aseneth*, Sheffield: Sheffield Academic Press, 1995.

Clines, D.J., "X, X ben Y, ben Y – Personal Names in Hebrew Narrative Style", *VT* 22 (1972), 282-7.

Cohen, A.P., *Boundaries of Consciousness, Consciousness of Boundaries*, plenary paper delivered at the conference on The Anthropology of Ethnicity: A Critical View, The University of Amsterdam, 15th-18th December 1993.

Cohen, G.D., "The Song of Songs and the Jewish Religious Mentality", in G.D. Cohen, *The Samuel Friedland Lectures 1960-1966*, New York 1966, 1-21.

Cohen, N.G., "The Greek and Latin Transliteration Mariam and Maria", *Leshonenu* 38 (1974), 170-80 (Hebrew).

---, "Jewish Names as Cultural Indications in Antiquity", *JSJ* 7 (1967), 97-128.

Cohen, S.J.D. (ed.), *The Jewish Family in Antiquity* (Brown Judaic Studies, 289), Atlanta, GA: Scholars Press, 1993.

Collins, J.J., "Marriage, Divorce, and Family in Second Temple Judaism", in L. Perdue (ed.), *Families in Ancient Israel*, Louisville: Westminster John Knox Press, 1997, 104-62.

Condor, S., "Social Identity and Time", in W.P. Robinson (ed.), *Social Groups and Identities: Developing the Legacy of Henri Tajfel*, Oxford: Butterworth Heinemann, 1996, 285-315.

Cotton, H.M. *et al.*, "A Greek Ostracon from Masada", *IEJ* 45 (1995), 274-7.

Cotton, H.M. and J. Geiger, *The Latin and Greek Documents: Masada I, The Yigael Yadin Excavations 1963-1965, Final Reports*, Jerusalem: Israel Exploration Society/The Hebrew University, 1989.

Crüsemann, F., "'... er aber soll dein Herr sein' (Genesis 3,16): Die Frau in der patriarchalischen Welt des Alten Testamentes", in F. Crüsemann and H. Thyen, *Als Mann und Frau geschaffen: Exegetische Studien zur Rolle der Frau* (Kennzeichen, 2), Gelnhausen: Burckhardthaus, 1978, 13-106.

Culpepper, R.A., *Anatomy of the Fourth Gospel: A Study in Literary Design*, Philadelphia, PA: Fortress Press, 1983.

De Vaux, R., *Ancient Israel: Its Life and Institutions*, Grand Rapids: Eerdmans, 1997 (trans. from French, 1958-1960).

Delitzsch, F.J., *Hoheslied und Koheleth* (Biblischer Commentar über das Alte Testament, 4/4), Leipzig: Dörffling und Franke, 1875.

Dibelius, M., *A Commentary on the Epistle of James* (Hermeneia), ed. H. Greeven, trans. M.A. Williams, Philadelphia, PA: Fortress Press, 1975, 1-11.

---, *From Tradition to Gospel*, trans. B.L. Woolf, London 1934.

Donfried, K.P., "The Cults of Thessalonica and the Thessalonian Correspondence", *NTS* 31 (1985), 336-56.

DuBois, P., *Sowing the Body: Psychoanalysis and Ancient Representations of Women*, Chicago: University of Chicago Press, 1988.

Dunn, J.D.G., "The Household Rules of the New Testament", in S.C. Barton (ed.), *The Family in Theological Perspective*, Edinburgh: T & T Clark, 1996, 443-63.

Earnshaw, J.D., "Reconsidering Paul's Marriage Analogy in Romans 7.1-4", *NTS* 40 (1994), 68-88.

Eilberg-Schwartz, H., *God's Phallus and Other Problems for Men and Monotheism*, Boston: Beacon Press, 1994.

Elliott, J., *Social-Scientific Criticism of the New Testament: An Introduction*, London 1995.

Epstein, J.N., *Mekilta d'Rabbi Shimon b. Yohai*, Jerusalem: Hillel Press, 1960.

Eshel, E., "Personal Names in the Qumran Sect", in A. Demsky *et al.* (eds.), *These Are The Names*, vol. 1, Ramat Gan: Bar-Ilan University, 1997, 39-52.

Eshel, H. and H. Misgav, "A Fourth Century BCE Document from Ketef Yeriho", *IEJ* 38 (1988), 158-76.

Esler, P.F., *Community and Gospel in Luke-Acts: The Social and Political Motivations of Lucan Theology* (SNTS MS, 57), Cambridge: Cambridge University Press, 1987.

---, "Family Imagery and Christian Identity in Gal. 5:13-6:10", in H. Moxnes (ed.), *Constructing Early Christian Families: Family as Social Reality and Metaphor*, London: Routledge, 1997, 121-49.

---, *The First Christians in Their Social Worlds: Social-Scientific Approaches to New Testament Interpretation*, London: Routledge, 1994.

---, *Galatians*, London: Routledge, 1998.

---, "Group Boundaries and Intergroup Conflict in Galatians: A New Reading of Gal. 5:13-6:10", in M. Brett (ed.), *Ethnicity and the Bible*, Leiden: Brill, 1996, 215-40.

---, "'House Members of the Faith': Domestic Architecture and Early Christian Identity", *Cosmos* 12 (1996), 223-39.

---, (ed.), *Modelling Early Christianity: Social-Scientific Studies of the New Testament in Its Context*, London: Routledge, 1995.

---, "*Social Identity, Group Conflict and the Matthean Beatitudes: A New Reading of Matt. 5:3-12*", a plenary paper at the British New Testament Conference in Nottingham, 16 September 1994 (in debate with Dr Francis Watson of Kings College, London).

Falk, Z., *Introduction to Jewish Law of the Second Commonwealth*, 2 vols, Leiden: Brill, 1972-78.

Fatum, L., "Brotherhood in Christ: A Gender Hermeneutical Reading of 1 Thessalonians", in H. Moxnes (ed.), *Constructing Early Christian Families: Family as Social Reality and Metaphor*, London: Routledge, 1997, 183-97.

Finkelstein, L., *Sifre on Deuteronomy*, New York: The Jewish Theological Seminary of America, 1969.

Fiore, B., *The Function of Personal Example in the Socratic and Pastoral Epistles* (AnBib, 105), Rome: Biblical Institute Press, 1986.

Fleischer, E., *Shirat-haqodesh ha'ivrit b'yame-habenayim*, Jerusalem: Keter 1975 (Hebrew).

Fokkelman, J.P., *Narrative Art and Poetry in the Books of Samuel*, vol. 1 (SSN, 20), Assen: Van Gorcum, 1981.

Foster, G.M., "Peasant Society and the Image of the Limited Good", in J.M. Potter *et al.* (eds.), *Peasant Society: A Reader*, Boston: Little/Brown, 1967, 300-23. (First published in *American Anthropologist* 67 [1965]).

Fraade, S.D., *From Tradition to Commentary: Torah and Its Interpretation in the Midrash Sifre to Deuteronomy*, Albany: State University of New York Press, 1991.

Francis, J., "Children and Childhood in the New Testament", in S.C. Barton (ed.), *The Family in Theological Perspective*, Edinburgh: T & T Clark, 1996, 65-85.

Frey, J.-B., *Corpus Inscriptionum Judaicarum*, vol. 2, Rome: Pontificio Instituto di Archeologia Christiana, 1952.

Goitein, S.D., "Nicknames as Family Names", *JAOS* 90 (1970), 517-24.

Gordon, C.H., "Fratriarchy in the Old Testament", *JBL* 54 (1935), 223-31.

Goshen-Gottstein, A., *God and Israel as Father and Son in Tannaitic Literature* (diss., Hebrew University), Jerusalem 1987 (Hebrew).

Graetz, N., "God is to Israel as Husband is to Wife: The Metaphoric Battering of Hosea's Wife", in A. Brenner (ed.), *A Feminist Companion to the Latter Prophets*, Sheffield: Sheffield Academic Press, 1995, 126-45.

Grant, R.M., "The Mystery of Marriage in the Gospel of Philip", *VC* 15 (1961), 129-40.

Greenspahn, F.E., *When Brothers Dwell Together: The Preeminence of Younger Siblings in the Hebrew Bible*, New York: Oxford University Press, 1994.

Grimme, H., "Inschriften und Ossuarien aus Jerusalem", *OLZ* 12 (1912), 529-34.

Grintz, J.M., "Jehoezer – Unknown High Priest", *JQR* 50 (1960), 340-5.

Groß, W., *Die Pendenskonstruktion im Biblischen Hebräisch: Studien zum althebräischen Satz*, vol. 1 (Arbeiten zu Text und Sprache im Alten Testament, 27), St. Ottilien: EOS Verlag, 1987.

Gruen, E.S., *Heritage and Hellenism: The Reinvention of the Jewish Tradition*, Berkeley: University of California Press, 1998.

Gudykunst, W.B. and Y.Y. Kim, *Communicating with Strangers: An Approach to Intercultural Communication*, 2nd edition, New York: McGraw-Hill, 1992.

Hachlili, R., "The Goliath Family in Jericho: Funerary Inscriptions from a First Century A.D. Jewish Monumental Tomb", *BASOR* 235 (1979), 31-66.

---, "A Jerusalem Family in Jericho", *BASOR* 230 (1978), 45-56.

---, "Names and Nicknames at Masada", *Eretz Israel* 26 (Cross volume)(1999), 55-63, (Hebrew, English Summary p. 229*).

---, "Names and Nicknames of the Jews in Second Temple Times", *Eretz Israel* 17 (Brawer volume) (1984), 188-211 (Hebrew).

Hachlili, R. and P. Smith, "The Genealogy of the Goliat Family", *BASOR* 235 (1979), 67-70.

Hagan, H., "Deception as Motif and Theme in 2 Sam. 9-20; 1 Kgs. 1-2", *Bib.* 60 (1979), 301-26.

Hammer, R., "A Rabbinic Response to the Post Bar Kochba Era: Sifre Ha'azinu", *PAAJR* 52 (1985), 37-53.

Hanson, A.T., "The Treatment in the LXX of the Theme of Seeing God", in G.J. Brooke and B. Lindars (eds.), *Septuagint, Scrolls and Cognate Writings*, Atlanta, GA: Scholars Press, 1992, 557-68.

Hasel, G.F., "זָעַק", *ThWAT*, vol. 2, Stuttgart 1977, 628-39.

Hauck, F. and S. Schulz, "praus, prautēs", *TDNT*, vol. 6 (1968), 645-51.

Hawley, R. and B. Levick (eds.), *Women in Antiquity: New Assessments*, London: Routledge, 1995.

Herzfeld, M., *Anthropology Through the Looking Glass: Critical Ethnography in the Margins of Europe*, Cambridge: Cambridge University Press, 1987.

---, "The Horns of the Mediterraneanist Dilemma", *American Ethnologist* 11 (1984), 439-54.

Hezser, C., "'Joseph and Aseneth' in the Context of Ancient Greek Erotic Novels", *Frankfurter Judaistische Beiträge* 19 (1997), 1-40.

Hofstede, G., *Culture's Consequences: International Differences in Work-Related Values*, Beverly Hills: Sage Publications, 1980.

---, *Cultures and Organizations: Software of the Mind. Intercultural Cooperation and Its Importance for Survival*, London: McGraw-Hill, 1994.

Hoftijzer, J., "Absalom and Tamar: A Case of Fratriarchy?", in *Schrift en uitleg* (FS W.H. Gispen), Kampen: Kok, 1970, 54-61.

Hogg, M.A. and D. Abrams, *Social Identifications: A Social Psychology of Intergroup Relations and Group Processes*, London: Routledge, 1988.

Horbury, W., "The 'Caiaphas' Ossuaries and Joseph Caiaphas", *PEQ* 126 (1994), 32-48.

Horowitz, H.S. and I.A. Rabin, *Mekilta d'Rabbi Ishmael*, Jerusalem: Wahrmann, 1970.

Horsley, R.A., "Spiritual Marriage with Sophia", *VC* 33 (1979), 30-54.

Howard, G., *Paul: Crisis in Galatia. A Study in Early Christian Theology*, Cambridge: Cambridge University Press, 1979.

Hugenberger, G.P., *Marriage as a Covenant: A Study of Biblical Law and Ethics Governing Marriage Developed from the Perspective of Malachi*, Leiden: Brill, 1994, 280-338.

Hunter, D. (ed.), *Marriage in the Early Church*, Minneapolis: Fortress Press, 1992.

Hyman, H.H., "Reference Groups", *International Encyclopedia of the Social Sciences*, vol. 13, 353-61.

Hyman, H.H. and E. Singer, *Readings in Reference Group Theory and Research*, New York: Free Press, 1968.

Ilan, T., "The Names of the Hasmoneans in the Second Temple Period", *Eretz Israel* 19 (1987), 238-41 (Hebrew).

---, "The Names of the Jews in Palestine in the Second Temple and Mishnaic Periods – A Statistical Research" (Unpublished dissertation, Hebrew University, Jerusalem 1984, Hebrew).

---, "New Ossuary Inscriptions from Jerusalem", *SCI* 11 1991/2, 149-59.

---, "Notes on the Distribution of Jewish Women's Names in Palestine in the Second Temple and Mishnaic Periods", *JJS* 40/2 (1989), 186-200.

---, "The Ossuary and Sarcophagus Inscription", in Avni, G. and Z. Greenhut (eds.), *The Akeldama Tombs: Three Burial Caves in the Kidron Valley* (Israel Antiquities Authority Reports, 1), Jerusalem: Israel Antiquities Authority, 1996, 57-72.

Ingholt, H., "Two Published Tombs from the SW Necropolis of Palmyra, Syria", in D.K. Kouymjian (ed.), *Near Eastern Numismatics, Iconography, Epigraphy and History, Studies in Honor of G.C. Miles*, Beirut: American University of Beirut, 1974, 43ff.

Jagu, A., *Musonius Rufus, Entretiens et fragments: Introduction, traduction et commentaire*, Hildesheim: Olms, 1979.

Jastrow, M., *A Dictionary of the Targumim, the Talmud Babli and Yerushalmi, and the Midrashic Litrature*, New York: Putnam's Sons, 1903.

Jellicoe, S., *The Septuagint and Modern Study*, Oxford 1968.

Jeremias, J., *Jerusalem in the Time of Jesus*, London: S.C.M. Press, 1969.

Jewett, R., "Tenement Churches and Communal Meals in the

Early Church: The Implications of a Form-Critical Analysis of 2 Thessalonians 3:10", *BR* 38 (1993), 23-42.

Joubert, S. and J.W. van Henten, "Two A-Typical Jewish Families in the Greco-Roman Period", *Neot* 30/1 (1996), 121-40.

Katz, M.A, "Ideology and 'the Status of Women' in Ancient Greece", in R. Hawley and B. Levick (eds.), *Women in Antiquity: New Assessments*, London: Routledge, 1995, 21-43.

Keel, O., *Das Hohelied* (ZBK, 18), Zürich: Theologischer Verlag, 1986.

Klein, S., *Jüdisch-Palästinisches Corpus Inscriptionum*, Berlin and Vienna: Löwit, 1920.

- - -, "To the Study of Names and Nicknames", *Leshonenu* 1 (1929), 325-50 (Hebrew).

- - -, "To the Study of Names and Nicknames", *Leshonenu* 2 (1930), 260-72 (Hebrew).

Kloner A., "A Tomb with Inscribed Ossuaries in East Talpiyot, Jerusalem", *'Atiqot* 29 (1996), 15-22.

Kloppenborg, J.S., "PHILADELPHIA, THEODIDAKTOS and the Dioscuri: Rhetorical Engagement in 1 Thessalonians 4.9-12", *NTS* 39 (1993), 265-89.

Konstan, D., *Sexual Symmetry: Love in the Ancient Novel and Related Genres*, Princeton: Princeton University Press, 1994.

Kottsieper, I., "Anmerkungen zu Pap. Amherst 63: Teil II-V", *UF* 29 (1997), 397-98.

- - -, "Bäume als Kultort", in U. Neumann-Gorsolke and P. Riede (eds.), *Das Kleid der Erde: Pflanzen in der Lebenswelt des Alten Testament*, Stuttgart 2000, part II.1.

- - -, "Die literarische Aufnahme assyrischer Begebenheiten in frühen aramäischen Texten", in D. Charpin and F. Joannès (eds.), *La circulation des biens, des personnes et des idées dans le Proche-Orient ancien: Actes de la XXXVIIIe Rencontre Assyriologique Internationale (Paris, 8-10 juillet 1991)*, Paris: Ed. Recherche sur les Civilisations, 1992, 283-9.

Kraemer, R.S., *When Aseneth Met Joseph: A Late Antique Tale of the Biblical Patriarch and His Egyptian Wife Reconsidered*, New York: Oxford University Press, 1998.

Krinetzki, G., *Kommentar zum Hohenlied* (Beiträge zur biblischen Exegese und Theologie, 16), Frankfurt a.M.: Lang, 1981.

Laniak, T.S., *Shame and Honor in the Book of Esther* (SBLDS, 165), Atlanta, GA: Scholars Press, 1998.

Lefkowitz, M.R. and M.B. Fant, *Women's Life in Greece and Rome*, London: Duckworth, 1982.

Lévi-Strauss, C., *The View from Afar*, trans. J. Newgroschel and P. Hoss, New York: Basic Books, 1985.

Lieberman, S., *The Tosefta*, vol. 4, New York: The Jewish Theological Seminary of America, 1988.

Lührmann, D., "The Beginnings of the Church in Thessalonica", in D.L. Balch *et al.* (eds.), *Greeks, Romans, and Christians: Essays in Honor of Abraham J. Malherbe*, Minneapolis: Fortress Press, 1990, 237-49.

---, "Neutestamentliche Haustafeln und Antike Ökonomie", *NTS* 27 (1980), 83-97.

Lütgert, W., *Gesetz und Geist: Eine Untersuchung zur Vorgeschichte des Galaterbriefes*, Gütersloh: Bertelsmann, 1919.

Lutz, C.E., *Musonius Rufus, 'The Roman Socrates'*, New Haven 1947.

Maisler, B., "The House of Tobias", *Tarbiz* 12 (1941), 121-122 (Hebrew).

Malina, B.J., *The New Testament World: Insights from Cultural Anthropology*, 2ⁿᵈ edition, Louisville: Westminster/John Knox Press, 1993.

Malingrey, A.-M., *"Philosophia": Étude d'un groupe de mots dans la littérature grecque, des Présocratiques au IVᵉ siècle après J.-C.* (Études et commentaires, 40), Paris: Librairie C. Klincksieck, 1961.

Margolioth, M., *Encyclopedia of Talmudic and Geonic Literature, being a Biographical Dictionary of the Tanaim, Amoraim and Geonim*, Tel Aviv: Yavneh, 1976 (Hebrew).

Margulies, M., *Midrash Wayyikra Rabba: A Critical Edition based on Manuscripts and Genizah Fragments with Variants and Notes*, New York 1993.

Maurer, C., "σκεῦος", *TDNT*, vol. 7, 358-67.

Mayer, G., *Die jüdische Frau in der hellenistisch-römischen Antike*, Stuttgart: Kohlhammer, 1987.

Mayer, L.A., "A Tomb in the Kedron Valley containing Ossuaries with Hebrew Graffiti Names", *Bulletin of the British School of Archaeology in Jerusalem* 5 (1924), 56-60.

McCarthy, C., "The Treatment of Biblical Anthropomorphisms in Pentateuchal Targums", in K.J. Cathcart and J.F. Healey (eds.), *Back to the Sources: Biblical and Near Eastern Studies in Honour of Dermot Ryan*, Dublin: Glendale, 1989, 45-66.

McKinlay, J., *Gendering Wisdom the Host: Biblical Invitations to Eat and Drink*, Sheffield: Sheffield Academic Press, 1996.

Meinhold, A., *Die Sprüche*, Teil 1: Sprüche Kapitel 1-15 (ZBK, 16/1), Zürich: Theologischer Verlag, 1991.

Meir, O., "Nose' ha-hatunah b'mishle hamalakim b'agadat hazal", in I. Ben Ami and D. Noy (eds.), *Studies in Marriage Customs*, Jerusalem: Magnes Press, 1974, 9-51.

Mélèze Modrzejewski, J., *The Jews of Egypt from Rameses II to the Emperor Hadrian*, Philadelphia: The Jewish Publication Society, 1995.

Mendelsohn, I., "Guilds in Ancient Palestine", *BASOR* 80 (1940), 17-20.

Merton, R.K., *Social Theory and Social Structure*, New York: Free Press, 1968.

Milik, J.T., "Le couvercle de Bethpagé", in A. Caquot and M. Philonenko (eds.), *Hommages à André Dupont-Sommer*, Paris: Librarie d'Amérique et d'Oriènt, 1971, 75-96.

---, "Trois Tombeaux Juifs récemment découverts au Sud-Est de Jérusalem", *Liber Annuus* 7 (1956/7), 232-67.

---, "Un contract juif de l'an 134 Après J.C.", *RB* 61 (1954), 183.

Moloney, F.J., *The Gospel of John*, Collegeville: Liturgical Press, 1998.

Moxnes, H. (ed.), *Constructing Early Christian Families: Family as Social Reality and Metaphor*, London: Routledge, 1997.

---, "Patron and Client Relations and the New Community in Luke-Acts", in J.H. Neyrey (ed.), *The Social World of Luke-Acts: Models for Interpretation*, Peabody, MA: Hendrickson

Publishers, 1991, 241-68.

---, "What is Family? Problems in Constructing Early Christian Families", in H. Moxnes (ed.), *Constructing Early Christian Families*, 13-41.

Müller, H.-P., *Das Hohelied* (ATD, 16/2), Göttingen: Vandenhoeck & Ruprecht, 1992.

Müllner, I., *Gewalt im Hause Davids: Die Erzählung von Tamar und Amnon (2 Sam 13,1-22)* (Herders Biblische Studien, 13), Freiburg: Herder, 1997.

Mussies, G., "Jewish Personal Names in Some Non-Literary Sources", in J.W. van Henten and P.W. van der Horst (eds.), *Studies in Early Jewish Epigraphy*, Leiden: Brill, 1994, 242-76.

Naveh, J., "Nameless People", *IEJ* 40 (1990), 108-23.

---, "The Ossuary Inscriptions from Givat ha-Mivtar", *IEJ* 20 (1970), 33-7.

---, *On Sherd and Papyrus: The Aramaic and Hebrew Inscriptions from the Second Temple, Mishnaic and Talmudic Periods*, Jerusalem: Magnes Press, 1992 (Hebrew).

---, *On Stone and Mosaic: The Aramaic and Hebrew Inscriptions from Ancient Synagogues*, Jerusalem 1978 (Hebrew).

Newcomb, T.M. *et al.*, *Social Psychology: The Study of Human Interaction*, New York: Tavistock, 1960.

Nickel, R. (ed.), *Ausgewählte Schriften, Griechisch-Deutsch: Epiktet, Teles, Musonius*, herausgegeben und übersetzt, Zürich: Artemis und Winkler, 1994.

North, H., *Sophrosune, Self-Knowledge and Self-Restraint in Greek Literature*, Ithaca, NY: Cornell University Press, 1966.

O'Brien Wicker, K., "First-Century Marriage Ethics: A Comparative Study of the Household Codes and Plutarch's Conjugal Precepts", in J.W. Flanagan and A. Weisbrod Robinson (eds.), *No Famine in the Land: Studies in Honor of John L. McKenzie*, Atlanta, GA: Scholars Press, 1975, 141-53.

O'Neill, J.C., *The Recovery of Paul's Letter to the Galatians*, London: S.P.C.K., 1972.

Ortlund, R.C., *Whoredom: God's Unfaithful Wife in Biblical Theology*, Leicester: Inter-Varsity, 1996.

Osiek, C., "The Family in Early Christianity: 'Family Values' Revisited", *CBQ* 58 (1996), 1-24.

Osiek, C. and D. Balch (eds.), *Families in the New Testament World: Households and House Churches*, Louisville, KY: Westminster John Knox Press, 1997.

Perdue, L. *et al.*, *Families in Ancient Israel*, Louisville, KY 1997.

Peristiany, J.G. (ed.), *Honour and Shame: The Values of Mediterranean Society*, London: Weidenfeld and Nicolson, 1966.

Peristiany, J.G. and J. Pitt-Rivers (eds.), *Honor and Grace in Anthropology*, Cambridge: Cambridge University Press, 1992.

Perkins, J., *The Suffering Self: Pain and Narrative Representation in the Early Christian Era*, London: Routledge, 1995.

Peskowitz, M., *Spinning Fantasies: Rabbis, Gender and History*, Berkeley: University of California Press, 1997.

Pitt-Rivers, J.A., *The Fate of Shechem; or the Politics of Sex: Essays in the Anthropology of the Mediterranean*, Cambridge: Cambridge University Press, 1977.

---, "Honour and Social Status", in J.G. Peristiany (ed.), *Honour and Shame: The Values of Mediterranean Society*, London: Weidenfeld and Nicolson, 1966, 19-77.

---, *The People of the Sierra*, 2nd edition, Chicago: University of Chicago Press, 1971.

Pomeroy, S., *Goddesses, Whores, Wives, and Slaves: Women in Classical Antiquity*, New York: Schocken Books, 1975.

Pope, M.H., *Song of Songs* (AB, 7), Garden City, NY: Doubleday, 1977.

Puech, E., "A-t-on redécouvert le tombeau du grand-prêtre Caïphe?", *Le Monde de la Bible* 80 (1993), 42-7.

Rabinowitz, Z.M., *Mahzor piyute Rabbi Yanai la-Torah vela-mo'adim*, Jerusalem 1985 (Hebrew).

Rahmani, I.L., *Catalogue of Jewish Ossuaries in the Collections of the State of Israel*, Jerusalem 1994.

Reich, R., "Ossuary Inscriptions from the 'Caiaphas' Tomb", *'Atiqot* 21 (1992), 72-7.

Reicher, S., "Social Identity and Social Change: Rethinking the Context of Social Psychology", in P. Robinson (ed.), *Social*

Groups and Identities: Developing the Legacy of Henri Tajfel, Oxford: Butterworth Heinemann, 1996, 317-36.

Reinhartz, A., "Parents and Children: A Philonic Perspective", in S.J.D. Cohen (ed.), *The Jewish Family in Antiquity*, Atlanta, GA: Scholars Press, 1993, 61-88.

Rimmon-Kenan, S., *Narrative Fiction: Contemporary Poetics*, London: Routledge, 1992.

Robinson P., (ed.), *Social Groups and Identities: Developing the Legacy of Henri Tajfel*, Oxford: Butterworth Heinemann, 1996.

Rogerson, J., "The Family and Structures of Grace in the Old Testament", in S.C. Barton (ed.), *The Family in Theological Perspective*, Edinburg: T & T Clark, 1996, 25-42.

Ropes, J.H., *The Singular Problem of the Epistle to the Galatians*, Cambridge, MA 1929.

Safrai, S., "Home and Family", in S. Safrai and M. Stern (eds.), *The Jewish People in the First Century: Historical Geography, Political History, Social, Cultural and Religious Life and Institutions* (CRINT, 1/2), Assen: Van Gorcum/Fortress Press, 1976, 728-92.

Sandnes, K.O., "Equality Within Patriarchal Structures: Some New Testament Perspectives on the Christian Fellowship as a Brother- or Sisterhood and a Family", in H. Moxnes (ed.), *Constructing Early Christian Families: Family as Social Reality and Metaphor*, London: Routledge, 1997, 150-65.

Satlow, M., "'Try To Be A Man': The Rabbinic Construction of Masculinity", *HTR* 89 (1996), 19-40.

Schäfer, K., *Gemeinde als "Bruderschaft": Ein Beitrag zum Kirchenverständnis des Paulus* (Europäische Hochschulschriften, 23/333), Bern: Lang, 1989.

Schechter, S., *Avot d'Rabbi Nathan*, Frankfurt 1888.

Schneiders, S.M., "John 20:11-18. The Encounter of the Easter Jesus with Mary Magdalene: A Transformative Feminist Reading", in F.F. Segovia (ed.), *"What is John?" Readers and Readings of the Fourth Gospel*, Atlanta, GA: Scholars Press, 1996, 155-168.

---, "Women in the Fourth Gospel and the Role of Women in the Contemporary Church", *BTB* 12/2 (1982), 35-45; published again in M. Stibbe (ed.), *The Gospel of John as Literature: An Anthology of Twentieth Century Perspectives*, Leiden: Brill, 1993.

Schott, S., *Altägyptische Liebeslieder*, 2nd edition, Zürich: Artemis, 1950.

Schottroff, L., "Important Aspects of the Gospel for the Future", in F.F. Segovia (ed.), *"What is John?": Readers and Readings of the Fourth Gospel*, Atlanta, GA: Scholars Press, 1996, 205-10.

Schroer, S., *Die Samuelbücher* (Neuer Stuttgarter Kommentar: Altes Testament, 7), Stuttgart: Katholisches Bibelwerk, 1992.

Schulte, H., *Dennoch gingen sie aufrecht: Frauengestalten im Alten Testament*, Neukirchen-Vluyn 1995.

Schürer, E., *The History of the Jewish People in the Age of Jesus Christ (175 B.C. – A.D. 135)*, A New English Version Revised and Edited by G. Vermes, F. Millar, M. Black and M. Goodman, 3 vols, Edinburgh: T & T Clark, 1973-1987.

Schüssler Fiorenza, E., *Jesus – Miriam's Child, Sophia's Prophet. Critical Issues in Feminist Christology*, London: SCM Press, 1995.

---, *In Memory of Her: A Feminist Theological Reconstruction of Christian Origins*, New-York: Crossroad, 1983.

---, *Priester für Gott: Studien zum Herrschafts- und Priestermotiv in der Apokalypse* (NTAbh NF, 7), Münster: Aschendorff, 1972.

Schwabe M. and B. Lifshitz, *Beth Shearim*, vol. 2, *The Greek Inscriptions*, Jerusalem: Massada Press, 1974.

Scott, M., *Sophia and the Johannine Jesus*, Sheffield: JSOT Press, 1992.

Segovia, F.F., "The Journey(s) of the Word of God: A Reading of the Plot of the Fourth Gospel", *Semeia* 53 (1991), 23-54.

Seifert, E., *Tochter und Vater im Alten Testament: Eine ideologiekritische Untersuchung zur Verfügungsgewalt von Vätern über ihre Töchter* (Neukirchener Theologische Dissertationen und Habilitationen, 9), Neukirchen-Vluyn: Neukirchener Verlag, 1997.

Seim, T.K., "Roles of the Women in the Gospel of John", in

L. Hartman and B. Olsson (eds.), *Aspects on the Johannine Literature*, Stockholm: Almqvist & Wiksell, 1986, 56-73.

Semple, E.C., *The Geography of the Mediterranean Region: Its Relation to Ancient History*, London 1932.

Sperber, A. (ed.), *The Latter Prophets According to Targum Jonathan*, vol. 3, Leiden: Brill, 1962.

Steiner, R.C. and C.F. Nims, "Ashurbanipal and Shamash-shum-ukin: A Tale of Two Brothers from the Aramaic Text in Demotic Script", *RB* 92 (1985), 60-81.

Stern, D., *Parables in Midrash: Narrative and Exegesis in Rabbinic Literature*, Cambridge: Harvard University Press, 1991.

Stern, M., "Aspects of Jewish Society: The Priesthood and Other Classes", in S. Safrai and M. Stern (eds.), *The Jewish People in the First Century*, vol. 2, Assen: Van Gorcum, 1976, 561-630.

---, "The Politics of Herod and Jewish Society towards the End of the Second Commonwealth", *Tarbiz* 35 (1966), 235-53 (Hebrew).

---, "Trachides – Surname of Alexander Yannai in Josephus and Syncallus", *Tarbiz* 29 (1960), 207-9 (Hebrew).

Sukenik, E.L., "The Earliest Records of Christianity", *AJA* 51 (1947), 351-65.

---, "A Jewish Hypogeum near Jerusalem", *JPOS* 8 (1928), 113-21.

---, "A Jewish Tomb on the Mount of Olives (B)", *Tarbiz* 1/4 (1930), 137-44 (Hebrew).

---, "Jewish Tombs in the Kedron Valley", *Kedem* 2 (1945), 23-32 (Hebrew).

Sussman, V., "A Burial Cave on Mount Scopus", *'Atiqot* 21 (1992), 90-5.

Tajfel, H., *Differentiation between Social Groups: Studies in the Social Psychology of Intergroup Relations*, London: Academic Press/European Association of Experimental Social Psychology, 1978.

---, "La catégorisation sociale", in S. Moscovici (ed.), *Introduction à la Psychologie Sociale*, vol. 1, Paris: Larousse, 1972, 272-302.

---, "Social Stereotypes and Social Groups", in H. Tajfel, *Human Groups and Social Categories: Studies in Social Psychology*, Cambridge: Cambridge University Press, 1981, part II.7.

Tcherikover, V., "Jewish Apologetical Literature Reconsidered", *Eos* 48 (1957), 169-93.

---, *The Jews in Egypt in the Hellenistic-Roman Age in the Light of the Papyri*, 2nd edition, Jerusalem: Magnes Press/The Hebrew University, 1963 (Hebrew).

Tcherikover, V.A. *et al.*, *Corpus Papyrorum Judaicarum*, vol. 1, Cambridge, Mass.: Harvard University Press, 1964.

Theodor, J. and C.A. Albeck, *Midrash Bereshit Rabba*, Jerusalem: Wahrmann, 1965.

Thiel, W., *Die deuteronomistische Redaktion von Jeremia 26-45* (WMANT, 52), Neukirchen-Vluyn: Neukirchener Verlag, 1981.

Thompson, M.M., " 'God's Voice You Have Never Heard, God's Form You Have Never Seen': The Characterization of God in the Gospel of John", *Semeia* 63 (1993), 177-202.

Torjesen, K.J., *When Women Were Priests: Women's Leadership in the Early Church and the Scandal of Their Subordination in the Rise of Christianity*, San Francisco 1993.

Trible, P., *Texts of Terror: Literary-Feminist Readings of Biblical Narratives*, Philadelphia: Fortress Press, 1984.

Tuker, N., "Shabbat v'yisrael k'ḥatan v'kalah: Hashabbat k'brit ben H' l'yisrael v'kesreah l'inyane ḥatunah", *Mahut* 18 (1989), 53-61 (Hebrew).

Urbach, E.E., "The Homiletical Interpretations of the Sages and the Expositions of Origen on Canticles, and the Jewish-Christian Disputation", in J. Heinemann and D. Noy (eds.), *Studies in Aggadah and Folk-Literature* (Scripta Hierosolymitana), Jerusalem: Magnes Press, 1971, 247-75.

Van Bremen, R., "Women and Wealth", in A. Cameron and A. Kuhrt (eds.), *Images of Women in Antiquity*, London: Croom Helm, 1983.

Van Geytenbeek, A.C., *Musonius Rufus and Greek Diatribe*, Assen: Van Gorcum, 1962.

Van Henten, J.W., *The Maccabean Martyrs as Saviours of the Jewish People: A Study of 2 and 4 Maccabees* (JSJ Sup, 57),

Leiden: Brill, 1997.

---, "The Martyrs as Heroes of the Christian People: Some Remarks on the Continuity between Jewish and Christian Martyrology, with Pagan Analogies", in M. Lamberigts and P. van Deun (eds.), *Martyrium in Multidisciplinary Perspective: Memorial Louis Reekmans* (BETL, 117), Leuven: Peeters, 1995, 303-22.

Van Leeuwen, R.C., *The Book of Proverbs* (The New Interpreter's Bible, 5), Nashville 1997.

Van Tilborg, S., *Imaginative Love in John* (Biblical Interpretation, 2), Leiden: Brill, 1993.

Van der Horst, P.W., *Ancient Jewish Epitaphs: An Introductory Survey of a Millennium of Jewish Funerary Epigraphy* (300 BCE-700 CE), Kampen: Kok Pharos, 1991.

Van der Woude, A.S., "Malachi's Struggle for a Pure Community: Reflections on Malachi 2:10-16", in J.W. van Henten *et al.* (eds.), *Tradition and Reinterpretation in Jewish and Early Christian Literature: Essays in Honour of Jürgen C.H. Lebram*, Leiden: Brill, 1986, 65-71.

Vellacott, P., *Aeschylus: Prometheus Bound, The Suppliants, Seven Against Thebes and The Persians*, translated with an Introduction, Harmondsworth: Penguin, 1961.

Vikan, G., "Art and Marriage in Early Byzantium", *Dumbarton Oaks Papers* 44 (1990), 145-63.

Vleeming, S.P. and J.W. Wesselius, "Preliminary Observations on the Revolt of Babylon", in S.P. Vleeming and J.W. Wesselius, *Studies in Papyrus Amherst 63: Essays on the Aramaic texts in Aramaic/demotic Papyrus Amherst 63*, vol. 1, Amsterdam: Juda Palache Instituut, 1985, 31-42.

Von Rad, G., *Das erste Buch Mose: Genesis* (ATD, 2-4), 12th edition, Göttingen: Vandenhoeck & Ruprecht, 1987.

Waithe, M.E., *A History of Women Philosophers*, 4 vols, Dordrecht: Nijhoff/Kluwer Academic Publishers, 1987-1995.

Wallace-Hadrill A., (ed.), *Patronage in Ancient Society*, London: Routledge, 1990.

Westermann, C., *Genesis* (BKAT, 1/2), Neukirchen-Vluyn: Neukirchener Verlag, 1981.

Wikan, U., "Shame and Honour: A Contestable Pair", *Man* 19 (1984), 635-52.

Wills, L.M., *The Jewish Novel in the Ancient World*, Ithaca, NY: Cornell University Press, 1995.

Winston, D., *The Wisdom of Solomon: A New Translation with Introduction and Commentary*, Garden City, NY: Doubleday & Co., 1979.

Wolfson, H.A., *Philo: Foundations of Religious Philosophy in Judaism, Christianity, and Islam*, vol. 1, Cambridge: Harvard University Press, 1968.

Yadin, Y., *Bar Kokhba*, Jerusalem 1971.

---, "Epigraphy and Crucifixion", *IEJ* 23 (1973), 18-22.

---, "Masada", in M. Avi-Yonah and E. Stern (eds.), *Encyclopedia of Archaeological Excavations in the Holy Land*, vol. 3, Israel Exploration Society/Massada Press, 1977, 811-2.

---, *Masada: Herod's Fortress and the Zealots' Last Stand*, London: Weidenfeld and Nicolson, 1966.

---, "Masada, Preliminary Report of the 1963/64 Season", *IEJ* 15 (1975), 1-120.

---, *The Message of the Scrolls*, New York: Grosset & Dunlap, 1962.

Yadin, Y. and J. Naveh, *The Aramaic and Hebrew Ostraca and Jar Inscriptions: Masada II, The Yigael Yadin Excavations 1963-1965, Final Reports*, Jerusalem: Israel Exploration Society/The Hebrew University, 1989, 1-68.

Yarbrough, O.L., "Parents and Children in the Jewish Family of Antiquity", in S.J.D. Cohen (ed.), *The Jewish Family in Antiquity*, Atlanta, GA: Scholars Press, 1993, 39-59.

Zakovitch, Y., "The Woman's Rights in the Biblical Law of Divorce", *JLA* 4 (1981), 28-46.

Ziegler, I., *Die Königsgleichnisse des Midrasch Beleuchtet durch die Römische Kaiserzeit*, Breslau: Schlesische Verlags-Anstalt, 1903.

Zlotnick, D., *The Tractate 'Mourning' (Semahot)*, New Haven: Yale University Press, 1966.

Indices

Index of Authors

Selective Index of Sources

BIBLE

Hebrew Bible/Old Testament

New Testament

Appendices

Netherlands School for Advanced Studies in Theology and Religion

Biblical Studies Subsections

in cooperation with

the Amsterdam School for Cultural Analysis and Felix Meritis

Colloquium, June 9th-11th, 1998

Felix Meritis House, Keizersgracht 324, Amsterdam (Tues.-Wed., June 9th-10th)

Bungehuis, Room 101, Spuistraat 210, Amsterdam (Thurs., June 11th)

Families in the Ancient Near Eastern World, the Hebrew Bible and the Judaisms and Christianities of Early Antiquity

PROGRAM

Tuesday, June 9th: Ancient Near East and Hebrew Bible (Dr. Jopie Siebert-Hommes presiding)

09.30-10.00	Welcome, coffee and registration
10.00-10.15	Opening: Prof. Karel van der Toorn (Dean, Faculty of the Humanities, University of Amsterdam)
10.15-12.00	Lecture, Prof. Michael Satlow (University of Virginia):
	"Marriage, Myth, and Metaphor: Marital Ideologies in Early Judaisms"
	Response, Prof. Judith Frishman (Catholic University of Utrecht)
	Discussion
12.00-13.00	Lunch
13.00-15.30	Panel Discussion:
	"Pregnancy, Birth, Birth Control and Related Issues in the Hebrew Bible, Jewish Sources and the Ancient Near East"
	Introductory paper, Prof. Marten Stol (Free University of Amsterdam):
	"Birth in Babylonia and the Bible"
	Panelists: Michael Satlow, Athalya Brenner, Judith Frishman, Rachel Hachlili, Marten Stol
15.30-16.00	Tea/coffee break
16.00-18.00	Lecture, Dr. Ingo Kottsieper (University of Münster):
	"'We have a Little Sister': Aspects of the Relations between Brothers and Sisters in Ancient Israel"
	Response, Prof. Arie van der Kooij (University of Leiden)
	Discussion
18.00-20.15	Reception and dinner

Wednesday, June 10th: Early Christian Literature
(Prof. Wim Weren presiding)

10.00-10.15 Welcome, coffee, registration

10.15-11.30 Project in Progress-paper, Drs. Bianca Lataire (Catholic University of Leuven): "Three Situations of Conflict in the Gospel of John"
Response, Prof. Henk-Jan de Jonge (University of Leiden)
Discussion

11.30-12.30 Lecture and Slide presentation, Prof. Rachel Hachlili (University of Haifa) "The Goliath Family"

12.30-13.30 Lunch

13.30-15.30 Lecture, Prof. Sjef van Tilborg (Catholic University of Nijmegen): "The Women in John: On Gender and Gender Bending"
Response, Prof. Reimund Bieringer (Catholic University of Leuven)
Discussion

15.30-16.00 Tea/coffee break

16.00-18.00 Lecture, Prof. Philip Esler (University of St. Andrews): "Keeping it in the Family: Culture, Kinship and Identity in 1 Thessalonians and Galatians"

Response, Prof. Jan Willem van Henten (University of Amsterdam)
Discussion

Thursday, June 11th: Early Judaism (Prof. Jan Willem van Henten and Prof. Pieter van der Horst presiding)

10.00-10.15 Welcome, coffee, registration

10.15-12.45 Lecture, Prof. Miriam Peskowitz (University of Florida): "Domesticity and the Spindle"
Response, Dr. Lieve Teugels (University of Utrecht)
Discussion

12.45-13.30 Lunch

13.30-15.45 Visit to the Portuguese synagogue, the Jewish Historical Museum, and/or the Rembrandt House

15.45-16.15 Tea/Coffee break

16.15-18.00 Lecture, Prof. Rachel Hachlili (University of Haifa): "Personal Names, Family Names, and Nicknames of Jews in the Second Temple Period"
Response, Dr. Gerard Mussies (University of Utrecht)
Discussion

18.00-18.30 Evaluation and departure

FAMILIES IN BIBLICAL TIMES, JEWISH AND CHRISTIAN
EARLY ANTIQUITIES

J.W. van Henten, A. Brenner, 3rd trimester, 1997/98.

Syllabus

1. **30.3.98** Introduction: Basic Terms (family; 'nuclear' and 'extended' families; 'conjugal'; household; clan; kin; monogamy-polygamy-polyandry-polygyny; exogamy-endogamy), celibacy, sexual mores; definitions/constructions of family and kin; reproduction ideologies

2. **6.4.98** Archaeological, geographical and anthropological aspects (urban and rural; space and architecture; material culture; comparative studies)

   Group Assignment: search the *Anchor Bible Dictionary* (or other Dictionaries or Encyclopedias), in the library or the Internet or CD, through the Net in the Delenus Institute), for material aspects of the family such as housing, burial customs, archaeological sites. Possible sites to look for: Hazor, Dan, Sepphoris, Jerusalem, En Gedi. Duration of search: one hour. A brief oral report about the findings to be given in class

3. **20.4.98** Economic management; general activities (labour and division of labour; 'public' and 'domestic'; resources; property and inheritance; reproduction; life expectancy, support of the elderly)

4. **27.4.98** Family religion and religious activities. Family spaces and relations with the 'external' world; families and larger communities

5. **11.5.98** 'Vertical' relationships: parents, children, education; hierarchies and their regulation; slaves and non-kin; incest regulations

6. **25.5.98** 'Horizontal' relationships: marriage and partnerships; levirate; sibling relationships

7. **8.6.98** Family roles and gender stereotypes (with visual representations)
   [**Workshop, 9-11.6.98.**]

8. **15.6.98** Summary; evaluation

Note: Participants in the course will attend the 'Families'
workshop/colloquium (at least one day), June 9-11, as part
of the course requirements

By 1.7.98 Paper/exam to be handed in

Source Texts
1. Gen. 1, 5, 24; Deut. 23:3-9; Ezra 9:10–10:17; Neh. 13:23-27;
    Judith 8:1-2; Philo, *Hypothetica*, 14-17; Josephus, *Jewish
    War*, 2.120-121; Josephus, *Antiquities*, 18.21; 1 Cor. 7;
    1 Macc. 2:49-70; 14:25-49; *CIJ* 741, Rufina of Smyrna.
2. Isa. 3:16–4:2, Amos 4:1-3; Judg. 17; Deut. 22:23-27.
3. Gen. 3; Ruth; Deut. 22:1-4; Num. 27:1-11 and 36:1-12;
    Testament of Job (for Job's first wife and the daughters'
    inheritance); Jewish inscriptions in Van der Horst, Index
    (see Bibliography).
4. 1 Kings 11; Jer. 7; 44; Ezek. 8:14 (cf. *Midrash Zuta* for
    Lam. 1:1); Lev. 25; Exod. 20=Deut. 5; Mark 7:1-13.
5. Prov. 1–9; 31:10-31; Deut. 21:15-21; Lev. 18; 20; Lev.
    19:33-37; 2 Sam. 13; Exod. 21; Lev. 25; (cf. *Talmud Babli
    Berakot* 5a; *Mechilta de-Rabbi Yishmael, Mishpatim* 1;
    Aboth de-Rabbi Nathan 17); Ben Sira 7:24-25; 22:3-5; 42:9-
    14; 4 Macc. 18; Philo about his apostate nephew.
6. Gen. 3; 4:1-16; 25:19-34; 34; Deut. 22–23; Ruth 1; 4; Deut.
    25:5-10; Judg. 14; 19–21; *Mishna, Yebamot* 1, *Kiddushin* 1,
    Gitttin 1; the Babatha documents; *Ketubah* from the Cairo
    Genizah; Ben Sira 36:20-28.

Select Bibliography

1. C. Lévi-Strauss, *The View from Afar*, trans. J. Newgroschel and P. Hoss, New York: Basic Books, 1985, 39-62; J. Bernardes, *Family Studies: An Introduction* (London and New York: Routledge, 1997), 1-49; *S. Bendor, *The Israelite Beth 'Ab*, ch. 1; S. Safrai, "Home and Family", in S. Safrai and M. Stern (eds.), *The Jewish People in the First Century* (Philadelphia: Fortress, 1987), 728-92; S. Joubert and J.W. van Henten, "Two A-Typical Jewish Families in the Greco-Roman Period", *Neot* 30/1 (1996), 121-40.

2. C. Meyers, "The Family in Early Israel", in L.G. Perdue et al. (eds.), *Families in Ancient Israel* (Louisville, KY: Westminster John Knox, 1997), 1-47; C. Osiek and D. Balch, *Families in the New Testament World: Households and House Churches* (Louisville, KY: Westminster John Knox, 1997), 7-47.

3. J. Blenkinsopp, "The Family in First temple Israel", in Perdue et al., *Families*, 49-57, 78-82; S.B. Pomeroy, "Some Greek Families: Production and Reproduction", in S.J.D. Cohen (ed.), *The Jewish Family in Antiquity* (Atlanta: Scholars Press, 1993), 155-63; Osiek and Balch, "Family Life, Meals and Hospitality", in *Families*, 193-214; P.W. van der Horst, *Ancient Jewish Epitaphs: An Introductory Survey of a Millennium of Jewish Funerary Epigraphy (300 BCE-700 CE)* (Kampen: Kok-Pharos, 1991).

4. K. van der Toorn, *From her Cradle to her Grave* (Sheffield: SAP, 1994; see also Dutch edition, 1987), 93-133; M. Peskowitz, " 'Family/ies' in Antiquity: Evidence from Tannaitic Literature and Roman Galilean Architecture", in Cohen (ed.), *The Jewish Family*, 9-36; Blenkinsopp, "The Family in First temple Israel", in Perdue et al., *Families*, 85-103.

5. Blenkinsopp, "The Family in First Temple Israel", in Perdue *et al.*, *Families*, 58-78; J.J. Collins, "Marriage, Divorce and Family in Second Temple Judaism", in Perdue *et al.*, *Families*, 104-40, 147-62; M. Satlow, "Reconsidering the Rabbinic Ketubah Payment", in Cohen (ed.), *Jewish Families*, 133-51.

6. O.L. Yarbrough, "Parents and Children in the Jewish Family of Antiquity"; A. Reinhartz, "Parents and Children: A Philonic Perspective"; R.S. Kraemer, "Jewish Mothers and Daughters in the Greco-Roman World"; "Slavery and the Ancient Jewish Family", all in Cohen (ed.), *The Jewish Family*, 39-129; C. Lévi-Strauss, "On Marriage between Close Kin", in *The View from Afar*, 88-97; A. Brenner, "On Incest", in *The Intercourse of Knowledge* (Leiden: Brill, 1997).

7. J. Annas, "Women and the Quality of Life: Two Norms or One?", in M.C. Nussbaum and A. Sen (eds.), *The Quality of Life* (Oxford: Clarendon Press, 1993), 279-96.

Assignments

1. Mid-Term: Short paper (3-4 pp.), analyzing a biblical/post biblical text on 'families' or 'a family', together with some bibliographical items.

2. Final : Examination/paper on bibliography.